D1617257

Life Forms and
Meaning Structure

The International Library of Phenomenology and Moral Sciences

Editor: John O'Neill, *York University, Toronto*

The Library will publish original and translated works guided by an analytical interest in the foundations of human culture and the moral sciences. It is intended to foster phenomenological, hermeneutical and ethnomethodological studies in the social sciences, art and literature.

ALFRED SCHUTZ

Life Forms and Meaning Structure

Translated, introduced, and annotated
by Helmut R. Wagner

Routledge & Kegan Paul
London, Boston, Melbourne and Henley

First published in 1982
by Routledge & Kegan Paul Ltd
39 Store Street, London WC1E 7DD,
9 Park Street, Boston, Mass. 02108,
296 Beaconsfield Parade, Middle Park,
Melbourne, 3206, Australia, and
Broadway House, Newtown Road,
Henley-on-Thames, Oxon RG9 1EN
Printed in Great Britain by
Redwood Burn Ltd, Trowbridge, Wiltshire

Library of Congress Cataloging in Publication Data

Schutz, Alfred, 1899–1959.
    Life forms and meaning structure.
    (International library of phenomenology and moral sciences)
    Translation of: Lebensformen und Sinnstruktur.
    1. Meaning (Philosophy) 2. Symbolism. 3. Social sciences –
    Methodology. I. Wagner, Helmut R. II. Title.
    III. Series.

B105.M4S3813   121'.68   81–22690
ISBN 0-7100-9201-6   AACR2

CONTENTS

ACKNOWLEDGMENTS

This volume was prepared with the consent and the encouragement of Mrs Ilse Schutz. Having made the Bergson manuscripts of her husband available to me for earlier scholarly purposes, she entrusted me with the preparation of the publication in English translation. I am deeply indebted to her for this opportunity to bring these early studies of Alfred Schutz to the attention of English and American readers. Further, my thanks goes to Professor John O'Neill, who originally suggested the inclusion of these pieces into the International Library of Phenomenology and Moral Sciences and smoothed the way for its acceptance by Routledge & Kegan Paul. Finally, Dr Ilja Srubar of Constance University, who took care of the preparation of the manuscripts for publication in their original German text, obliged me greatly by making available to me both the completely documentary transcripts of them and the editorially prepared texts which were submitted to the German publisher.

INTRODUCTORY PART

Editor's introduction

In the years between 1924 to 1928, Alfred Schutz worked on a book project which, in scope and intent, anticipated his major work, 'Der sinnhafte Aufbau der sozialen Welt,' which he wrote in 1930 and 1931 and which was published early in 1932. The earlier project had no overall title; I selected the title Schutz gave to the first main part of the study as general title: 'Lebensformen und Sinnstruktur' (in translation, 'Life Forms and Meaning Structure').

At the outset, he had considered but rejected the idea of seeking a philosophical basis for his undertaking in Husserl's earlier work, notably the 'Logical Investigations' (1900-1) and 'Ideas I' (1913). Instead, he seized upon various works of Bergson, most of all 'Time and Free Will' (1889) and 'Matter and Memory' (1896).[1] For reasons which I have discussed elsewhere,[2] he found himself compelled to abandon the whole project and to return to Husserl, whose writings of the middle period, in the meantime, had become available, and to re-orient his undertaking by accepting the latter's phenomenological psychology.

Thereby, he did not disavow Bergson; rather, he made him a quite important second foundation of his work. For this reason, the manuscripts of his Bergson period are not obsolete. In fact, they remain valuable documents of the germination of fundamental conceptions which entered his work of 1932 and remained with him throughout his scholarly activities. In addition, they contain observations, insights, and theoretical considerations which remain genuine contributions to his life work. Even though the whole project and most of its pieces remained unfinished, these manuscripts add to the scholarly stock of the intellectual inheritance which he left to the growing international circles of his followers. Their publication, then, is not merely a tribute to his memory; it is offered as a service to the phenomenological movement.

Dr Ilja Srubar, of the University of Constance, has taken care of the preparation of the German original manuscripts, for publication in 1981. Since space limitations prohibit the inclusion of an extensive theoretical introduction into the present volume, the editor plans, in collaboration with Dr Srubar, to publish a companion volume containing an expository and critical appraisal of Schutz's thinking during his Bergson period.

THE MANUSCRIPTS

The manuscript collection of the Bergson period consists of four textually coherent manuscripts; three of them definitely unfinished. In addition, there exists a collection of shorter manuscripts, containing sundry preparatory matters. In my - as yet not published - annotated bibliography of Schutz's writings, they fall under the group of unpublished manuscripts (UM) and are individually identified by the approximate year(s) in which they originated. The list of these titles is the following:

UM 1924-1925 'Soziale Aspekte der Musik als Artform'
               'Meaning Structures of Drama and Opera'
UM 1925   'Spracharbeit'
               'Meaning Structures of Language'
UM 1925-1926 'Goethe: Novelle'
               'Meaning Structures of Literary Art Forms'
UM 1925-1927a Preparatory materials for an untitled book
UM 1925-1927b 'Lebensformen und Sinnstruktur'
               'Life Forms and Meaning Structure'

The key to the planned structure of the whole project is found in the preparatory materials. The sequence in which the manuscripts are presented in this volume follows the given outlines; that means, it differs from the chronological sequence of the previous list.

CHARACTERIZATION OF THE MANUSCRIPTS FOR THE MAIN BODY OF THIS VOLUME

(1) *The outline of the project*
A comprehensive outline for the whole project was put together by me by telescoping four separate but overlapping outlines of altogether 7 handwritten pages. At the beginning of the main body of this book, I will render a shortened translation of the major items of this outline.

(2) *'Author's introduction'*
Three coherent shorter manuscripts, belonging to the collection of preparatory materials, are offered sequentially under three different sub-titles. Together, they comprise 10 handwritten pages of the German texts.

(3) *'Life Forms and Meaning Structure'*
This is by far the largest of the manuscripts of the Bergson period. It comprises a typescript of 168 pages legal* size yet breaks off unfinished. Schutz designated it as the first of three

*About 14 inches long.

main parts of his study. For reasons explained in the technical
introduction to this part, the translation contains a number of
condensations of more or less elaborate and rather technical
passages.

The next three manuscripts originated in Schutz's Bergson
period but were not written as chapters of the planned book. At
least two of them originated as, or became background material
for, oral presentations. In their substance, however, they fall
within the range of the second main part of the Bergson project;
they touch upon a number of themes relevant for this part.

(4) *'Meaning Structures of Language'*
This unfinished manuscript consists of 41 handwritten and 10
typed pages. Its purpose was to establish the relationships between language and other life forms.

(5) *'Meaning Structures of Literary Art Forms'*
This unfinished manuscript consists of 42 typewritten pages,
legal format. It is concerned with the symbolization of experiences
in literary language. Its original title was 'Goethe: Novelle.' It
was not appropriate to maintain it because the manuscript broke
off before Goethe was introduced and the art form of the novella,
the story inserted into a novel, was discussed.

(6) *'Meaning Structures of Drama and Opera'*
Although with 39 typewritten pages (legal format) the shortest
of four major manuscripts, it is the only one which gives the
impression of being finished in itself. However, the original title,
'Social Aspects of Music as Form of Art', is much broader than the
one imposed by the editor as more adequate. It is possible that
Schutz considered it as merely one part of a larger study, which
he failed to execute. He took up the topic of music in considerably
greater depth later.[3]

The titles of these three manuscripts of the second part of the
study have been provided by the editor. The general designation,
'meaning structures,' was chosen for all of them in order to emphasize their substantive relevance for the central theme of the whole
project. The specification of the titles was chosen not in accordance with the central topic Schutz had intended to treat in each
manuscript, but in agreement with the actual content of the existing fragmentary texts.

(7) *'Object and Method of the Social Sciences'*
This is a token representation of the third main part of the project.
It consists of a seven-point outline of the major topics which
Schutz intended to treat in the last part of his study. It was taken
from one of the manuscripts which provided the overall outline of
Schutz's Bergson project.

STYLE AND FORM OF THE TRANSLATION

The German edition of the original texts of Schutz's Bergson manuscripts, as prepared by Dr Srubar, is a documentary edition
which preserves Schutz's formulations faithfully. Anyone who
seeks text-critical exactness and literal correctness will have to
refer to this edition.

The existence of this documentary edition has allowed me to
treat the task of preparing this English-language edition with a
certain amount of freedom. Such freedom was the more desirable
as Schutz's texts themselves provide particular difficulties for
their translator and, in a sense, resist translation. Essentially,
the manuscripts available were first drafts. That is, they were
not subjected to the careful process of correction and rewriting
which Schutz used to prepare his publications, doing his drafts
three to five times over. What he originally pinned down on paper
were formulations of thoughts jotted down without any regard for
style. In consequence, a dual problem arose. On the one hand,
many of his coherent expositions were full of complex sentences,
beset with inserts and inserts within inserts whose meanings were
sometimes difficult to figure out. On the other hand, he resorted
to a telegram style: jotting down words and phrases, leaving their
expansion to coherent sentences and paragraphs for later.

The main purpose of the English-language edition of Schutz's
Bergson manuscripts is not that of a literally faithful translation -
an impossible task - but a faithful rendering of their meaning in a
form which allows the maximum of understanding by English and
American readers. Therefore, I have not hesitated to take Schutz's
compound sentences apart, making two or three sentences out of
one, whenever necessary. With a few exceptions and in reverse,
I have expanded outline terms and phrases into complete sentences.
In this, I based myself on the immediate textual context, or on the
larger context of the manuscript in question, or finally on my
knowledge of Schutz's later work.

On occasion, a singular noun in the texts has been changed to
the plural when the more consistent rules of English grammar
advised it. The definite article has been omitted from some nouns,
especially when they were used in abstract or typified form.

In the texts, Schutz was sometimes given to the abundant use
of prepositions which, when rendered in English, would sound re-
dundant. In this and some other respects, the translation has
been simplified in accordance with English-language usage.

In dealing with the compound sentences of Schutz, I have sometimes linked as well as separated two parts of a statement by a
colon (:). Often, the colon simultaneously replaced conjunctions
and transitional expressions, such as, 'because,' 'to wit,' 'namely.'

NOTES ON TERMINOLOGY

A few explanations will have to be given concerning the selection of terminological equivalents for Schutz's theoretical or philosophical terms, for the handling of foreign phrases or sentences in his texts, and finally about the selection of some particular expressions by Schutz.

The words chosen for rendering the many specific terms of the texts in English, as far as possible, follow the terminology of Schutz's English writings. In a few cases, Schutz used two terms homonymously. In this case, I have taken the term most consistent with his theories, so: 'conduct' instead of 'behavior' if intent and deliberation is involved. Only in one case did I deviate from Schutz's terminology. He - and most other English-writing phenomenologists - rendered Husserl's term, *die natürliche Einstellung,* with 'natural attitude.' As sociologist, I find myself unable to follow this example; in my field, attitude means not a general disposition to respond to all phenomena coming to attention within a broad era of experience - especially of the life-world - but a specific mode of responding to specific types of objects, situations, or persons. Therefore, I have rendered Husserl's term by 'natural stance.'

According to the custom of Central-European scholars with an intensive humanistic education, Schutz occasionally inserted Latin and Greek phrases or sentences into his texts. I have tried to render their meaning, as emerging from the given textual context, rather than to aim at an essentially literal translation. It would have served no specific purpose, to render the original Latin or Greek formulations in parentheses or otherwise mark the translated passages from the classical languages in every specific case. However, when the terms in question were of a flavor which I could not adequately catch in English, I added the original expression to the text.

A few expressions, which Schutz used frequently, became standard equipment of his expositions without being explicitly defined. Obviously, he found the latter unnecessary because they were standard equipment also of those of his intellectual contemporaries in Central Europe who worked in the areas of the *Geisteswissenschaften.* Five of them, however, call for comments either because he largely abandoned them in his American writings, or he maintained them in their English equivalent but used them with a different meaning. They are: Law, Logic, Material, Phenomenon, Symbol, and their derivative forms.

In the exaggerating manner of his period, Schutz occasionally referred to 'laws' pertaining to social and cultural matters. Thus, he spoke of 'laws of artistic creation.' In contrast to positivist sociologists, adherents of the German *Geisteswissenschaften* used the concept of 'law' not in deference to the model of the natural sciences but in defiance of positivist philosophers. In spite of our sharp separation of the human sciences from the natural ones, we too are scientists in our fashion. Thereby, they referred to their adherence to the principle of impartiality ('objectivity' in common terms), to their rationally controlled procedures, and to the claim of the validity of their findings, subject to the same condition as the validy of the findings in the natural sciences: valid as long as no counter-evidence was found which challenges them.

While, in the opinion and practice of most scholars working in the fields of the so-called social sciences, the same criteria obtain today, the need for asserting the 'scientificity' of their under-takings has greatly lessened. The aggressive prestige of Science, fostered both by the triumph of Evolutionism and the breathtaking progress of Physics in the last decades of the nineteenth and the first decades of the twentieth centuries, has long since been broken by a growing scepticism about the validity of the simplistic principles that Science has the answer to every answerable ques-tion and that questions which are unanswerable by Science are devoid of meaning. It is no longer important to decide whether or not the criteria of scientific operations, as mentioned above, are both necessary and sufficient conditions for calling humanistic disciplines 'sciences'.

In any case, where Schutz in these texts spoke of laws in the scientific sense, while referring to matters of the analysis of consciousness and/or social relations, he spoke according to the intellectual usage of his time. In all cases in which he used the term positively, that is, not critically, we could replace it by the term, rules, in accordance with a more adequate present-day understanding of the nature of the regularities involved.

Schutz also followed the usage of his European contemporaries, who, in the early decades of the century, tended to speak of 'logic' and of 'logical conclusions' not only when they actually referred to the strictly formalistic correctness of deductions and propositions, but also when they were concerned with the sub-stantive consistency of empirical comparisons and conclusions. Schutz sometimes used the terms logic and logical in the narrow technical sense, and sometimes in the loose sense of judgments about the factual context and content of a theoretical argumentation.

A further conspicuous term in the present manuscripts is that of 'material'. The term was generally accepted at the time as a label for the substantive subject matter to which a scholar directed himself. Schutz used it in this fashion. Thus, the term may point to anything which makes for the content of any kind of experience, the given phenomenological data in Husserl's manner. In the 'Meaning Structures of Literary Art Forms,' it also denotes the contents of literary creations as linguistic expressions of imagined experiences.

Occasionally, Schutz spoke of 'phenomenon' or 'phenomena'. At the time he wrote the Bergson manuscripts he had not accepted the specific meaning these terms have acquired in Husserl's philosophy. He used these terms operationally and in the loose fashion of most of his intellectual contemporaries. Thus, they indicate not merely anything which appears to our senses or in our consciousness, but also general categories which label whole groups of data and observations. Thus, Schutz spoke of the 'phenomenon of memory' as if the ability to remember and to recall were of the same quality as a concretely appearing 'memory image.'

Finally, Schutz made use of the term 'symbol' in the same omnibus fashion in which his contemporaries used it. In the light of his later elucidation of the problems of signs and signification, symbols and symbolization,[4] his expositions do not bring out the for his purposes relevant distinctions between the 'symbol system' of language and the 'symbol systems' of life forms or realms of meaning constructed with the help of linguistic 'symbol' systems, and finally the distinction between the symbolizations of everyday life and those of the spheres of artistic experiences.

These short remarks on some of Schutz's terms ought not to be read as a critique. Rather, these terminological characteristics are pointed out because they are indicators of the transitional stage of Schutz's work during the period of 1924-8. He tried to deal with the problems of subjectivity and consciousness to a large degree with the terminological equipment he had acquired prior to his involvement with Bergson's writing which, in turn, were not entirely free from traditional, especially biological and evolutionary, conceptions. What he achieved in the direction of a phenomenal psychology of consciousness, even though with the help of Bergson, demands all the more respect because it was achieved with partially inadequate means.

EDITORIAL CHARACTERIZATION OF INSERTS IN THE TEXT

(------------)   Either passages set in parentheses by Schutz or rendering of the German original term for which a translated term stands.

(--------, HRW)   Short explanatory term or phrase added by the editor.

[------------]   Passage or paragraph crossed out by Schutz in the original manuscript but preserved in the translation.

[[-----------]]   Passage or paragraph which has been either condensed or added by the editor.

ABBREVIATIONS IN NOTES

In order to distinguish notes written by the author and such added by the editor, the following identifying letters appear before the note text:

   AS: Alfred Schutz
   HRW: Helmut R. Wagner

Where all notes in a part of this book originated either with the

author or the editor, this identification of individual notes is
omitted. Instead, a corresponding note is given on top of the
relevant notes section.
   Only two other abbreviations occur in the text of notes:

E.T.   English translation
MS(S) Manuscript(s)

SHORT OMISSIONS IN TEXTUAL PASSAGES

According to generally accepted usage, I have indicated the
omission of words and phrases or short sentences in the text by
three dots (ellipses). Such abbreviations were made most of all
in the case of terms and phrases which repeated statements made
shortly before but which, in the differently arranged English
text, did not require repetition.

BIBLIOGRAPHICAL INFORMATION

In the present publication, the compilation of a list of all bibliographical references occurring in texts and notes would hardly
serve any tangible purpose. The necessary information, at least
in the Introductory Part, can be found in the text: for the manuscripts of Schutz, it has been given in notes attached to the
actual textual places at which hints at the corresponding publications appear.

NOTES
(written by HRW)

1 As far as I could ascertain, Schutz worked exclusively from
   the French original texts of Bergson's writings.
2 See Helmut R. Wagner, The Bergsonian Period of Alfred Schutz.
   'Philosophy and Phenomenological Research' 38, 1977: 187-99.
3 See Alfred Schutz, Fragments on the Phenomenology of Music.
   Edited by Fred Kersten. 'Music and Man' 2, 1976: 5-71. This
   manuscript was written in 1944 and exists in mimeographed
   form.
4 See Alfred Schutz, Symbol, Reality and Society. Chapter VII
   of Lyman Bryson et al. (editors), 'Symbols and Society'.
   New York, Harper, 1955: 135-203.

The outline of the project

EDITOR'S INTRODUCTORY NOTE

The documents from which the comprehensive outline of Schutz's project of 1925-1927 was composed consist of a short indication of the over-all content of the planned three main parts of the study, and three other manuscripts specifying in considerable detail the content of an introductory part and of the first main part, drafts for both of which have been executed. My combination of these documents covers nine pages, typed single-spaced. The outline is reproduced here with the omission of overlap and lower-level details. The latter abound but, in part, would call for comments and explanations which would serve the purposes of the analysis of the scholarly-historical background of Schutz's approach but are not needed for the comprehension of his undertaking itself.

The titles and points of this outline are rendered in Schutz's formulation and arrangement. On a few occasions, I have added titles which were missing in the documents. They are marked by my initials, added in parentheses.

The greater part of the points and sub-points of the outline manuscripts carry identification marks in forms of Arabic or Roman numerals or else lower and upper case letters. The systems used in different documents are not necessarily consistent with one another. I have given the outline without these auxiliary identifications.

LIFE FORMS AND MEANING STRUCTURE (HRW)

Main Overview

INTRODUCTION

Life and cognition

Sciences of Life and *Geisteswissenschaften*

Crisis of epistemology and logic

Approaches and objectives (HRW)

Applicability of modern epistemological tendencies to the social sciences

Subject matter and method of the investigation

Positing of meaning and interpreting of meaning

Meaning as complex symbol structure

PART II   THEORY OF THE STRUCTURE OF THE
         OBJECTIFICATION OF MEANING

PART III OBJECT AND METHOD OF THE SOCIAL SCIENCES

NOTE

1 An alternate title was given as 'Theory of Life Forms and
   Analysis of Symbol Strata.' Both forms differ from the title
   of the major manuscript for the first main part: 'Life Forms
   and Meaning Structure.' It was written along the left margin
   of the first page of manuscript UM 1925-1927b. As stated at
   the beginning of the 'Editor's Introduction,' the same title
   was given to the present volume.

Author's introduction

EDITOR'S NOTE

It was not possible to ascertain the dates at which the three pieces of this introduction were written. It stands to reason that they originated in the first preparatory stages of the project and in conjunction with the outlines. However, these outlines show that they definitely belong to the introductory sections of the projected book. Every one of them has its specific characteristics. The one rendered first starts with historical-philosophical considerations of the development of a traditional position which has closed the door to the understanding of the phenomena of daily life. Attempts to open this door have been made by Ernst Cassirer, Henri Bergson, and Max Weber. Postulating his objective as that of dealing with 'the pre-scientific materials of life as totality,' Schutz changed to an outline style in order to set down the last four points of his introduction: the difficulties and the expected results of the planned investigation, and the discussion of the proposed methods and their justification.

The second introductory piece is of theoretical-philosophical character. It deals with the problem of 'founding,' in Scheler's sense, the point of departure and central over-all problem of the planned study. It stresses the significance of Bergson for the solution of this problem but also mentions the incompleteness and shortcomings of his attempts. In continuation, he subjects Kant's position to a more extensive criticism. Finally, he begins a discussion of his concept of life forms. He contrasts the idea of an undetermined multiplicity of such life forms to both Kant's antithesis of sensuality and cognition and Bergson's opposition of duration and reason. Further, he underlines the basic unity of the experiences of the undivided I in the face of theoretically set limitations of single life forms. But he simultaneously explains that the life forms occur as a hierarchical order with a generally fixed characteristic mode of linkage between each of two adjacent ones. The text offers a detailed explanation of this.

The third piece of Schutz's introduction turns to Bergson in particular, characterizing his conceptions of duration and memory, linking them to symbolization, and contrasting the planned analysis as mere reflection about life to 'life itself.' These indications, too, have found fuller explanation in the text of the first main part of the project.

Obviously, the three pieces of Schutz's introduction were segments of a first draft. I have arranged them in an order which seemed substantively most consistent. This, of course, does not mean that Schutz, had he proceeded toward a final version, would have done the same; I even doubt that he would have maintained the three pieces in their preliminary structure. The title for the second one, 'The Theory of Life Forms and the Analysis of Symbol Concepts,' was provided by Schutz; the other two have been labelled by me.

(1) THE OBJECTIVES OF THE INVESTIGATION

Philosophy, as developed during the last half-century, was unable to achieve anything for the *Geisteswissenschaften*. The cause for this is as follows:

Kant, to whom all systems can eventually be traced back, started from mathematical physics. Since then the prevailing ambition has been to subsume the object of cognition under a minimum of categories according to formal procedures. (This has been done in two major ways, HRW.) There is the neo-Kantian assertion of the production of the object by the method, combined with the postulate of the purity of method and the prohibition of syncretism;[1] that is, a way of chopping-up the unitary object of experience into the objects of uncounted special sciences. And there is the establishment of ultimate spheres of irreconcilability by Husserl's essential ontological analysis, the search for formal laws being unconditionally and generally valid for the forming of categories and their use in categorizing, and the establishment of the universal science.

Both procedures are of high value for the mathematical natural sciences; their cognitive goal is to find lawful regularities in the inanimate world. They are useless where one deals with the areas of knowledge of the *Geisteswissenschaften* and their animated and understandable objects. Therefore, these sciences vacillate between (a) empirical-historical collections of materials; (b) attempts at constructing methodologically pure theoretical systems which, however, do not serve the cognitive goal of the social sciences because they already alter their object so that it loses any connection with the real reality; and (c) mystical or misunderstood metaphysics on the basis of 'a prioristic' valuations and ethic-political postulates.[2]

Consequences of (b) are: ever-growing remoteness from life; no attempt at explaining the most fundamental phenomena of our daily life with the help of these methods: awakeness - sleep; Eros, music, understanding, Thou; dualism, syncretism, etc.

(Discuss the example of, HRW) Russel(1)'s hypothesis of the intelligence of other humans which is both nonprovable and nonrefutable.

(Consider the hopeless alternatives of accepting, HRW) either solipsism as necessity or pre-established harmony or occasionalism[3] (as interpretation of the reciprocity of mind-body relations, HRW).

Misgivings about this situation are felt in philosophy itself. Attempts at bridging the opposition of life and cognition have been made: Cassirer referred to Goethe's conception of the possibility of a non-mathematical recognition of nature. Simmel gained insights into the transcendence of life. Bergson demonstrated that, in principle, the methods and conclusions which were gained from and applicable to an inanimate subject matter do not apply to an animated subject matter.

The last-named attempt is particularly significant. Through the introduction of the conception of duration, it is shown that a philosophy which is constructed on the time basis of inanimated matter is a special case. There are really experienceable yet essentially unreal worlds. Attempts at grasping the phenomena of duration with the methods of the natural sciences are fruitless. The central concepts of Bergson are: life, duration, and a particular conception of consciousness.

Bergson realized the stream of duration as the central problem. Next to this achievement, Scheler's last writings must be mentioned. In them, he emphatically designated as main problems of the *Geisteswissenschaften* the understanding of others and the evidence for the existence of the Thou.

Weber's sociology, too, places understanding in the center; it demonstrates that the cognitive goal of the social sciences is different from that of the natural sciences. Without naming it, he moves the Thou problem into the center. In addition, he introduces the eminently important concepts of the interpretation of meaning and of subjective meaning; and he refers to the empirical merely in the concept of the objective chance.

Common to all of these three attempts is the following: Rejection of the cognitive goals of the natural for the social sciences; emphasis on central concepts characteristic for the *Geisteswissenschaften* (or sciences of life): duration - Thou. Occupation with what is offered by everyday life; the so-called pre-scientific material which is scorned by methodologically pure sciences and which every one of the empirical sciences declares the responsibility of other sciences. Reality of life as totality. (Natural-science, HRW) cognition is arbitrary for the problems of the social sciences and pointless because it produces irreal segments (of the indivisible totality of life, HRW).

From this follows the postulate of an occupation with the pre-scientific materials of life as totality, of an attempt at its analysis according to duration and Thou, and of applying the results thus gained to a theory of the *Geisteswissenschaften* which are always social sciences.

Difficulties of this investigation
(a) The habits of thinking in the social world of daily life are already highly complex constructions of the data of experience.
(b) The instrument of language is supposed to penetrate beneath language.
(c) The intimate person, who alone could elucidate the depth

strata (of the human psyche, HRW), is ineffable.
(d)   Recognition of self already presupposes duration and the
positing of the Thou.
(e)   In consequence, unavoidable paradoxes result.

Expected optimal results of the investigation
(a)   Demonstration of the identity of duration and Thou as
exclusively primary facts of consciousness.
(b)   Analysis of the formative strata leads from life to thinking.
(c)   Discovery of a kind of regularity in the relationship (of life
and thinking, HRW) to one another.
(d)   Discovery of the step-by-step transformation (of experience
into thinking, HRW), shedding light upon the epistemological
problems of the in theory 'methodologically pure' systems and
demonstrating the impossibility of realizing their postulate (rejection of the theory of dualism) and showing their uselessness for
the social sciences.
(e)   Clarification of a few essential connections thus far left
obscure (language-conditioned thinking, Thou-conditioned
language, etc.).
(f)   Obtaining a theory of founding *(Fundierungstheorie)* in the
sense of Scheler.

Proposed methods
Arbitrary construction of ideal types of the facts of consciousness
which are experienced undifferentiated and as a whole in the
totality of life. The artifical analysis of these ideal types. Investigation of individual events and their mutually reciprocal effects.
Establishment of the mechanism of symbolization.
     From the results gained will be derived the nature of the object
of the social sciences. The consequences of the executed analysis
for the theory of methodology and basic concepts of the sociology
of understanding will be shown.

Justification of this method
(a)   The how of artificial analysis: Since it is ideal-typical, it is
exclusively justified by its purposiveness, its output of results.
(b)   The why of the analysis: synthesis by way of constantly
relating individual spheres to each other and through the respective reconstruction of the unity of the experiencing I.
(c)   Contrast to logic: solution of all apparent paradoxes in
generally conscious integrations which, in the end, will be recon-
cilable with logic as a special case.
(d)   To penetrate through language beneath language: demonstration by way of data of daily life whose images are vaguely
described by language (Eros, music, dance, breathing, sleep,
etc.), even though only in form of 'parables.' But language itself
is nothing else.

(2) THE THEORY OF LIFE FORMS AND THE ANALYSIS
OF SYMBOL CONCEPTS

The point of departure is Scheler's problem of 'founding.' In
'life' this question cannot come up because all experiences are
equally spontaneous, regardless whether they are apperceptions,
sensations, or in any way symbolically preformed matters. Now,
what significance has to be granted, from the view point of actual
experience, to the problem of the separation of individual realms
of experience and the relation of these realms to one another?
  Bergson's attempt at a solution: The realm of inner duration,
accessible to intuition and even instinct, is juxtaposed to the
realm of time-space, of objects, of action, of the social sphere –
accessible to concept and intellect. He deals with the relation of
these two realms to each other in the totality of daily life: degrees
of tension, of attention toward life as regulating agent. He shows
the tyranny of the acting I, toward which the intellect fashions
objects, concepts, etc.

Significance of Bergson's formulation of the problem
It is a first attempt of constructing ideal types of consciousness;
a pointing-out of the inadequacy of the intellect to grasp the problem of duration; a dissolving of the polarity of the unity of the
experiencing I and, through this, an overcoming of dualism of
every kind, for instance: body/soul, spirit/matter, finalism/
vitalism, causality/teleology, freedom of will/determinism.

Critique of Bergson's execution (of the investigation of the
problem HRW)
Bergson is satisfied with singling out *two* planes. While his theory
is suitable like no other for overcoming dualism, it apparently
re-introduces it. His dualism, far from being accidental, becomes
a constructive principle. (He chooses this way, HRW) instead of
deliberately and methodologically becoming a *pluralist*. One could
object that Bergson's problem formulation, which alone justifies
the usefulness of such an ideal-typical construction, demands
only two planes. Therefore, intermediate stages could be ignored.
However, this is not the case.
  The following presuppositions make for the incompleteness (of
Bergson's theory, HRW):

    The historically conditioned limitations of the sciences of his
      time;
    A taking-for granted of 'the givens' (so of the social world) which
      today, becomes more and more problematic;
    The selection of a biological natural-science orientation as path
      into metaphysics, emphasizing most of all things relevant for
      a biological conception of life and development;
    The overrating of *action*, in no way justified, as constituent
      of (a) memory, (b) intellect, (c) the material world and thus
      of time and causality.

Where is the realm of drives, of values, of the Thou?

Bergson knows that contexts are concealed through symbol formations, particularly through language, and he puts into account the fact of 'symbol deception'; but he does not investigate the origin and growth of these symbol systems in their relevance for the planes of consciousness. (Is the 'symbol' experienced in the same fashion as the fundamental phenomena of consciousness, so duration, or different - and if so, how?) Therefore, he does not recognize intermediary stages. Only an unambiguous distinction of the latter will make it possible precisely to circumscribe the 'problem of founding' and therewith Bergson's problem formation as well as to find solutions to other questions which occupy philosophy and in particular epistemology.

The problem of founding is an old problem of philosophy
It occurs in various disguises. Two main examples - many could be cited - are: (a) the problem of apriority, and (b) the 'primacy' of practical reason. Both demonstrate that the basic problems cannot be solved when reduced to one plane. Their investigation merely in terms of the logical-cognitive formation of concepts must needs conflict with all data which are directed upon experience.[4]
Kant limited metaphysics to the epistemological question: How are synthetical judgments a priori possible? He also confined religion to the sphere of mere reason. These restrictions show the limits of the intellectualization of these realms but not the boundaries of the realms themselves. They all are open to experience on the far side of these limitations. Likewise, the apriori itself was relativized through epistemology. We point to deeper areas which are inaccessible to an epistemological formalism. This clearly manifests itself, for instance, with regard to all essential questions of *life* which are encountered, by pure reason, merely as antinomies or contradictions. Finally, the Kantian 'moral imperative in me' and its derivative, the primacy of practical reason, merely show the renunciation, by the intellect, of the foray into the realm of life.
But is it truly the inadequacy of our intellect which leads us to this partial agnosticism? Kant himself answers this question. He formulates the synthetic unity of apperception as the uppermost principle of every use of reason and he differentiates between the objective unity of self-consciousness and the subjective unity of consciousness, considering the latter a mere designation of the inner sense. Having done this, he feels compelled to admit that the manifold must needs be given in apperception before Reason can accomplish the synthesis; it is independent of it. However, it remains undetermined ('Kritik der reinen Vernunft' and earlier):

Because should I imagine a reason who apperceives himself, like maybe a divine one, who not only imagines non-existing objects but through whose imagination the objects themselves would be

simultaneously given and created, the categories - in the face
of such a realization - would have no significance whatsoever.
They are rules for a reason whose whole capacity exists in
thinking, that is, in the action which brings into the unity of
apperception the synthesis of the manifold which, otherwise,
was given him in perception. Therefore, for himself he *recognizes* nothing; he merely connects and orders the materials of
cognition, the perception of which has to be given to him
through the object.

In this sense, Kant also executes the separation between 'inner
sense' and apperception (pp. 165ff). The first occurs as a mere
form of apperception without connection with the manifoldedness
of perception, the latter as source of all connections with 'the
manifold of perception as such under the label of the categories
prior to all sensory perception of objects as such' (p. 166).[5]
    These passages show that the whole (Kantian, HRW) transcen-
dental logic is tailor-made for cognition. Yet, by definition, the
latter has already cut out a well-defined sector from reality,
selected according to the same principles which are postulated a
priori as ultimate logical necessities *(Denknotwendigkeiten)*.
According to Kant, the free creative life which produces the
'apperceived' simultaneously in 'apperception' lies beyond the
categories. If applied to these realms, they become meaningless
and purposeless. It is characteristic of reason to make certain
selections from that which is given and to symbolize these selections as if they were the whole. To symbolize means to execute
certain changes on the 'givens' of our life for specific purposes.
The selection of materials is determined by this purpose. Therefore, the question of an Apriori, an immediacy, is relativized to
a degree which makes the answer relevant only for a very small
area of real life.
    Seen from this angle, the Apriori turns from a differentiation
between the mediate and the immediate into a differentiation between that which can be communicated and that which cannot be
communicated. Different gradations are possible; therefore, the
Apriori, in principle, remains capable of relativization. The self-
contemplation of reason, the subsumption of the sensory manifoldness under categories, the transcendental schematism of pure
rational concepts - all are obviously of symbolic character. That
means they are abbreviations for more complex events which,
through extraction of one aspect, become simpler because easier
to comprehend rationally. Further, it is uncontested that language,
the basis of all logical-cognitive operations, represents in itself
a symbol system. This system transforms the true stock of life
data in a highly complex manner. Therefore, logicians should
treat it only with great caution. What is situated beyond these
two symbol systems, seems to be immediate or non-communicable.
Thus, for logic, the sensory manifoldedness already becomes a
given which cannot be reduced further. Likewise, individual
experience as such, which cannot be identical with the experience

accessible to a multitude, becomes ineffable for language - and
the more so the closer it is situated to the boundaries of the
'intimate person.' In the light of this, it can be easily established
that there are, (1) on the one hand, a series of experiences
which, being ineffable, cannot even reach the threshold of
language; and (2) on the other hand, a series of 'modes of communication' which - because situated beneath language - seize
experiences which occur in a layer deeper than that which is
accessible to language. Under (1) fall all phenomena of duration,
body consciousness, the Thou; and (2) communication through
the given body (body as 'field of expression,' erotic relations,
etc.), music, dance, pitch of voice, etc.

It seems that there exist, between the Kantian antithesis of
sensuality and cognition or between Bergson's duration and
reason, a series of *intermediate stages*. Each of them is adequate
to a different 'symbol sphere'; the relation among them is that of
relative non-communicability. It is just for this reason that they
are accepted as 'immediate.'

Non-communicable, here, shall mean that the experiences of the
deeper (= less complex) intermediate stage, although understandable in its own characteristic symbol system, are non-transferrable
into the higher (= more complex) sphere. It is even possible, by
following the boundary lines of these symbol systems, to make
cuts through the totality of life.

Here an important correction is necessary. Just below the realm
of language, 'communicability' loses its meaning as criterion -
provided one is not inclined to designate as communicability the
ability to make one's own experience evident in consciousness.
Here, completely clearly, the significance of the Thou problem
manifests itself. However, those relations which we designated as
'communicable' do not stop with the accentuation of the Thou.
Even within the most intimate sphere occurs the continuation of
the stratification (of layers of experiences and symbols, HRW),
accompanied by adequate symbol systems through which the
evidence of these experiences enters consciousness. For this
reason, we will call these individual planes appropriately not
planes of communicability but planes of consciousness. And this
also because in them manifests itself a particular stance of the I
do to the world: the I in an actually given place of consciousness
(= this is always only an artificially selected part of the total I =)
the life form of the I.

Of course, an infinite number of such planes of consciousness
of life forms can be projected into the totality of the real ego.
Which of them is selected remains a question of purpose.

The following basic considerations prevail. The total world as
object of experience stands opposite to each life form. In principle,
all experiences of the total I enter into *every* life form. But each
experience (gains awareness, HRW) only in the life form which is
adequate to the actual given consciousness. That means, the
experiences undergo different changes within the individual planes
of consciousness in which they attain evidence. We designate as

symbolization that process of transformation to which experiences
are subjected when they enter into the specific stance of life
which we call consciousness. And we designate as symbols the
transformed experiences which have been turned into evidence.

Evidence is the experience of being Now and Thus affected by
experiences. It is the sole aprioristic presupposition of our
speculations but not of our life. This life, as *our* life, is accessible to us even in the lowest life forms. On the strength of its
existence, it re-enters the Now and Thus of the evidence.

The principal thesis is that all experiences of the total I enter
into every life form. It is subjected to the restriction that all
experiences enter into the given life forms only as symbols. The
changes thereby affected have the following consequence: The
experiences of the deeper life forms enter into the higher ones
only after passing through innumerable processes of symbolization; thus, their Now and Being-Thus no longer affect the consciousness of higher planes. It is only by their *existence* that
they give a specific coloring to life or the total stance of the I.

In reverse, it is impossible for the symbol system of higher
forms of life to affect the Being-Thus of deeper experiences;
they can do no more than state their existence. On their part,
deeper experiences express the evidence of their Being-Thus
through the symbol system adequate to a deeper layer. The tension between experiences as existing and as Being-Thus is a
trade mark of the artificial ideal-typical structure of the introduced
concept of life forms. This is so because life itself finds ever
only that which is Now and Being-Thus; it does not grasp existence without Being-Thus.

The totality of life demands a characterization of the I who be
becomes cognizant of this totality. Kant's difficulties in ascertain-
ing this I (necessitate the choice of, HRW) our point of departure:
the Bergsonian duration.

(3) ON DURATION, SYMBOLIZATION, AND LIFE

Bergson offers several metaphorical images for describing the
flow of duration: it is like a tune without music, a rubber band,
a course or stream (see his 'Introduction into Metaphysics').

Characteristics of the stream of duration are: (a) continuity
(transcendence of the Now and Thus), (b) manifoldedness,
(c) irreversibility, and (d) stream as that which streams. These
characteristics are said to be testable through intuitive meditation
about one's own duration. This has to be countered by the argument that 'pure duration' remains an unexecutable hypostasis
because the last stratum to which we can penetrate is already
'memory-endowed.' This is so because:

(a)   Consciousness of the 'past,' that is, continuity and trans-
      cendence of the Now and Thus already presupposes

memory. Otherwise, I would have only many 'Now and
Thus' experiences placed side by side without cohesion.
I could not reach the continuity into the future (past and
anticipation).

(b) A manifold exists only for *memory*; without it, the differentiation between homogeneous/heterogeneous would be
meaningless.

(c) 'Irreversibility,' too, can only be ascertained in memory;
it could never become 'evident' within 'pure' duration
although continuity exists within it.

(d) The 'stream of that which streams' becomes meaningful only
if juxtaposed to the achievements of memory.

Actually, duration and memory are by Bergson in principle coordinated; they are reciprocally founded by each other. Bergson's
starting point is a life form which is more complex and symbol-
penetrated: that of memory-endowed duration. This is not a fault
because it merely contains the admission that *pure duration* can
only be deduced with the help of the symbol system of the more
complex life form (memory): it is impossible immediately to *experience* pure duration, even by intuition. Nevertheless, the givenness of memory presupposes the presence of the four characteristics, as stated above, in deeper (that is, memoryless, HRW) life
forms. I do not intend to assert the impossibility of pure duration
without memory (so, the duration of plants) but only the impossibility of experiencing it *immediately* in the sense of 'evidence.'
This merely means that evidence (as 'Being-Thus' experience of a
'Now and Thus') can only appear in a least complex symbol sphere
which can occur in memory. Pure duration is a necessarily marginal
concept, an unexecutable postulate, like its counterpart immor-
tality. Thus, in this investigation, I can only speak of a 'relative
approximation of duration.' The reason for this is the necessity
to assume the existence of a symbol-free life form below memory
combined with the impossibility to reach below memory.

(Pure duration is a postulate of a symbol-free life which is
inaccessible to our symbol-conditioned thinking, nay, even to our
still symbol-conditioned intuition.) Every symbolization has to
step out of duration because:

(a) an experience is grasped as Now and Thus which is
transcended in the mere stream of duration.

(b) Unity (homogeneity) is posited in place of the manifold
(heterogeneity).

(c) That which did pass is maintained; this could not happen
within the irreversible stream of duration.

(d) Therefore, experience is posited as having passed.

Symbolization begins already with 'being conscious' of the past
(continuity) of our duration; thus, with memory. Also duration
as stream is *relative* for every life form; if not for the immediate
experience so for every *conscious* experience and thus also for

primary *evidence* as *experience of experiencing*.[6]

The characteristics of 'memory' are in truth characteristics of every *symbol*. This is so because memory in itself has already symbol character. To wit, every symbol is tension between what has passed and what is passing relative to that life form whose 'content' becomes the foundation of the process of symbolization.

This is linked to the attempt at positing a system of relevance for the 'momentarily actual I.' Every analysis of consciousness . . . finds itself compelled to make this attempt in so far as each of these systems of relevance are relatively 'pre-given' to the super-ordinated symbol system.

It must be remembered that the analysis (to be offered in this book, HRW), with all its difficulties is merely a reflection about life, never life itself. *Life itself* does not need a 'system of relevance' . . . and a regress to deeper planes of consciousness: all states of consciousness are contained in the momentarily given Now and Thus of the total I and constitute it. There is no difference between experience and symbol because the latter too becomes experience and constitutes the Thus of the Now. There is no positing of the having-passed (the dead) in the possibility of that which lives Now. Due to this, life *as streaming experience* is simultaneously *meaning-free* and necessarily *meaningful* because it is symbol-related in *looking-back* (reflection). If I were alive only as streaming I, 'consciousness' of 'I' would solely occur in the form of 'I stream' *(Ich dauere)*.[7]

Now, we reflect constantly in the sphere of the total I. This is because consciousness is already = reflection = interpretation, we can posit 'I' *meaningfully* only as 'I stream.' *Meaning* is solely contained in the transformation of selected past experiences into becoming symbols. 'Now' is only meaningful in relation to 'earlier'; 'Being-Thus' is only meaningful in relation to a different 'Being-There' *(Dasein)*. For this reason, all meaning and symbol systems are relative because they (a) are coming from a Now and Thus and (b) are directed upon a past experience. . . . In every case, however, they are meaningful only in contemplation and for the I who surrenders to the stream of life.

NOTES
(written by HRW)

1   The term syncretism is usually used negatively as a label for an uncritical mixing-together of elements from various philosophical systems. Schutz seems to introduce it here with a positive connotation, meaning a treating-together of 'things' which have been arbitrarily separated by the criticized analytical method.

2   The figures 1, 2, 3 were written at the end of this paragraph. They could have been meant as indicators of successive footnotes, since three notes were set down at the bottom of the

page. However, it seems more likely that the three notes indicate three additional points Schutz intended to insert between this and the next paragraph. Leaning to the second explanation, I have placed them in the text.

3 According to the Cartesian theory of occasionalism, seemingly causal relations (e.g. between spirit and body) are merely occasioned by a third agent; they do not originate in the necessities of the corresponding phenomena themselves.

4 During his years of study, and possibly up to 1924, Schutz subscribed to a neo-Kantian position. The following para-graphs mark his radical departure from this philosophical approach.

5 I was unable to ascertain which edition of Kant's writings Schutz was using.

6 This short paragraph has been lifted from a different short manuscript of UM 1925-1927a.

7 In ordinary German language, the verb *dauern* means to last, to persist. In this context, Schutz plays on his translation of Bergson's term, 'durée' by the noun *Dauer* but links the corresponding verb *dauern* to the meaning of the French noun. To translate the statement 'Ich dauere' literally by 'I persist' would be grossly misleading.

PART I
Theory of Life Forms and Symbol Concept

Editor's note

According to Schutz's outline, the first part of this project was to serve three purposes. The first was to introduce the concepts of life form and symbol in their general ideal-typical structure. Secondly, it was to offer the analysis and discussion of six specific life forms, representing cross-sections of an actually continuous life of consciousness and forming a hierarchy of ideal types in ascending order, ranging from the spontaneous flow of inner duration to the highest forms of rational thinking. Finally, a general treatment of the concept of symbol relations and the concept of meaning was foreseen.

The first main part is the only one which Schutz managed to execute to a substantial degree. Yet, it was broken off before the analysis of the fifth life form had been finished. Nevertheless the themes of symbol relations and meaning have found considerable attention in the given text, since they were needed for the treatment of the relationship of adjacent life forms to one another.

Schutz sectioned off the manuscript into numerous parts, separated by dividing lines. I have numbered these sections and provided them with adequate sub-titles.

This manuscript offered the relatively greatest difficulties for the translator and posed serious problems for the editor. After careful consideration, I decided to circumvent the seven quasi-mathematical diagrams and their algebraic denotations which Schutz introduced into the manuscript and discussed at considerable length. In justification of this circumvention, I state the following: The 'mathematization' of parts of Schutz's expositions served merely illustrative purposes. It cannot possibly serve any function in the development of the substantive argument. To the contrary, it shows Schutz resorting to extreme quantitative means for the description of by definition unquantifiable happenings and experiences, all located in or connected with 'inner duration.' This purely qualitative concept of Bergson, for instance, is in utter opposition to the linear conception of a mathematical continuum which, in addition, consists of an infinite series of discrete points laid out in space.

As the reader will learn from remarks of Schutz, found both in the text and in notes, he himself was highly concerned with undoing the unwarranted effects of his quasi-mathematical illustrations. He was, of course, completely aware of the general paradox of speaking about inner duration in a language which, as Bergson said, laid out everything in space, and knew that the language of a mathematical formalism drives the spatialization of time to its uttermost extreme.

That there was no inner necessity for making use of this formalism is demonstrated by Schutz's discussion of duration and inner
time in 'Der sinnhafte Aufbau' of 1932. Here, he expressed the
gist of his earlier expositions in terms of a language which, in
spite of its pragmatic character, at least allows for description
with the help of qualitatively-descriptive terms.
    I suggest that Schutz, in the mid-1920s, used quasi-mathematical
illustrations for pedagogical reasons. He planned to address himself to fellow intellectuals who, like him, had a good general
mathematical training and could be expected to gain an easier
access to the strange considerations of Bergson if they faced it
first in, for them, convenient mathematical terms and made the
corrections later. Whether such expectations were justified, I am
unable to decide. In any case, fifty-five years later and for an
English-speaking audience - at least in North America - the effect
of an illustrative mathematization would likely to be the opposite
of that expected at the time from a German-Austrian readership.
It would confuse the issues even more than any ordinary descrip-
tive language could.

In this part as well as the second part, consecutive page numbers
(p. 1, p. 2, etc.) appear in the margins. They indicate the pages
on which the given text begins in the German original manuscripts.
They will be helpful to anyone who wishes to compare the translation with the original text in the German edition of these studies
or with the original manuscripts on microfilm.

Life Forms and Meaning Structure

(1) IMAGES, DURATION, SPACE AND TIME

My experiencing I is placed into the cosmos. I may allow the latter   p.1
to affect me; and I may take the world into myself, without cognitively objectifying it, simply as stuff of my being-here and as
material of my existence: accepting, processing, and transforming
it. If I accept the World not as mental representation but as experience, the abundance of its phenomena yields to me 'images'
which, although differentiated, are not at all heterogeneous.[1]
   They are differentiated: when I move, within finite spheres, in
various directions, I seem to move toward the infinity of that
which is forming itself. Nevertheless, these differentiations are
unitary; all these experiences belong *to me*. The experiences of
my environment are different in quality, quantity, and possibly
also in intensity; they are most differentiated in their intentional
content. Yet, they unify themselves in the experience of my own
I in a manifold unity which is not merely the unity of my consciousness (in the logical sense). Between nature and art, God and
world, feeling and spirit, the sensuate and the supernatural, I
experience this many-colored life colorful and undifferentiated as
a constant change in the mode of succession. I differentiate it
only afterwards and artificially on reflection. Only conceptually
do I grant the quality of coexistence to the separate phases of my
ideal I.
   Many dreams leave in the awakening person at first nothing but
the vague feeling of having experienced something. The situation   p.2
which caused - or more accurately accompanied - the dream experience reveals itself only after some reflection. Similarly, all
that which is observed, felt, and enjoyed during the experience
of a summer evening, remains closely bound to this experience in
its unity - even though only for its duration. That which is
remembered differentiates itself into mountain and lake, sun and
tree, ringing of the bell and conversation, movement of the row-
boat and color of the woods only for the consciousness which turns
back (to an experience after it has passed away, HRW) and now
forms sharply delimited images. Established in retrospect, their
simultaneous side-by-side makes the experience, 'summer evening,'
comprehensible and easily remembered. But, nevertheless, reflection is not capable of bringing back the experience.[2]
   What resulted for us originally was only an ever-changing but
steady succession, a unitary but manifold development of the
experience of the I. For reasons still to be given, it cannot be

31

communicated in concise form, and therefore not at all.

The first philosopher who forced modern philosophy to accept
this basic difference between experiences as such and the reflection about experiences - a difference important for many reasons
- was Bergson. He showed, for the first time, the unity of the
manifold in the stream of duration whose criterion is continuous
change of quality. He was the first to make matter, as an order
of memory images, into a function of memory.

But already Bergson has pointed out that we are rarely allowed
to self-contemplate the experiencing I, to become absorbed in pure
duration. Our I-experience is banished into time and space; it is
tied to consociates through language and emotions; it is accustomed
to thinking, that is, to spatialize streaming changes of quality
p.3   and to form them into concepts. Therefore, we have to push aside
the whole layer of our habits of thinking and living in order to
achieve a first primitive surrender to duration. This is so because
our world of thinking, our concepts, our science demonstrate
their time-space character at every move. Nothing, however, can
suppress the experience of continual change of quality more than
the constant reflection on the world around us. Reflection represents a realm of side-by-side quantities; even movement, which
most resembles duration, is spatialized through concepts. Our
adaptation to commerce with the external world and our acquisition
of habits of thinking have forced us to replace our experience of
duration by the experience of space and time, and to remain en-
tangled in reflection and thinking. Our experiencing is almost
ever coupled with reflection about the experience. We control ourselves by our thinking; often we are unable to see the image on
account of the concepts. Our consciousness of the stream of duration holds on only timidly to the unambiguous 'now' and 'thus',
using them as rigid boundaries between which we squeeze our
experiences-turned-into-concepts.

At first glance, it seems to be most of all one circumstance
which forces me to exchange the subjective experience of duration
with the conceptual experience of time and space, nay more, to
project duration into time and space. This is the fact that I live
in duration not alone. I am surrounded by objects which exist
simultaneously with me. I know about consociates, that is, of
other egos who experience their own duration and whose consciousness flows similarly to mine. Initially, we shall examine this dual
experience of the object and the knowledge about a Thou and we
shall investigate whether and in what way we are thereby forced
to modify our experience of duration. Further, we will examine
p.4   the means at our disposal for unifying in our consciousness the
two realms of our existence: the experience of the I in duration
and the Thou experience in space and time. Further, we will try
to ascertain, within the realm of science, the systematic possibility
of the recognition of this state of fact.

(2) THE PASSAGE FROM DURATION TO SPACE-TIME

The experience of space and matter became a major problem of
philosophy long before Kant. The central point of the Aristotelian
logic and of the whole medieval scholastic is the concept of substance. Since Kant, the problem received a different formulation,
but did not lose anything in significance. The 'Kopernican turn'
of Kant did not concern the question of the essence of the object
but our possibility of cognitively realizing the object. This reversal of the question subsequently proved itself extremely fruitful.
But it presupposed a fundamental insight into the nature of the
world outside ourselves which was apriorily given and relegated
the conception of the 'phenomenon' into a pre-scientific sphere.
Thus, the transsubstantiation of the sensorily perceptible into a
conceptual-categorical recognizable had to be made possible
through the mystery of the transcendental schematism. The experience which, according to the system, was focusing on the
external world, could only in this way be brought in agreement
with the (neither denied nor considered) discrepancy between
the intensive experience of continuous quality changes and the
quantifiable discontinuum (of space and time fulfilled). Now, when
the Kantian philosophy demonstrated space and time as pure forms
of our thinking, it deliberately banned from its field of vision
the experience of the concept of space (and thus of matter)
through apriorization. It limited itself to demonstrating that   p.5
phenomena are given to our senses and that space and time are
a-priorily given prior to all thinking and, in fact, making the
latter possible. Starting with the configuration of experience of
science, and especially of mathematical natural science, it made
the latter possible and produced a critique of pure reason, that
is, of scientific experience. It demonstrated the laws of scientific
experience which themselves were conditioned in many ways. It
had to renounce the efforts to assume that scientific experience
is secondary and that space and time is relative. And it was right
in doing so. It found as object of its investigations an intellectual
world in which, indeed, space and time were postulated as a-
priorily given. In the course of our investigation, we hope to
show why this is so: the world of space and time, into which we
are placed in the experience of our inner duration, is socially
conditioned by way of memory and Thou experience; and our
'concepts' (in the sense of the original materials of our experience)
are erected upon the socially conditioned fundament of the linguistic symbol. The transition from the world of the inner I experience
to the outer world of the Thou is already executed in memory
image and symbol.
   To clarify this difficult linkage, we will initially try to retrace
the path from the inner experience of pure duration to the concept
of space. We will do this on hand of Bergson's conception, especially as formulated in his later writings. Thereafter, we will
speak about the phenomenon of memory and, after closer inspection of this fundamental factum, to derive the symbol from it.

Having made ourselves familiar with these basic factual complexes,
we may calmly return to the social world of space and time, of
p.6   concepts and experience. But more, we have to do it if we want
to come close to the actual purpose of these investigations: the
grounding of the social sciences in the Thou experience. Practis-
ing science, we will intentionally move within the sphere of the
'space-timely' conditioned concept. In reverse, it will therefore
be our task to investigate in what way is possible a science, that
is, a conceptually-categorically comprehensible 'series of experiences' of the Thou. The experience of the thou by far precedes
conceptual-categorial comprehension. The former conditions the
latter and makes it possible just by resisting it. We will ask which
method such a science would have to use in order to lift the
irrational fundamental experience of the thou out of its own
specific sphere and to transfer it into the rational realm of science
without abandoning the circle of 'symbols,' to wit, the language-
directed concepts of experience.

(3) DURATION OBSERVED

When I lock out all sensory impressions and turn completely into
myself, I become aware of a steady and continuous change, a
continuous transition of qualities which is comparable to a melody.
I distinguish an altered Before which through change became a
Now. This Now itself, however, having become noticed by me,
passed at that very moment into a Before by way of a change of
which I became conscious with the help of my memory. But, by
making these considerations, I already have left the sphere of
the pure experience of duration. Only by remembering a Before
have I been able to get hold of the qualitatively different Now. I
have 'made present' the immediately following Now only through
letting it become rigid, through fixation by fiat as the Now which
just was, as one qualitatively different from the other. Intentionally disrupting the eternal stream, I formed an image of my
p.7   inner 'condition' out of the Now, which is just forming itself, and
the Now which just had been. This image was preserved in my
memory; through comparison, it shows to me my present 'I am'
in contrast to my 'I was.' Thus, if I wish to distinguish the
qualitative change in my sphere of the stream of duration, I have
to fixate, as it were, some points in the course of my inner experience. I will have to have noticed the second-last tone of the
melody in order to know whether the tone sounding now is higher,
lower, stronger, weaker, or of different timbre – in short, whether
it is different from its predecessor. I achieve this by an artificial
process, through an image which I form in my memory.
  If I now open my eyes and look around, I notice images of
objects which are in movement or in rest, which are changeable
or, apparently, non-changeable. I become aware of my body as
an image in the outer world. While writing these lines, I see my
hand executing movements on this paper; I remember that I in-

tended to make these movements. Now, they participate in my
inner duration as well as they are perceived by me in the outer
world. At first, these images are for me mere qualities of my I,
states of my duration. If I lift my eyes from a piece of paper,
covered with letters, and look through the window at the landscape, 'paper' and 'landscape' are only conspicuous qualities of
two moments of my being.

Nevertheless, I can co-ordinate exactly several such qualities
with every moment of my duration. While writing this down, I see
my hand slide across the paper; I hear the scratching of the pen;
I smell the smoke of my cigar; I feel the warmth of the stove; and
I am aware of the position of my body at the desk. All these
moments, and many others neither named nor countable, constitute the experience of my being-Now-and-Thus. In a minute, a   p.8
comparison of them will enable me to establish the quality differences between the moment which had been a Now but did just
pass, and the moment which just now became a Now.[3] However, if
I frequently make such comparisons among the images which I
find as qualities in my experience of duration, I notice series of
images which remain unchanged. That means, they codetermine
the quality of my earlier Now as well as that of my present Now.
First of all, I notice this quality of belonging-to-the-moments-of-
my-duration on my body. Always in a different position, it is
always sensed by me as an image of the outer world and as an experience in my duration. Thus, it is most of all that I know my
body to be everlastingly coordinated to every phase of my being.
But, strictly speaking, I know this also only by comparing a Now
with a Before, the latter having been preserved in my memory.

This comparing activity of memory becomes still clearer with
regard to objects which, in contrast to my body, are not consistently coordinated with the course of my inner duration. For the
contemplation of my inner being there is not yet an 'object'; for
it, there exists no being-outside at all but only images of changing quality. It is exactly the task of this investigation to pursue
the process in which we project these images into the outside,
thereby discovering the realized *(erfuellten)* space and, with
and in it, the qualities of matter and time.   p.9

We mentioned earlier already that the comparison of the phases
of our duration shows a series of qualities which are common to
several of its phases.[4]

By way of mathematical analogy we may say that we 'take out'
and 'put in brackets' these unchanging qualities. Through this
activity of our comparing memory, we obtain groups of qualities
which belong together and of which we can say that they partake
in our duration. We grant these groups persistence in the always-
changing stream of our experiences in duration. Therefore, they
will have to show a continuity similar to that of our duration;
they must have something in common with this duration. On the
other hand, they must also be basically different from our duration: with the exception of our body, they signify for us quality
experiences only in stretches. In fact, there exists a common

quality in all these groups by virtue of which they are different from the quality of our experiences of duration. This is the quality of extension of matter.

In stating this, we anticipated a result supposed to be produced by our investigation. We recognized and identified the quality of

p.10

matter, with the help of our memory, as something extended, and extension as similar to our duration. Therewith, we have already abandoned the experience of our duration. Duration is manifold and unextended; yet it is a continuum. It can get hold of extension and discontinuity - the two criteria of the space-time world - only in the artificial process of remembering. Thus, the formulation attempted above seems to be paradoxical. But this paradox is merely apparent. It disappears in the closer investigation of the mechanics of the process in which our memory transforms the flowing and becoming of mere continuing qualities into the concepts of extension and matter.

(4) MEMORY PARTICIPATES IN DURATION

We said already: our duration is a continuum of changing experiences of quality. We cannot force the stream of our experiencing into form without thereby abandoning the realm of duration. Embossed form is opposed to living unfolding. We transform being-becoming into being-of-that-which has-been-formed. That which has been formed, however, belongs to the existing and delimited realm of concepts. There is nothing stable in the course of duration. Speaking exactly, there is not even a 'Thus and Now' because, as statement, 'Thus and Now' appears in time. As an activity, it claims a fraction of the time, while my inner duration continues to flow.

How do we recognize differentiation in the flow of our duration? This question was posed in the previous section where we tried to follow the comparative activity of memory on hand of the example of the body. But this formulation was provisional, and less precise as required. We clarified only that we become aware

p.11

of a preceding change through the comparing function of our memory. As yet, we did not speak about the fact that our memory itself participates in the manifoldedness of our duration. Nay, more: on the one hand, it effects the change of quality; on the other hand, like anything immediately given in consciousness, it changes itself differentiatingly and continually with and in duration. We intend now to investigate these two phenomena but state already now that our formulations will come closer to the actual state of affairs but will represent still provisional states of transition.

Let us imagine a concentration of our attention exclusively on a single object. For the sake of simplicity, we choose an unanimate object, maybe an ancient coin which a researcher scrutinizes under a magnifying glass. He prefers to use artifical light in order to avoid being distracted by the play of sunlight on metal from his observation of the coin itself. For the time being, we abstain from considering the inscription of the coin which would have to be deciphered. Our researcher does not know the meaning of the signs in an unknown language; he merely wants to make a drawing of this coin in order to reproduce its character as faithfully as possible. A first glance allows him to see a blurred, scrambled mixture of lines, little differentiated from each other. But, in concentrated prolonged scrutiny, the structure of the inscription becomes clear and impressive; it is simple to transfer it exactly on the drawing. One says, the eye has accustomed itself to the observed object. What did happen? How can one explain that the same object under unchanged external conditions (light,　p.12 position, etc.) provided two different images?

The following hypothesis may provide a plausible explanation. We said, no 'moment' of our inner being can be equal to the one which preceded it. If we want to convince ourselves of this fact, we have only to consult our memory. It has faithfully registered everything 'before'; now, it offers us the occasion to compare this memory report with the actual state of things of the 'Now.' Of course, we have to recall our memory image; but does this recall consist in the re-experience of the Before? Does 're-presenting' mean to enter the image of something past into the book of our memory, or do we merely consult this actual diary in order conveniently to re-read the notice we find there? Everything speaks against the second, many things against the first assumption. Because, if every 'remembering' indicated a new experience of the image, it would be impossible for us to distinguish between that which is actually experienced and that which is remembered. In reality, we can do this at any time.[5]

A still other phenomenon shows clearly that the first thesis does not apply. I refer to the enigmatic and still unclarified roles played in our inner experience by fantasy, be it of artistic or otherwise conceptive nature. Great similarities exist between fantasy experience and memory image; both functions of our I provide 'virtual' images. The factual circumstances become still more complicated through the fact that there are memory images of fantasies as well as of any other experience. Nevertheless, each of us clearly knows the difference between memory, directed toward the past, and fantasy, directed toward the future. In particular, artistic fantasy seems to offer important elucidations.　p.13 Starting with given materials, it takes a path into the future. The I of the artist follows it on this path in vicarious experiences. By contrast, our memory has absorbed only our experiences. Therefore, memory too belongs only to us and our earlier experience. It belongs, so to speak, totally to the I whose identity for us is beyond doubt by virtue of the experience of duration. By contrast, fantasy anticipates something in the future. It is as if it explodes the boundaries of our I; it seems to participate in the great enigma which all metaphysics left behind unsolved.

In particular, these circumstances seem to demonstrate that our memory, even without our asking, participates in, and registers every phase of our I. Every moment of our duration is the memory image of the preceding one plus an X. This X constitutes that which is essential for this moment; in fact, it is responsible for the unending variations of duration. In the case of our numismatic researcher, does possibly the same visual impression add itself once more to all already accepted visual impressions of the same object which have been stored in his memory? The same? Not at all. Apparently, nothing has changed. The coin still lies in the same place under the magnifying glass, which has not been moved. The light remained unchanged. Now as before, the attention of the researcher is undividedly aimed at the character of the inscription. He sees the same and he sees it anew. The experience of the inscription of the coin under the magnifying glass joins the memory images of many moments of inner duration, each of which had as its content the experience, 'inscription of the coin under the magnifying glass.' *For this reason,* a new image results; it did not exist before.

p.14   This observation is familiar to all of us. From experience, we all know enough examples for the fact that adding what is 'similar' means a change of quality in our experiencing.[6] One may only recall a noise which regularly repeats itself (ticking of a clock, miller and mill) and which we at first perceive as unpleasant; later, we 'do not hear it' any more. Again, if the noise grows in intensity with repetition, we experience it with a constant level of pain (judged by its cause).

To recapitulate: every moment of our duration contains, as virtual memory image, all earlier moments of our I. Memory makes duration into a manifold experience and thus conditions our actual inner life.

But, one may object, in how many cases does the appeal to memory fail? How little do we really remember? This objection is in no way justified, because our 'experiences' are falsified, materialized, socially conditioned - in short, they are conceptual. We think, that is, we live in our environment a totally different life as that of pure duration. Our habits of thinking suppress our *mneme* (*mens,* 'minne') and transform it into memoria. The German language took the same path from 'remembering' *(Erinnerung)* to 'memory' *(Gedaechtnis).* But if we succeed in transposing ourselves again into pure duration, we will be able again to 'become aware' of those experiences which belong to our own duration.

p.15   The recognition that our memory preserves a complete and continuous image of our inner duration, however, explains the fact that it partakes in our inner duration and changes with and in it.

I recall an experience of my school years which, at the time, deeply shook and tormented me but now, my remembrance is friendly. I came across a letter which I wrote years ago, and which renewed the pain of this experience. Both times I thought of the same event. But how much has it changed! How did it become, for him who escaped the tormenting and fear-ridden atmosphere of the school, an idyllic image? In the intervening time, I have lived through much; I have become 'older' and 'more mature, and my memory with me.

Here, I have intentionally used a phenomenon of the emotional
life as an example; the discrepancy of memories becomes especially
clear in the case of affectual experiences. But the memory of
specific objects of the outer world, too, shows changes of this
kind. Countless examples for this are provided in daily life.

However, now we must ask whether, by introducing this dual
function of our memory, we again go beyond the circle of our
problem configuration. On the one hand, we asserted that it is
our memory which conditions the manifoldedness of our duration.
On the other hand, we stated that our memory changes with us
and our duration. In short, it also is duration. As in the case of
our body, we stated now that a moment of the flow of our memory
is coordinated to every moment of our duration. Did we, then, not
artificially double our I by transposing all functions of duration   p.16
to memory, which belongs to but is not identical with it? With this
dualization, did we not rob the I of its existence? Is there, maybe,
duration *only* in the flow of memory?

At the present stage of our considerations, this serious objection cannot be refuted. We merely set it down. It will still occupy
us in various contexts. Hopefully, it will allow us to show that the
problem arose from the intermingling of the sphere of pure duration with the sphere of the world which evolved in space and
time. However, already now will we have to point out that this
objection will become indispensable for the solution of our problem.

(5) REALITY IMAGE AND MEMORY IMAGE: THE PROBLEM

After these statements, we will take up the preliminary formulation
of the existence of space and objects and the provisional derivation
of the 'concept' extension at the point, at which we interrupted
it. We will check whether we are already in a position to replace
the provisional formulation by another one - not less problematic
but nevertheless closer to the truth.

Starting with the change of quality, we had observed that we
become aware of these changes only through what we called the
comparative function of our memory. Only the combination and
ordering of these comparisons leads to the establishment of the
fact that several quality groups (my body, 'objects of the outer
world') display a 'steadiness' which is adequate to that of my
inner duration. We saw just now how this comparing function
operates. We realized that our memory absorbs all moments of
duration. This More is added to a Given. Through it, the 'reality
image,' which joins a 'memory image,' brings about that continuous change which forms the essence of our duration-experiences.   p.17
Now, we know how much the manifoldedness of our experience-
impressions depends on our memory; but we do not know anything
about the nature of the images as such. Originally, we assumed
that we will arrive at the 'object' through a comparing function
which, so to speak, provides us with unchanging groups of images
which, again, among themselves have in common certain 'quality

groups,' for instance, expansion. After the investigation of the
mechanism of our flow of memory, we have to realize that this path
does not lead to the object, to space, to time, in short, to anything external. This is so because these 'qualities' of extension,
of time, etc., enter so to speak automatically and without our
help into our memory images. They are contained in the image of
our 'Now' and 'Thus,' but just as qualities, as virtual and unextended images. We still have not broken through to the essence
of matter. We have not even clearly enough comprehended how
the reality image unites itself with the memory image and how, on
its part, it becomes memory image. Still less clear for us is the
capacity of establishing the 'sameness' of the two images of two
states of our I, or better, of establishing that certain quality
groups are common to several images.

Indeed, it seems that every speculation encounters here unsur-
mountable difficulties. The relation between image and object,
duration and spacetime, sensation and concept, in one word the
problem of cognition itself, shows itself here completely inaccessible. We cannot comprehend how that which is not extended could
stand in any kind of relationship to that which is extended. All
attempts at explaining this mystery are either a humbly believing
p.18   credo, like the theory of the pre-established harmony, or hypotheses which aim at reducing that which is incomprehensible to
something which is no less incomprehensible. It is characteristic
of philosophy that its history displays a constant wavering between these two poles of explanation. Thus, modern philosophy,
tired from the Kantian struggle for a rational solution of the
problem, accepts as given the linkage between our mind and the
objects. It merely attempts to examine the functions of such
'recognition of essences' or 'relatedness to meaning,' 'value-
surrounded reality' or 'value experience,' or whatever complicated
names are assigned to the investigation of the epistemological
problem of judgment and concept, method and system.

Up to now, this study has tried to rather faithfully follow the
genial investigations of Bergson. He, too, had to face this question. But it occurs to me that he did not seek its solution. On
the contrary, he availed himself of several auxiliary means in
order to reject as irrelevant for his investigation the question:
'how does that which is extended reach that which is unextended,
the sensation the image, the object the concept, the outer the
inner?' The world presents itself to him as ultimately 'given' as it
does to Kant and all others. This, in fact, seems to be last resort
of all speculation. We live 'in' the world and we 'experience' 'the'
world. The world is 'object' only for our experience. Placed into
it, we use it as a 'circumstance of space and time.' Only the renun
ciation of the possibility of recognizing this state of things allows
us to recognize what is basic to it: the relations of our 'images,'
p.19   our 'concepts' among themselves on the one hand, and the relation
among the objects of the outer world on the other.[7]

This extended space-time world, into which we are placed, becomes in various ways perceivable to our I. This I experiences

inner duration, even if it may be denied to the human mind to
explain it rationally. Most of all, our body mediates between the
I, tied to pure duration, and the outer world which simply exists
for every consciousness. And this in two respects: First - as already said above - a quality image of our body is coordinated to
every moment of pure duration. However, this body has one
characteristic which it has in common with all other 'objects' of
the outer world: it is extended. Being evenly coordinated to our
inner I and the outer world, the body offers a particularly suitable link between the I and the outer world. It is an image among
other outer images, but it is very special and uniquely privileged
image; it is privileged because it is, for our I, more than an image
because it partakes in our duration. This leads to the second
function of the body which makes the recognition of the outer
world possible to a still higher degree. Our body is tool or carrier
of the *acting I*. However, for this acting I, in contrast to the
reflecting I, there no longer exists, according to Bergson, the
problem of the Inner and the Outer, even though it still belongs
to pure duration. For it, every apperception and every image   p.20
transforms itself immediately into movement which acts into the
outer world and, thereby, partakes in space, time, and matter.
Therefore, for this living, that is, acting, I exists no conflict
between pure duration and extended space-time, between that
which becomes and passes away in the flow of duration and that
which exists in space. It belongs equally to both spheres through
the transformation of that which is apperceived into action. Nay
more: apperception, subsumed under the powerful primacy of
action, already selects among the images. This selection is determined by the apparently potential action which is supposed to
release just this apperception in the I. Moving and moved, the
acting I places its duration twofold into the space-time world.
Therefore, for Bergson, movement must mean two things because
it must partake in inner duration as well as in the space-time
world. This, in fact, is so: movement, as flow, is that which
moves, belongs to inner duration; movement, as path followed
and as space traversed, is something external and extended and
thus quantifiable and measurable - in contrast to movement in
inner duration, which is continuous change of quality.
    In this way, Bergson tried to ignore the solution of the epistemo-
logical problem, in its usal form, in the formulation of his questions. He did this not inadvertently. He started with the correct
presupposition that the epistemological problem, in form of an
inquiry into the relation of the Inner to the Outer, is only possible
in a sphere which approaches the experience of our duration with
the help of language and concepts, and thus with the equipment
of the world conditioned by space and time. He only hints at that
which forthwith will occupy us most of all: word and concept as   p.21
tied to space and time. As Bergson thinks, the acting I may not
know of the contradiction because it participates in space and
duration. We are most of all interested in how and whereby the
'apprehending' (a reflecting, HRW) I or the I as such partakes

in the outer world by creating or acquiring concepts and language. We do not doubt that an outer world exists; as Berkeley did. We also do not investigate the relation of our duration, and of the images which unwind themselves in this manifold continuum, to the outer world and the objects which are located in discontinuous space. We do not pretend to solve the epistemological problem; we do not even try to do so. On the contrary, we will find justification in the avoidance of two dangers which the attempts at solving this problem contain in themselves: either to dissolve the world in Berkeley's ideas or else to postulate an Absolute Thing behind our sensations. We will try to demonstrate that the epistemological problem in this form has its solution in its presuppositions. That means, that the solution becomes possible at all only when we are sure of our belonging to the realm of duration as well as to that of the Extended. Therefore, we do not ask: how enters the extended object into my unextended apperception? How turns that which becomes and passes away into an Existing? But, at first, we ask: which path is traversed by the image when moving from pure duration to concept? What, for our consciousness which belongs to pure duration, differentiates becoming and passing-away from existing?

As stated, we will have to justify this event in two ways. We will have to demonstrate that the question of the relation of the object to the I, in fact, is only meaningful for a thinking which has already absorbed the elements of time and space yet, nevertheless, knows about the flow of inner duration. And further, p.22 we will have to investigate whether our I-in-duration is connected with the outer world also by another bridge aside from that of action and movement. One demonstration will yield the other, but we will reach it only after various discussions. However, before discussing the transformation of the image into the concept, we want to stop a bit in order to recall our aim, once more to review the path we have gone thus far, and to make sure of the direction in which we want to proceed.

(6)   THOU AND MEANING AS CONTENT OF EXPERIENCE:
       THE PROBLEM

This study aims at investigating the methods of the sociology of understanding. Max Weber had made this sociology into a science. He was sure of his method and his aim as only a few others were. Thus, he did not find it necessary to say much about the preconditions of his scientific undertaking. But he speaks all the clearer about his method as derived from his investigations. He abstained from constructing a concept of Society and from hypostatizing social relations into an 'as such.' Only the Thou, the consociate, was given to him. And further the fact that this Thou can be understood as being meaningful to himself and also to the person who asks him. The Thou, then, stands in the center of Weber's considerations. He intends to comprehend the Thou and

his meaning scientifically, that is, conceptually. However, this
Thou is different from all other objects of experience in that it
can be understood. Therefore, his comprehension demands a particular method. To exactly formulate this method is the purpose
of the main part of this study.

However, with the conceptual grasp of the Thou, understandability is presupposed but not clarified. We discover meaning contexts. But, as long as we remain in the sphere of sociology, we
cannot know more about 'meaning' as its existence, its forms, its   p.23
recognizability.

This study starts with the notion that 'Thou' and 'meaning' are
not primarily objects of experience but contents of experience.
Therefore, it places a deliberately 'pre-scientific' investigation of
the experience of duration and of meaning before the scientific-
conceptual analysis of these contents as objects of experience. It
hopes, from the realized uniqueness and specificity of these experiences, to gain knowledge for answering the question: according to the opinion of the author of the sociology of understanding,
which method has to be used by an experiential science of the
Thou.

However, this pre-scientific investigation is directed upon an
experience, and thus upon an experience which belongs to the I
and is widely remote from concept and object of experience. As
Bergson demonstrated, this I has pure duration as primary content. Therefore, we have to check the Thou experience of the I
and to establish how this experience becomes known to the I:
whether it still belongs to pure duration or to the realm of concepts; whether it is conditioned by the concept or whether it
conditions the concept which, certainly, is not primary; whether
'meaning' becomes possible only through the experience of the
Thou or whether the 'Thou' experience presupposes meaning
already.

However, the form of experience of the I, pure duration, had
to be considered. We had to start with the experiences of the I,
while ever anticipating the results, without paying attention to
the Thou and to 'meaning' relatedness. We have attempted this in
the preceding chapters.

The experience of pure duration as continual change of duality
was our starting point. Already here arose two questions: first,   p.24
the manifoldedness of pure duration as such was not recognizable:
By what means do we convince ourselves of the difference between
the 'Now' and 'Thus' and that which just has been? Provisionally,
we answered, through the comparing function of our memory. The
second question, however, concerned the cause of this manifoldedness itself. Also provisionally, we found the cause of this manifoldedness in our memory which preserves our memory images and
adds the experienced images to them.

Still, we had not yet reached the outside, matter, space, and
time. We tried first to explain the phenomenon of expansion in
terms of a group of qualities which, due to the comparing function
of our memory, had to be unchangeable and were as such kept in

memory. This attempt foundered pitifully on the recognition that
our memory maintains all experiences evenly without a specific
comparing function. In addition, the assertion of something 'remaining the same' in duration was coarsely inaccurate. Therefore,
we stopped trying to find a way from the experience of pure
duration to the outside of space and time. We noticed that we were
facing a form of the epistemological problem as such. Now, we
had to decide in which direction we should pursue our investigation next. We decided to leave aside the question of an Outer
and an Inner. Should we succeed in this, we will direct our attention again to the function of memory because we hope to find here
a partial answer to the last posed question of the path from image
to concept.

(7)   SCRUTINY OF THE RELATION BETWEEN EXPERIENCE
AND MEMORY: MEANING

p.25   Each of us who reflects about his life will be able to remember a
series of events which gave direction to his later fate. As a rule,
this is a matter of circumstances whose full significance transpires
only in retrospective survey. At the time, they were submerged
by other events, apparently being without significance or else
of no greater significance than many other events. How does it
come to pass that just these 'accidents,' seemingly irrelevant, gain
in retrospect importance for the total course of our life?

This example will bring us to a consideration of the nature of
the 'significance' of 'meaning.'

Analyzing our faculty of remembering, we stated two things:
First, memory stores the events of our inner duration without
our help. Second, it partakes in our inner duration and changes
with and in it. Now, what happens when we remember a specific
event of our life? Obviously, we direct our attention upon that
image of our experience which our memory picked up and registered. However, this memory image displays significant deviations
from the experience – a fact which we already mentioned and
which has several causes. Most of all, the irreversibility of the
flow of our inner duration conditions the discrepancy between
experience and memory image. We had defined inner duration as
continuous manifoldedness, stating thereby that, in every phase
of this flow, an as yet not existing x must be added to that which
is given.

Since anything which passed away has been integrated into our
memory, this new x can only consist of an additional experience.
Our duration flows unequivocally and continuously. While we add
new contents of experience to the experiences which we stored in
memory, we are getting older. It follows that an identity of
p.26   experiences with memory images is impossible. Such an identity
would have as precondition the reversibility of duration. Remembering a specific event consists essentially in the reproduction of a
memory image which has been removed from the flow of our duration.

[[The phenomena of memory are complex events. Let us depict inner duration mathematically as a semi-ray[8] propagating itself unilaterally from zero toward infinity. On it specific points are indicated, marking a specific 'moment' of experience turned into a memory image (B) and other points as later 'moments' of remembering the event for which the memory image stands (A, A^1, etc.). Any memory image is embedded into a long chain of memory images, some of earlier, others of later origin. Due to the continuity of inner duration, the memory image itself is a kind of combination   p.27 of all preceding experiences. It appears from an experience which itself changes the totality of the previous memories. By the same token, it changes with every moment of re-remembrance because in each interval new experiences have been added to memory. At face value, a certain image seems to be fixed by past experiences and memory images; yet, it varies with every new retrospective glance since new experiences have been made in the meantime. The retrospective 'moment' is actually a whole set of 'moments' no matter how short the time-intervals between them. Thus, the 'moment' of remembering itself flows along and changes; it too is variable.]]

Let us free ourselves of the diagram, which served only illus-   p.28 trative purposes. It contains an eminent danger for our problem: it spatializes the flow of duration.[9] Let us transfer the given considerations into the terminology which we have used so far.

Our memory has preserved for us all experiences of our inner duration up to the (present, HRW) Now and Thus and, therewith, also the experience which I now intend to evoke. However, at the moment of concentrated attention, my memory contains more and different images than those it contained at the moment of the experience which I want to take in focus. I have expressed myself here imprecisely. The nature of inner duration is constant change of quality. Hence, we cannot speak of 'more' images because inner duration does not allow any kind of quantification. I can only say that my memory image 'now' is different and more differentiated. And more, the flow of memory has something in common with the flow of inner duration, which it conditions: it too consists of a mesh and mixture of changing moments of quality. It is continu-   p.29 ous and manifold, and we become aware of our inner duration only through our memory. Therefore, I intentionally interrupt the flow of this continuum as soon as I 'pick out a point,' say the experience B. This experience has been absorbed into uncounted other experiences. Together with these, it has been carried forth in my memory; it has become part of my 'Now' and 'Thus.'

How do I pass from my (present, HRW) 'I am' to 'I was'? Obviously, my memory image B has not been completely absorbed by the memory images which followed it. My memory does not mechanically register the experiences of my inner duration; it affects them also in a different form: it *integrates* them.

In the moment A of my inner duration, actually I have not been able to recall the naked memory image of my experience B. Because this experience was a condition for moment A, it is contained in it.

I am not able to analyze the experience of the 'Now' and 'Thus' (of moment B, HRW) in order to arrive at B (the memory image, HRW). This would mean to grant the reversibility of pure duration (which is impossible, HRW). Yet, I am capable of remembering the experience. If memory had no other faculty than to register the images of my experiences, the dilemma would be insoluble. In fact, the problem cannot be solved as long as we continue to identify memory with pure duration. But let us pay undivided attention to the dual activity of 'memory.' On the one hand, we called memory the condition of the manifoldedness of our inner duration. As such, it seizes every experience; it flows 'with us' and it makes duration 'conscious' for us. On the other hand, we

p.30   spoke of the memory images of a specific experience. Thus, we lifted this specific experience out of the flow of pure duration. We have intentionally interrupted the continuous flow; actually, we spoke about something which no longer occurs in the pure experience of duration which is constant change of quality. The experience remembered is something which has been given a stable form; as such, it is only conditionally subject to quality change.

Nevertheless, we believe that we did not make a mistake when we used the term 'memory' for both phenomena: Absorption in the Now and Thus is common to both. The Now and Thus consists not merely of something different from something which was earlier. In it, too, I am conscious of the continuity of my duration. I am aware of the individual experiences which *I* have experienced. The unity of the I is a quality of every 'Now' and 'Thus.' This unity, however, consists of the awareness of that 'I was' as much as that 'I am.' We believe, then, that we have to justify the unity of memory by resorting to the most primary experience of pure duration, the experience of the unity of the I. What, at first, we encountered as two forms of memory now represents itself – in view of the unity of the I – as two functions of one and the same phenomenon.

As discussed, the function of memory is to make the continuum of pure duration into a manifold. It ties together the different moments of our being, which are differentiated in quality: *It is the awareness of the ongoing I.* With regard to its other function, to allow us to remember individual quality experiences of our I, we can only form a hypothesis. Its soundness will have to be demonstrated in the course of this investigation.

p.31   We do not assume that our memory preserves our experiences unchanged. A quality experience, in itself, is not necessarily determined in any direction. Precisely on account of the changes in the continuum of pure duration, there is no delimitation of a former 'Now' and 'Thus' from the 'Now' and 'Thus' which – figuratively speaking – follows it. In its function of consciousness of the ongoing I, however, memory affects this change; it achieves something else. So-to-speak, it delimits the quality experience by isolating it as a 'Now and Thus.' It achieves this not only by changing the Before to the Now but also by freezing it. In other words, memory as consciousness of the ongoing I proceeds in a specific direction which is given in duration. It is this *conscious-ness of direction* which enables memory to freeze the changed individual experience and contrast it with that which follows. But more, it freezes the quality image of this experience only so far as it passes from one Now and Thus to a later Now and Thus. What our memory preserves for us as the quality image of something before is the change of this image seen from the moment of a new Now.

In order to illustrate this event,[10] we [[modify our earlier illus-tration. We assume that experience B immediately precedes ex-perience A; the distance is infinitely small. Experience A consists   p.32 of the quality experience of the memory image B, modified by the time elapsed. As consciousness of the ongoing I, memory froze the image B. It will absorb the change brought about by the time elapsed and refreeze the image thus obtained. The same recurs when the newly frozen image is viewed at a moment later than A. Yet, we do not obtain an addition of changes in the memory image. Different moments of remembering the 'same' event represent different quality experiences; they are incommensurable and can-not be reduced to each other]].

[[At the moment at which memory absorbs changes occurring in time, the experiences themselves have disappeared; now they are only memory experiences of the ongoing I. The *becoming* memory image of a past quality experience contains a memory image of the original quality experience and the quality experiences of the succeeding moments. A *passed-away* memory image holds in primary givenness only past quality experiences of passed-away moments. This does not mean that the memory correlate[11] of the first experience has been lost. Successive memory images of the same event belong to one duration, are mine and have been pre-   p.33 served in memory for me. But this memory image is not commen-surable with the original experience. Memory posits two acts with the absorbtion of the experience of remembering an earlier experi-ence. They are similarly significant for the *passing-away* experience and the *becoming* later experience. The earlier is seen from the perspective of the later moment: the memory image exists only in so far as it underwent a change in time. Thus, our memory does not maintain an experience which has passed-away but only a be-coming memory experience. It preserves a memory image of the earlier experience as viewed in the perspective of the later moment.]]

Here, we find the actual confirmation of our earlier second pro-position, saying that our memory changes with the flow of dur-ation (example: school experience). This connection will gain on clarity when we free ourselves from algebraic examples and draw the results of our investigation together.

Our memory does not maintain our experiences unchanged, after they have passed away. It itself both evoked and underwent the change which occurred in the passing-away of the experience. It does not preserve the experience; instead, it preserves a *symbol*   p.34 of it. Like any symbol, this symbol is not absolute; it is valid only for a specific Now and Thus. In other words: our memory does not preserve the experience but its *meaning*; that is, exactly

the meaning which it acquires in the Now and Thus which emerges
out of it. Every experience is meaningful for retrospective memory.
This is guaranteed by the indivisible unity of the I in the flow of
inner duration. That means, it is guaranteed by memory itself.
For *becoming* duration, it is awareness of the ongoing I.

  To become interpretable, every meaning calls for a frame of
reference. Thus, the meaning, which our memory bestows upon
a passed-away experience in the flow of pure duration and which
is directed upon a *coming* quality experience, demands and owns
a reference system. It inheres in memory itself, representing the
consciousness of the ongoing I. Therefore, our experiences become meaningful for us only after they have gone. To ask about
the meaning of an experience means to look for the place of an
experience-having-past in the flow of pure duration. It means
asking how a past experience of ours fits into the general line of
our life. In becoming experiences, that is, in pure becoming
duration, there is no question of meaning. Inner experience exists
exclusively in pure awareness of its quality. However, as soon
as this quality has been 'experienced,' it is submerged in a new
experience of a new quality. What remains is only a symbol of our
experience - a memory-bound meaning relation to our inner duration. This duration with its experiences, which emerge and
develop from passing-way experience, is still meaning-free. The
question about the meaning of a Now and Thus no longer belongs
to the Now and Thus.

p.35   While we investigated this, our duration carried us to new
moments in which meaning was absent. But the Now and Thus,
which just was meaning-free, became a symbol for us. It became
meaningful and interpretable in terms of the direction followed
by our duration in its flow into that which (as yet, HRW) has no
meaning.

(8) MEANING AND SYMBOL RELATION

The concept of 'meaning,' as introduced here, needs further
clarification. The latter is important for the symbol relation itself.

  Prevailingly, Psychology and Metaphysics assume that abstraction is the existence of pure images of perception. One is concerned with isolating an 'image' from pure duration and to analyze
it without any connection with what went before and came after
the pure Now and Thus. And this is done only partially, for
instance, according to a visual impression which corresponds to
this Now and Thus. Of course, if one does this, he abandons the
only way of reflection which is adequate to pure duration. In
pure duration exists no Now and Thus which could create the
isolated 'visual space' in which alone purely visual perception
exists. For the moment, we could forget that, in pure duration,
our 'pure awareness' apperceives only the totality of the quality
experience of a Now and Thus and that any other conception signifies an artificial disruption of the eternal flow which characterizes

pure duration. We still have demonstrated that pure perception cannot at all exist when we assume that inner duration is endowed with memory. The memory images of our whole life have become determining for the quality experiences of each and every Now and Thus.

Nevertheless, we are not inclined to deny the possibility of 'pure' awareness – even though we are cognizant of the question-ability of such an attitude – for the purpose of establishing the difference between apperception and memory image. However, we understand by 'pure awareness' the quality experience of any given Now and Thus as offered in our apperceptive image – for now intentionally ignoring the part which memory plays in such an image. Assuming the possibility and existence of such an apperceptive image, we appose it to the memory image of pure awareness, which forms its base. We know clearly that such an apposition cannot be made within pure duration, simply because the apperceptive image is awareness image only as *becoming* experience of quality. *Having passed away,* it must already have been turned into a symbol.
p.36

Now, we assert that the memory image of pure awareness acquires symbol character when apposed to the apperceptive image. Thereby, we intend to state that between the two exists a certain difference whose causes we have just tried to clarify. Obviously, we mean that we can ascertain a commonness between them in spite of the established discrepancy. This commonness enables us to ascribe both a memory and an apperceptive image to one and the same quality experience of a specific point of our pure duration. What we called symbol must be different from what it symbolizes in the same sphere of experience, yet the symbol became possible thanks to a higher identity of both spheres. Apperceptive image and meaning image are images of one and the same quality of a Now and Thus of our pure duration. The one is actually experienced, the other is seen from the perspective of a later Now and Thus, filtered through the intervening quality experiences. In our earlier investigation, we clarified the origin of the discrepancy between the symbol and that which it symbolizes, between apperceptive image and memory image. We formulated the hypothesis that our memory does not preserve our experiences unchanged. It absorbs the quality experience of a Now and Thus only in so far as it is transferred from this Now and Thus to a later Now and Thus. If this hypothesis holds, it also must provide an explanation of the fact that we recognize the 'higher identity' of the memory image with the 'apperceptive image.'
p.37

Above, we indicated a possible explanation for this. . . .: the function of the same memory which, through change, determines the manifoldedness of inner duration as awareness of the ongoing I. The sphere of 'higher identity,' which is essential for any symbol function, exists exclusively in the unity of the I. It is this indivisible I, identical with itself and yet different at every different moment of inner duration, which creates the paradox of the identical yet different symbol function. But, here too, the

paradox is only apparent. It springs from our attempt at approach-
ing the experience of inner duration with linguistic-conceptual
means. Doubtlessly, we experience our I as unity within our
duration. The experience of changing quality belongs to the I.
Reason, however, attempts to carry into pure duration a precon-
ceived object relation which originated in the sphere of the concept and thus in space-time. The unity of the I experience becomes
a dualism for Reason only. On the one hand, it splits the experience of the I who experiences himself, in his own duration, as
continuum. On the other hand, it breaks up the experience of
qualities, which constitute the manifoldedness of duration. That
the habitual subject-object relation is applied to duration is very
curious but deeply rooted in the nature of conceptual thinking.
The question of the subject-object dualism does not arise in the
primitive experience of pure duration. Every I experiences quality
changes as belonging exclusively to himself; he is not tempted to
interpret quality experiences as *states of the I*. The latter, however, is done by Reason which is bound to space and time and
operates with concepts even when it seeks out the I who experiences his own duration. It arrests duration; that is, it places
it in the space-time sphere to which it is accustomed. It assumes
that quality experiences exist and identifies them with an existing
I; but it declares them to be *states* of the I and separate experiences of the I. Conceptually, operating Reason robs inner duration of its manifoldedness and its flowing. Thereby, it obtains
an unanimated I tied to space and time. Thereby, it cuts this I
into states and juxtaposes it to the states of rigid qualities. The
latter are thought to belong to the I and yet to be something
different from it. In this way, Reason imputes to pure duration
matter, space and time, language and concept, and symbol. Thinking, again, asks about its own presuppositions. All solutions of
problems of pure duration, which it pretends to have found, have
themselves as presuppositions.

(This is fallacious, HRW) because in pure duration there is no
externality and no outer existence: there are only becoming and
p. 39   passing-away experiences.[12] However, due to memory, the passed-
away quality experience is re-experienced by the I. I enter pure
duration as new quality experience; yet, both belong to the indivisible and unitary I. This makes possible the identity of symbol
and that which it symbolizes. However, to assert such an identity
is already a concession to the conceptual sphere. By the dual
function of memory as awareness of the ongoing I and as a trans-
former of quality experiences, the symbol function is secured as
a life form. From this follow very significant consequences for the
differentiation between apperceptive image and memory image.

As said before, [[only for passed-away quality experiences
exist memory images of the original experience and the quality
experiences of later moments. These are given in primacy as a
succession of memory images of the quality experience of earlier
memory images. By contrast, a becoming memory image is the pure
apperceptive image of the event which is absorbed by memory,

functioning as awareness of the ongoing I. As soon as the experience passes away, it turns into a memory image proper.]] Thus,
the pure apperceptive image exists in exactly the same way in
which a quality experience 'exists' in pure duration. It becomes
and passes-away in memory, functioning as awareness of the
ongoing I. *Becoming, it is apperceptive image; passing-away, it
is symbol (meaning image).*

In other words: the earlier assumption of pure apperception in
memory-endowed duration contradicts itself. The question concerning the relation between apperceptive image and meaning   p.40
image of a quality experience is an incorrectly formulated question.[13]

Within pure duration, there is no existence as such but only
becoming or passing-away of quality experiences. Becoming quality
experiences are absorbed by memory as awareness of the ongoing
I. These images are apperceptive images but never pure apperceptive images, because they are conditioned by memory. Passed-
away quality experiences are meaning images, that is, memory
images of apperceptive images which were received in becoming
quality experiences. Now, the identity of the symbolized with the
symbolizing phenomena manifests itself clearly in the unity of the
I to whom belong becoming as well as passing-away. Yet, the
discrepancy between that which is symbolized and that which
symbolizes shows itself no less clearly in the tension, in the
change of attention from that which is passing-away to that which
becomes. When saying that we concentrate our attention on a
passed-away experience, we indicated a change in the direction
of our view. The meaning image is the passed-away apperceptive
image of passed-away quality experiences. *Meaning is the tension* p.41
*between that which becomes and that which passes-away. This
tension resolves itself in the unity of the I: due to the function
of memory, it enters into our duration as function of the ongoing
I.*

Yet, the assertion stands that the memory image, the meaning
image of one of our quality experiences, is not congruent with
the 'apperceptive image' of this quality experience. Its justification
derives from the irreversibility of inner duration. Meaning does
not originate within the flow of our experience merely by the
acceptance of quality experiences as apperceptive images. Only
an arrest, brought into our life by 'remembering,' allows us to
experience anew passed-away quality experiences in memory
images. The concentration of attention, however, does not hamper
the flow of inner duration.

From this follow important consequences: first, for the nature
of symbol relations; second, for the relation between I and
memory; third and most of all, for the insight that memory-
endowed duration . . . is only one among many forms of our consciousness. Simpler forms precede memory-endowed duration;
more complex ones follow it. But it is the most primitive form
which we can grasp conceptually and which is symbol-conditioned:
it alone creates the symbol.

Prior to our investigation of the phenomena of memory, we hinted at the world of pure, memory-free duration. Now, we have to pay attention to it: It is possible to an explanation of the phenomenon of the symbol in the relationship between pure duration and the form of consciousness of the memory-endowed I.

p.42   (9) THE PRIMARY FORM OF MEANING PROBLEM AND SYMBOL RELATION

Up to now, we have spoken only of the symbol relation within the memory-endowed duration of the living I. Not only the method of our investigation but also the content of the concepts of 'meaning' and 'symbol' will gradually change with the introduction of the acting I, with the experience of the Thou, with the birth of the word, with the origin of the conceptual sphere and with living and thinking in the purely spatial-temporal world. The more 'material' (in a totally primitive sense) is grasped by our experiences, the more manifold will be the possibilities of grouping the materials interpretingly, the more varied become the relations among the materials on the one hand, and between materials and the I on the other. The meaning problem - a major problem of sociology - and the symbol relation will be basic to all these relations. They will occur in many forms, themselves transformed innumerable times and transforming the materials, but also reducable to one primeval form.

We shall carefully attempt to find this primeval form. We will single it out in every phase of our prior investigation, and we will inquire into its continuation within (more complex, HRW) symbol and meaning concepts. It will be necessary to demonstrate that the expected changes and expansions of the meaning concept spring from that sphere of our life form with which the changed meaning concept is coordinated.

(1) *The nature of the symbol relation is rooted in the identity of symbol and that which is symbolized in a more primitive sphere of the I, and in the discrepancy between symbol and symbolized in the respective life form.* By life form - presently not quite understandable for the reader - we understand a stance toward the world which I-consciousness assumes.

p.43   If one starts with the most fundamental experience of the I, when inquiring into the significance of I consciousness, the content of this experience reduces itself to the experience of unity. Posited unity is addended by the awareness of pure duration as an expanded life form. Looked at in itself, this duration signifies at first only the continuous and ever-changing awareness of qualities. The memory-endowed I presents another life form. Here, the pure apperceptive images have disappeared. Neither pure awareness nor pure memory (both are conceptual, irreal abstractions which cannot be experienced) represent themselves as life forms to the memory-endowed I. Pure duration, as unity of the I, em-

braces both.[14] It undertakes the mixing of awareness and memory
in the meaning image on the one hand, and it adds images, acquired in awareness, to pre-existing meaning images on the other
hand.[15] These forms, and most of all that of memory-endowed
duration, have been treated in previous sections.[16]

In the course of this study, other life forms will be encountered: p.44
the acting I, which experiences its body not only as a quality in
pure duration but also as 'extended in expansion'; the Thou-
related I, who knows of an other duration and is capable to experience it; the speaking I, who experiences meaning relations in
the same manner in which the acting I experiences realities; the
thinking I, whose experiences are spatial-temporal and conceptual.[17]

This series of life forms does not claim completeness. They are
nothing but ideal types, formed for purposes of this investigation.
The series is characterized by a strict polarity of its extreme
members. This bipolarity becomes especially clear when one ignores
the primary I as unity (beyond pure duration) which, in a manner
of speaking, has been posited as mathematical point of origin. A
few key phrases will contribute to the understanding of the continuous series:

I in pure duration	conceptual, logical I
pure duration	pure world of time and space
pure quality experiences	everything quantifiable
realm of the unextended	realm of extension
continuum, eternal flow	discontinuum, continuous formation
indivisible manifoldedness	divisible homogeneity
freedom	necessity
image	concept
free of meaning in itself prior to birth of symbol	complicated construction of meaning systems and dissolving of meaning systems in pure logic
value-free in principle	completely value oriented
solitary	essentially social
world as experience	world as form ('representation')

p.45

For the time being, these pairs of opposites are set down hypo-
thetically, and without proof, for purposes of illustration. They
shall convey an idea of the bipolarity of the life forms. On occasion
of the discussion of the individual life forms, each pair of opposites will have to be carefully examined.

Living in all life forms simultaneously, we sense this bipolarity
as the limiting points of a continual transition flowing though un-
countable gradations. We would not at all notice the contrasts were
it not for a specific phenomenon which forces us to reflect about
them: our inability to gain access to extended spiritual realms
through rational thinking as long as we bow to the primacy of
conceptual thinking. Amidst the rational world of our categorical-
conceptual cognition of experience, the non-rationality of our I
experiences seems to entitle us only to the assumption that certain
functions of our I do not reach into the highest and most powerful
life form - that of categorical-conceptual thinking. Rather, these

functions lose their particular character when subjected to habitual and necessarily conceptual formulation - in so far as they are
not completely pushed aside and diverted. In reverse - and the
theory of life forms is based on this assumption - these functions
reach not down into the more primitive life forms. To a relatively
more primitive life form is added a new function of the I which
cannot be derived from the earlier form. Provided one could
experience life forms in isolation all by themselves, one could not
experience the new I function in the more primitive form. Therefore, thanks to the unity of the I, a new, more complex and more
differentiated, life form originates; we call it higher without
p.46   intending an evaluation. In this higher life form, the 'function'
of the preceding stage can be experienced - further: in this form,
it becomes the dominant experience.

These are preliminary considerations made in order to clarify
the first postulate of the symbol relation. Returning to this postulate, we divide its dual thesis into its two components.

(1a) *Symbol and symbolized are one in the awareness of the*
life form which precedes the symbol experience.
This thesis is justified in terms of the following difference between pure and memory-endowed durations: Within the sphere of
pure duration exist no symbol relations but only changing quality
experiences and pure apperceptual images of every 'Now' and
'Thus.' Each of them is replaced by an other Now and Thus which
has nothing in common with the earlier one aside from the I who
experiences both. The images of quality experiences in pure duration - still assumed to be memory-free - can be called pure
apperceptive images without falsification and hypostatization -
provided we understand by 'apperceptive' the pure influence of
the qualities of a given 'Now and Thus' upon an ongoing I. We
have little more to say about the nature of memory-free pure duration, in which alone exist apperceptive images in purity, except
that this life form is not ours even though we know about it
through the phenomenon of the continuity of pure duration. Most
of all, memory-free duration cannot be a necessary manifold like
ours, from which we started and beyond which to go is denied us.
The former presents pure continuity in itself; the latter signifies
a continuum of manifold quality changes.
p.47   As we tried to show above (coin and researcher), memory is the
actual condition of our manifoldness. Yet, the same memory also
produces the symbol. The sphere of pure duration lies beyond
all symbols; our symbol-conditioned thinking cannot penetrate it.
No more can we grasp, in our original experience of manifoldness,
the idea of a homogeneous continuum without the simultaneous idea
of a homogeneous discontinuum, namely, 'empty space.' However,
the apperceptive image as such does not exist in memory-endowed
duration; it cannot be experienced as pure apperceptive image.
Memory preserves all quality experiences which preceded the particular 'Now and Thus.' This memory image, earlier identified as
meaning image, becomes a quality image of the 'Now and Thus.'

It corresponds to the meaning images of all the quality experiences which preceded this 'Now and Thus,' but also to the pure apperceptive image of the correlate of *pure* duration which corresponds to the same Now and Thus. However, it is no longer a pure apperceptive image in itself. If one speaks of pure apperceptive images within the memory sphere, one introduces a hypostasis. Intentionally or not, with its help one excludes from consideration the memory-bound character of quality experience.

How did we conceive of the function of our memory? At one occasion, it appeared as awareness of pure duration. At another occasion, we stated that it does not preserve our experiences pure and unchanged; it *interprets* them while transversing intervening changes and reduces them to their meaning. Thus, for the first time, we encountered symbol concept and meaning image. However, what is a meaning image? Obviously, an already passed-away quality image which is 'reproduced' at the present moment (hypostatized apperceptive image). In memory-free pure duration, p.48 this image would have been a pure apperceptive image. Thereby, the identity of the symbol (meaning image of a former Now and Thus in the present Now and Thus) with that which it symbolizes (actual quality experience or hypostatized apperceptive image of a Now and Thus) would be resolved *(beschlossen)*. However, no pure reality pictures exist in the sphere of memory-bound life. Thus, the quality image of a Now and Thus can only be a 'quality image,' that is, a meaning image of all earlier phases plus an actual quality experience. Or, in grossly simplified terms, a hypostatized apperceived image is produced. . . .

[[If meaning images of quality experiences[18] were diagrammed, they could not be placed along a single line because, then, they would be indistinguishable from quality experiences. Thus, they have to be placed on a deviating line of memory-endowed duration p.49 which, for its part, would oscillate between the quality image of the apperceptual boundary and the realm of meaning; it would continue into the realm of the latter. The lines of meaning would be tangents on the curve of memory-endowed duration. The mean- p.50 ing images of a passed-away experience would be projected upon one tangent of meaning-endowed duration, and this image at a later moment upon another such tangent.]]

This means that, in the factual context of symbol relations, the p.51 unity of the I is refracted in the same fashion in which the prism refracts white light into the colors of the spectrum: symbol relations become recognizable only in a so-to-speak optical diversion from the direction of pure duration in the same fashion in which a prism is required in order to bring about, by refraction and deflection, the colors of the spectrum. Therefore, the task of the investigation of the symbol has to pay full attention to the phenom- p.52 enon of the refraction of pure duration in the actual life form through symbolic relations as well as through the synthesis of the symbol relations in the flow of the next higher life form. It is necessary to find the rhythm in which life forms follow each other, in the dominating unity of the I, by focusing on symbol construction and symbol dissolving. It follows that every investigation, which aims at symbol construction, needs to operate within the sphere of the actual life form. Yet, it will have to find these phenomena in the next lower life form, although not in order to demonstrate that they do not appear there. This is precluded by the theory of life forms. The aim is to reach, through the pursuit of the colored rays, the prism which causes the deflection and refraction. We intended to express this in the thesis that symbol and symbolized are identical in the lower life form. In our case, all meaning images of an experience B are reducible to a pure apperceptive image B in the life form of pure duration in the same manner in which all colored light rays, no matter how far deflected, can be reduced to an unrefracted white ray which enters the prism.

The pure apperceptive images of pure duration, refracted by memory, create meaning images and spread their color over the whole sphere of the memory-endowed world. The phenomena of *this* life form become recognizable only in the reflection *(Abglanz)* of these meaning images. In the higher life form, these colors are reunited as in a concave mirror and the spectrum is reconverted into a white ray. Thus, the actual life form appears in the white light of the perspective of the higher life form. But the colors of p.53   these symbols remain in the perspective of the higher life form, thanks to the unity of the ongoing I which in himself unites all life forms.

One may distance oneself from such abstractions which are of a mere methodological value. Yet, the colors of these symbols remain, flow into each other, change into colors which are produced by a new medium in the new life form: The world of the I becomes more colorful, richer, and more articulated with every new life form. This is so on account of the ongoing I. . . .[19]

After scrutinizing the incident ray, we inquire now into the nature of spectrum and prism while investigating the second part of our first major proposition.

(1b) *Symbol and symbolized are discrepant. This is mainly due to the difference between the points ascribed to them in the flow of duration. The symbolized passes into the symbol like becoming glides into passing-away.*

An intermediate remark, concerning that which is symbolized, has to be inserted here. Part of the nature of the symbol is belonging simultaneously to two life forms. More exactly, since we cannot present the 'life form' as preceding the symbol, we state that the boundary between two life forms can be symbolized at p.54   each point of experience. This does not affect the assertion of the 'identity of the symbol with the symbolized in the lower life form.' In order to be symbolized, the experience 'B' can and has to belong to two different life forms. In our case, one of them is *pure* duration. Its concomitant experience occurs as *pure* apperceptive image. The other life form is memory-endowed duration; experience enters it as qualitative or hypostatized apperceptive image. This dual position of the symbol is logically necessary because symbolizing consists ever in selection from multiple possibilities of interpretation *(Mehrdeutigkeit)* (namely in the direction of pure duration and in that of the line of symbolization).

This dual position is nothing but a *logical* postulate. After all, the whole theory of life forms consists of a series of logical hypotheses concerning the analyzability of consciousness. The theory of a specific life form will have a claim to validity only if, time and again, it can be reduced to the unity of the I and the ongoing consciousness. By the same token, it is not paradox to speak of a dual unity of the symbolized experience. This dual interpretability shows itself as a purely analytical-logical phenomenon. The unity is evident to the experiencing I. . . . Nevertheless, it makes theoretical sense to pose the completely abstract and essentially non-practical question of the dual interpretability of that which has been symbolized. . . .

The symbol[20] . . . remains unequivocal (regardless of its rela-   p.55 tivity, which ties it to a specific Now and Thus). . . .

Another difference stands up under any approach. Symbolized and symbol are ascribed to different points of inner duration, be the latter seen as pure or as memory-endowed. The discrepancy between the points of coordination manifests itself whether I place my experience B on the line of pure duration or whether I add it to already preformed meaning images of past experiences occurring either as qualitative or as hypostatized apperceptive images. . . .

In my opinion, this difference is decisive. It is the reason why the symbol relation cannot yet occur in pure duration but, most of all, presents a function of memory. The constitution of the character of the symbol is (essentially influenced by HRW) the dis-   p.56 crepancy between that Now and Thus to whose duration belongs the image of that which is symbolized . . . and the Now and Thus to whose duration belongs the symbol or the meaning image of the symbolized. This discrepancy can only be established in memory. It cannot appear in the life form of pure duration as succession of not even necessarily manifold quality experiences. . . .

The symbol relation is already tied to the flow of memory phenomena by one fact. In the becoming Now and Thus only the passed-away quality experience (as that which is symbolized) acquires meaning (as symbol). Thus, the quality experience becomes interpretable only through its passing-away. But it is interpretable only in a Now which, just through the acceptance of something passed-away as quality experience, becomes a Thus. Here, the correlativity of the symbol relation manifests itself clearly: *Something which has passed-away becomes symbolizable only in a becoming Now and Thus; the symbol-experiencing Now becomes a Thus only with respect to a passed-away Now and Thus.* Here, the dual thesis of our first major proposition manifests itself especially clearly. Symbol and symbolized are one in the consciousness of the lower life form. The symbol becomes visible only in that which has passed away. . . . Symbol and symbolized are discrepant already by virtue of the correlativity of the various quality

experiences whose 'Thus' they represent in relation to the 'Now'
at the moment in which this 'Thus' enters duration.

p.57   A still other phenomenon appears in this linkage of the symbolized with that which has passed away, and of the symbol with that
which becomes. We cannot ignore this dependence of the symbol
function on the 'direction' which is pursued by our becoming,
our inner duration. As said before, the symbol relation can be
recognized only if one considers it outside of the duration of the
actual life form. . . . Our present problem does not touch upon
this question. At present, we do not inquire into the recognizability of the symbol; we seek criteria for the relativity of this
recognizability of the qualifications of a quality experience as
symbol. In short, we look for the possibility of interpeting a
symbol. Two such criteria have to be stated:

First, there is the already postulated discrepancy between the
symbolized and the symbol as the discrepancy between something
passed-away and something becoming. From this follows that
every symbol relation is relative to a specific Now and Thus.[21]
Second, as just stated, there exists a relation between symbol
function and flow or 'goal direction' of inner duration. This results
necessarily from the experience of the irreversibility of inner
duration. . . . It allows us to draw important conclusions concerning the nature of the symbol itself. If the relation between
symbolized and symbol is embedded into the tension between that
which has been experienced (symbolized) and the present symbol
experience, this function itself depends directly on the direction
of inner duration. Therefore, the possibility of experiencing the
symbol rests necessarily and exclusively in the Now which be-
p.58   comes a Thus. It will never become 'actual,' that is, experienced
as something passed; it will always remain 'potential' as something
continuously becoming. In other words, everything which has
passed away and was symbolized will be symbolized time and again.
Although the symbol enters the quality image of every Now and
Thus, the symbolized is not thereby disposed of. The Now and
Thus which follows, too, forms a symbol of the same passed experience, and so on.[22]

One can speak of the actual experienceability of the symbol only
by identifying the symbolized with the symbol, that is, in a lower
than the actual life form. Only there does the symbol pass away
with and in the symbolized. The potential continuation of the symbol
is extinguished only in the actual experience of this passing-
away. The symbol originates only in the passing-away of the
symbolized; yet, the symbolized never passes away in the higher
life form. The symbolized always transform that which has passed
away, but it itself does not pass away. It is never actually experienced. Potentially, it always changes what has already passed
away through its transformation into something continuously
becoming. In other words: *No experience simply passes away. Although it passes away as quality image; at every point of inner
duration, it becomes anew a meaning image.* It passes away merely
in the artificial isolation of the life forms from each other, because

it can never yield a meaning image. It can never be elevated
from actuality into potentiality. It does not constitute passing-
away when, in the higher life form, quality images become mean-   p.59
ing images, and when these again transform themselves into
quality images. This is so because, according to our definition of
memory, every quality image of every Now and Thus as consciousness of inner duration creates a meaning image of every passed-
away Now and Thus.[23] - These considerations may be reformulated
in the second proposition about the symbol relation.

(2) *The symbolized (as having passed away) can be actually*
experienced only in the more primitive life form. In the present
one it is symbol. For this reason, it is only potentially experience-
able. This means, it becomes with our inner duration.
The third proposition about the symbol follows from this:

(3) *To turn to the symbol means to move in the direction of*
inner duration within a specific life form as totality of becoming.
To inquire into the symbolized (that which is meant) means to
search for that which has passed away in a different life form.
A conflict for pure experience occurs in all life forms in which
we encounter the symbol, particularly in the higher ones in which
complicated symbol systems exist: a conflict between surrender
to inner duration and the deliberate transfer into a realm outside
of pure duration, that of time and space. This conflict of the
experiencing I can theoretically be solved without resorting to
the symbol problem. But it also appears in the sphere of the   p.59a
symbol. Since everything symbolized can become a quality image
which, in turn, can be symbolized, it follows with necessity that
every quality image can be dually interpreted. We intentionally
speak of dual *interpretability*. In immediate pure experience, in
pure duration, the symbol lacks the possibility of interpreting
quality images. 'Interpretation' itself presupposes a superstructure
of symbol systems. This superstructure conceals the facts of
pure experience - in so far as we mean by the latter quality experience within pure duration.
But we must stress once more that our 'life forms' represent
artificial types of ideas, constructed for the purposes of this
investigation. Even as heuristic principles, they are only service-
able when we assume that we all live in them simultaneously.[24]
Due to our symbol-conditioned thinking, pure, simple, memory-
free duration is absolutely unimaginable. Every other life form
comes in contact with the symbol; in it, every experience is
paralleled by interpretation. But interpretation itself enters into
the experience and evokes a new interpretation. This will have to
be considered further. We have already sufficiently explained
the function of interpretation in the sphere of memory-endowed
duration: memory does not preserve a fact of experience without
change; it merely preserves a meaning image. As we know from
our second major proposition, this meaning image can be interpreted
in the direction of our flow of duration in the given Now and Thus. p.60

In the sphere of memory-endowed duration, in which alone the symbol originates, it was impossible to recognize the problem about which we will speak now. In memory-endowed duration, we deal with the interpretation of primitive quality experiences. In higher life forms, by contrast, we deal with the interpretability of *symbols* which on their part became quality experiences of a specific nature. They became interpretable and symbolizable in a process similar to that in the primitive sphere of memory-endowed duration. In higher life forms, as we will demonstrate, the symbol *system* originates in a most characteristic act of consciousness. More correctly, this act constitutes the symbols. In it, the quality experiences of the next lower life form are interpreted in the same fashion in which memory interprets primitive quality experiences in pure duration. The superordinated symbol series originates only in such an act of consciousness. And this symbol series enters the Now and Thus as quality experience, which serves as basis of interpretation. This occurs in the same fashion in which memory images (symbols) enter into the given Now and Thus of memory-endowed duration. The difference is the following: in a symbol *system*, the experience can direct itself consciously to the symbol series or to the experience series of the lower life form. This is solely possible because, in more complex meaning systems, the symbolized level (quality experience of the next lower life form) rests already on a solid substructure of symbol relations. It is much closer to the life form of the cognitive space-time world, which we have acquired in education, than the lower life forms whose symbol character we can unravel only through difficult self-scrutiny and the artificial exclusion of the higher life forms.

p.61   Here results a dual possibility. Either we hold on to the symbol which is 'just in the process' of entering the given quality image of our Now and Thus; or, by an artificial act, we turn our attention to the passed-away quality experience in our former life form, which has been symbolized in the symbol. In the first case, we accept the symbol, like any other quality experience: as a datum, an ingredient of our becoming, an event which moves exclusively in the direction of our flow of life. In the second case, it seems, we abandon pure duration. We turn away from the realm of the ever-becoming and toward that which has passed away. Yet, we can approach that which passed away only through the medium of all qualities which have been experienced since then.

What has passed away is not something absolute; it is relative to our consciousness. As we said before, it cannot be re-experienced, except 'potentially.' That means: through and in its symbols. It has never been actually experienced in the life form to which the symbols belong; in it, it never *became*. It merely entered the life form, which is adequate to the symbol series, by way of transformation. By contrast, it belonged completely to the more primitive life form; in it, it became. In it it was actual experience and as such identical and united with the symbol series. Thus we could state in our third proposition that, to inquir

into that which is symbolized means to look for it in a different
and – to be sure – lower life form.

But, does this thesis not contradict the assertion made in our
second proposition, which said that the symbol becomes with our
inner duration? Does not what has passed away, the symbolized,
re-become in its transformation within our higher life form (which   p.62
is adequate to the symbol)?

This objection is justified. It forces us to make more precise
what we have said about the symbol.

Up to this point, we used the terms 'symbol' and 'symbolized'
indiscriminately as designation of two processes of consciousness.
Now we will have to separate them. Let us remember that we first
encountered the symbol concept while considering the phenomenon
of memory. Conspicuously, we found that memory does not preserve quality images in purity but in changed states. They are
conditioned both by the given Now and Thus and by the goal
direction of the flow of inner duration. On this occasion, we said
that memory preserves for us meaning images; it reinterprets
quality experiences. This is imprecise and the source of the apparent discrepancy between our second and third propositions.
Our second proposition started with uninterpretability of all
quality experiences; the third proposition presupposed the avail-
ability of symbol series for the phenomenon of interpretation. The
latter was justified if one did not wish to do violence to linguistic
usage. We felt entitled to avail ourselves of this usage. Now,
however, we will have carefully to substantiate our point of view.

When memory preserved a quality experience in pure duration . . .
it executed an act of interpretation by transforming this quality
experience, viewing it from the perspective of the given Now and
Thus and the direction of the flow of duration. However, it did
not interpret a meaning context but a quality experience. The
meaning image originated exclusively in this 'interpretation,' if
this term is at all acceptable to reason. The act of interpretation   p.63
constituted a meaning or symbol relation between experience image
and meaning image. Here, memory executed an act of *positing
meaning or positing a symbol*. In the future, this will be our designation for the transformation of something *symbolized* into a
symbol. With the exception of that passage in which we spoke of
the dual interpretation of everything symbolized, in this investigation so far we have always spoken about the act of positing
meaning.

However, when speaking about dual interpretability, we thought
of a different process of consciousness – one which for our field
of work, Sociology, is of fundamental significance: the process of
interpreting already posited meaning contexts or symbols. Such
an 'interpretation' occurs outside the context of the act of positing
meaning. It is so-to-speak complementary to it; it is the reduction of the colored ray to the white ray of light. The act of positing meaning, to which the interpretation of the symbol refers,
may be most different. The following possibilities present themselves to the external and superficial view:

(a)   The positing of the symbol occurs in the same life form as that of symbol interpretation.

(b)   The positing of the symbol as well as its interpretation occur in the next lower life form.

(c)   The positing of the life form occurs in a remote life form.

(d)   The positing of the symbol does not occur in my life form; it presents itself to me as already 'posited.'

These possibilities will have to be checked painstakingly. The propositions, which we have formulated thus far, will have to be reinvestigated in terms of the applicability of these possibilities.

p.64   After all we said before, it can no longer be taken for granted that 'positing the symbol' occurs in the same life form in which 'symbol interpretation' occurs. This is the less likely as, up to now, we have made a close scrutiny only of the life form of memory-endowed duration. Yet, we believe that, in this life form, we encounter a typical case of positing the symbol in the life form of the interpretation of the symbol. Let us assume any quality experience at all which suffered specific changes in our memory over a period of time.

As a child, I had been anaesthetized during an operation. For a long time, I preserved this unpleasant event with all its details in memory. Often, I dreamed the whole event night after night: I am put on a stretcher. I am examined by men in white robes. I am tied down. One man pulls my tongue out of my mouth and ties it to my chin. I want to fight back but I cannot do it. Another man steps next to me with a mask in one hand and a curiously formed bottle in the other; he holds the mask upon my face and demands that I count. I count to three; I inhale the obnoxiously sweet smell of the liquid. I cannot inhale the vapors and think I will suffocate. Somebody - I do not know who - orders me to breathe deeply. I do. More and more do I feel the pressure on my chest. It breaks my resistance; and I count - count - count till I lose consciousness completely. Vomiting, and with a heavy headache, I awake in my bed; and I see the face of my mother who bends over me.

I described the whole and rather common event in such detail
p.65   because I think that it roughly corresponds to the quality experience, 'anaesthesia.' This experience will serve as object of my investigation. I know definitely that, for several reasons, my presentation is not completely adequate to the quality experience. First, I use language and operate with concepts with which the 5-year-old could not have been familiar. Second, I take an event, which consisted of uncounted quality experiences, as having been *one* quality experience, 'anaesthesia.' Who would be able to characterize in words even one single quality experience, not to mention to lift it completely out of the flow of duration, in which it had been conceived, into which it entered and in which it passed away. Third, while penning down the event, I do not remember the event itself but only a memory image of it, an image which my memory, to my tenth year and later, preserved, relived

dreamed, etc.[25] Fourth, intentionally or unconsciously, I integrated
into my representation everything I have since heard, read,
thought, or otherwise 'came to know' about anaesthesia.

For the moment, let us ignore those unavoidable sources of   p.66
error and assume that the quality experience anaesthesia[26] occurred as represented, as far as possible, with the means of
language. Now, from my recollections, I will recount the memory
images of the event as quality experiences, not the memory images
(of other recollections of it, HRW). Of course, I am aware that,
in each single case, I will commit the same errors which I could
not avoid in my account of the (original, HRW) quality experience.

Up to my tenth year or so, I relived this event, at regular
time intervals, in a fashion described here with almost complete
details. In particular, the 'man in white' played a big role in my
thinking and my dreams. At that time, he was truly characteristic
of the event as remembered by me. Later, the vivid *(plastisch)*
remembrance of the preparation of the anaesthesia faded away
more and more. The memory of the smell of the liquid alone remained conspicuously. For long years, I had to fight nausea whenever I smelled ether (in a drugstore or during chemical experi-
ments in high school). Later, I retained merely the memory of
counting. Still today,[27] this memory returns sometimes before
falling asleep; I 'breathe deeply' and lose consciousness.

Thus, in my recollections, I imputed three memory images to
the quality experience of anaesthesia: man in white, smell of
ether, counting. They occurred at different periods of my inner
duration. It is worth noting that, successively, each of the three
memory images were felt to be characteristic of the event.

How did I at all arrive at the fixation of these three types of
memory images? Was it not, in reverse, 'association' during the   p.67
smelling of ether which made me think about anaesthesia? This is
well possible and even probable, but it does not appear as a contradiction to me. Up to now, the nature of 'association' has remained most obscure. Maybe some light can be shed on it from the
perspective of the theory of the symbol, which we offer here. In
any case, it remains possible that every 'memory image' is provoked by one association or other. We will have to speak clearly
about this possibility later.

Let us assume that we can reliably ascribe three memory images
to one and the same quality experience. (In the initial example,
the three memory images . . . are not meant to exhaust the
totality of my memory of the event 'anaesthesia.' Certainly, I also
remembered other features. But, without doubt, the three elements
named are characteristic for the typical divergence among memory
images of one and the same event.) Let us further assume a
memory image which, as 'hypostatized apperceptional image,'
corresponds to a quality experience. . . .[28] In pure duration, the   p.68
issue would be a pure apperceptual image; in memory-endowed
duration, it would be a meaning image of the hypostatized apperceptual image. At an initial moment, a quality experience would
have been ascribed to a given moment of time. In the next moment,

memory executes an act of positing meaning; in the resulting
memory image, it interprets the original quality experience by
integrating it into the life form of memory-endowed duration. . . .
Our first main proposition applies to the act of positing symbols;
it was executed by our memory. In the life form of pure duration,
symbol and symbolized are one. Yet, they are not one in meaning
context; they are not related to meaning. . . . When we say that

p.69 symbolized and symbol are one in pure duration, we resort to a
linguistic representation which itself rests on a most complicated
symbol system. Nevertheless, there are good reasons for starting
such a representation at the symbol.

The positing of meaning belongs exclusively to the life form of
memory-endowed duration. It realizes itself through integration -
or, as said earlier, through interpretation - of the quality experience according to known determinants. The symbol of a quality
experience is different from the latter because it is posited a
moment later in inner duration, even if the two moments are experienced as one. A *becoming* quality experience entered at a
specific moment into pure duration. At the next moment, it was
elevated to a *becoming* symbol in the sphere of memory-endowed
duration. Thus, also the second part of our first major proposition
has been confirmed.

It must be kept in mind that the transition from becoming to
passing away takes place in the sphere of simple duration; it
occurs as quality experience. But what has passed away can be
re-established only by a new becoming, that is, by what is posited
as symbol in the next-higher life form. In our first major proposition, we said that the symbolized passes into the symbol just
as becoming leads into passing away. This makes good sense.
Only, we have to add that the symbol itself is something becoming

p.70 - although not in the sphere of quality experience but for the
consciousness of a higher life form which, at the least, does posit
symbols. . . .

If a direct apperceptive image enters into the memory-endowed
sphere as something becoming, would it not also have to pass
away in this sphere? This is a decisive question for the investigation of the difference between (a given symbol, HRW) and a just-
posited symbol, which is applied in the interpretation of this
already given symbol.

According to our theory it is possible - nay, necessary and
automatic - that we posit at every point of our memory-endowed
duration a meaning image of one and the same quality experience
assigned to a particular moment. This meaning image enters into
duration, thereby making for the manifoldness of this duration.
Were our memory images - man in white or smell of ether, referring
to the quality experience anaesthesia - posited at the moment they
occurred? Nothing speaks against this assumption which we, in
general, used as a basis for the derivation of the symbol concept.
Accordingly, the memory image 'man in white' is the later meaning

p.71 image of the original quality experience, anaesthesia. . . . Our
second major proposition also speaks for this assumption.

I could also assert that my memory image does not, or not primarily, refer to the original experience; rather, it is an interpretation of the symbol of the quality experience. This would mean that my quality experience stands in a meaning relation with the memory image, which was established later. . . . Then, the memory image, 'man in white,' would not go back to the actual visual experience of the 'surgeon,' but only to the remembrance of the actually experienced event of anaesthesia. Maybe, the 'man in white' was something the child had dreamed. Should this be so, we must investigate what the phenomenon of interpretation consists of.

The answer would be less difficult, had we not based our investigation of the symbol on the fundamental phenomenon, the symbol function of memory instead of choosing an example from a complex meaning system: language, work of art, law. But the primitive sphere of the memory-endowed I can reveal many important things about the phenomenon of interpretability - provided one tries to reflect exclusively on the data which are provided by memory-endowed duration while maintaining some distrust of language and spatial-temporal logic.

The data of memory-endowed duration present us with the following factualities:

(1) A quality experience 'anaesthesia' was reinterpreted as a p.72
memory image of an original experience. I remember that I have been anaesthetized. That means, a man in white stepped close to the operation table, in one hand a mask, in the other a bottle, etc.

(2) The quality experience, 'anaesthesia,' passed away into my simple pure duration. Assumedly, I was operated on after the anaesthetic took hold. In the chosen example, the fading-away of consciousness is identical with the moment of the quality experience 'anaesthesia,' or better, of the complex of all those experiences which have been summed up under the label 'anaesthesia.'

(3) My memory image of the event, the remembering of the man in white who stepped close, etc., entered into my memory-endowed duration. This remembrance became meaningful for me and is this today as much as it was for the 5-year old. Meaningful by virtue of what? Through the circumstance that this scene has been experienced by *me*, that I was involved as acting or suffering participant.[29]

(4) The meaning image created by me enters into my memory- p.73
endowed duration in the same way as the quality experience, anaesthesia, into my pure duration. Only: the quality image became and passed away, but the memory image (meaning image) lives on in me. I say 'lives on,' although I have yet to justify this expression. It is a fact that my memory of the experience 'anaesthesia', in the long-range course of my duration, accentuated different moments as characteristic: man in white, smell of ether, counting. All these moments are continued in my experience of 'anaesthesia' as well as in the first memory image of this experience. Do my later memory images then appeal to the original

quality experience? Do they symbolize the experienced anaesthesia on their own, or do they not refer to the quality experience? And, should the latter be the case, do they reach back to the first meaning image in order to 'interpret' it? That means, do they reach back in order to single out aspects relevant for the direc-

p.74 tion of the flow of my duration and the Now and Thus of later moments? To assert this means to assert the reversibility of the flow of duration and thereby to void the unity of consciousness. Thus, we are forced to conclude that, in fact, meaning images issue from the original quality experience. Exactly as the original meaning image, they are determined by the given Now and Thus and the direction of the flow of duration – only with the difference that the Now and Thus is adequate to the later memory image. This Now became a Thus only because in a former Now the quality experience had already become a memory image. Further, through the memory image, the event had already been integrated – and that means meaningfully integrated – into the flow of pure duration. On its part, the latter determined the later meaning image.

The first memory image is especially important because it enters into the determinant factors of these meaning images. Without the first, a second meaning image cannot be imagined; but the first can exist without the second (so, for instance, if the patient had died during anaesthesia).[30]

Thus, we can say that the original memory image lives on in us, 'becomes' constantly in our duration. Two conclusions follow from this:

(A) With regard to memory-endowed duration, one cannot speak of a contrast between symbol positing and symbol interpretation. Every symbol interpretation is a new symbol positing, that means, a regress to the original quality experience and integration into the flow of duration. But the following difference obtains: The original quality experience was already meaningfully integrated into the two determinants for every positing of meaning: the respective Now and Thus and the direction of the flow of duration.[31]

p.75 It is again 'meaningfully' integrated.

The discrepancy between the originally posited and a later memory image can be explained by the discrepancy between the earlier and later Now and Thus involved and the direction of the flow of duration between them. This is valid not only for memory-endowed duration but for any life form whatsoever. Thus, we can now formulate the fourth major proposition of the theory of the symbol:

(4a) *In the same life form, every symbol interpretation is the positing of a symbol out of the Now and Thus which became a Thus by way of a preceding symbol positing of the same quality experience.*[32]

We will have to return to the significance of the difference between symbol positing and symbol interpretation in those cases in which symbol positing belongs to another life form than the symbol interpretation. However, before doing so, we shall draw the consequences of our results, so far, for the concepts of becoming and passing-away.

(B) We see clearly . . . that, taken absolutely, 'becoming-and-passing-away' do not belong to pure duration. They are only auxiliary means of representation, used to make the phenomena of continual flow comprehensible to our reason, which is conditioned by time-space and which is bound to conceptions. There is no having-passed in itself; there can be no existence itself for duration. Strictly speaking, there also exists nothing having passed away within the same life form. Because, in pure duration, I would not know anything of anything having passed away. And in memory-endowed duration, I know about anything having passed away only by way of the constantly becoming positing of symbols. Seen from here, of course, the symbolized 'has passed away'; this, however, in the next-lower life form of pure duration. Thus, we have to state that becoming-and-passing-away can never occur within the same life form. To assert this would be completely meaningless. The becoming can be separated from the having-passed-away only from the viewpoint of a higher life form. This indicates nothing else but the tension between symbolized and symbol: change of perspective; arrest brought into our life through 'attention.' Every symbolized must needs be a having-passed-away. Only that which has passed away can be symbolized. However, that it has passed away I know only in the superordinated life form. The latter allows me to experience becoming symbols; in them I can infer, by conceptual and spatial-temporal means, that something symbolized is something having passed away. However, this assertion is of no consequence for immediate life. All investigations of the symbol are - and can only be - of theoretical significance. p.76

Due to the unity of the I, we move simultaneously in all forms of life and consciousness: we think, speak, act, and remember, and are affected simultaneously by quality experiences. To our experiencing I, the difference between becoming and having passed away is not at all given as a datum - in contrast to sensory apperception. The difference is ascertainable merely, but at all times, in reflection. Yet, the contrast of becoming and passing away is conditioned by the tension between the life forms - in other words, by the 'meaning' of our life. And this 'meaning' is given in the fact that - in spite of the unidirectional flow of our duration - we know about experiences outside of the quality experience of our Now and Thus. Just for this reason, we call them 'having passed away.' p.77

However, the strict correlativity of becoming and passing-away on the one hand, and symbol and symbolized on the other, is of mere conceptual nature. The concept, like thinking as such, is conditioned by an 'a priori' of time. The assertion of the rigid correlativity of the two pairs of concepts gains greatest significance for the study of this a priori. We may let matters rest with this statement. It has been circumscribed in our second and third propositions, and it has been unequivocally discussed during the investigation of the symbol-producing function of memory. *Every-thing having passed away becomes in the symbol; everything which became passes away in experience.*

After this digression we may return to the four types of mean-ing positing and meaning interpretation, as set down earlier. We have now to derive the justification for the unity term, 'symbol-ized symbol,' from proposition (4a), at least to the degree necess-ary for the present state of our investigation. Proposition (4a) also answers the question about the relationship between symbol positing and symbol interpretation in different life forms. At present, we can make only general statements about this problem in order to round out the theory of the symbol. Anything more definite will have to be stated after the discussion of the individual life forms.

p.78   We may assume a symbol context which reaches into several life forms, such as the symbol context of language, the arts, the natural sciences. . . . We notice that in every one of these symbol systems a problem arises which is of equal significance in all of these heterogeneous areas: the problem of subjective and objective meaning, of the intended (posited) and the interpreted symbol.

To select a few examples: in jurisprudence arises the problem of the discrepancy between considerations of the law-giver, de lege ferenda, and the practitioner of the law, de lege lata. All present day esthetics waver between laws which presumably determine the production of the creative artist, and the demand to seek 'rules immanent in the work of art but unknown to the artist.' The latter would be binding not for the artist but for viewing a work of art. The natural sciences, for example physics, accept the world as positive meaning context which has to be interpreted according to the specific methods of physics. Medieval philosophy and theology knew of a still different problem: the theodicy in form of cosmogony; the world not as something created but something to be created; not a positive meaning context but a meaning context which has to be posited by the Creator; the world as symbol of the creative will of God which to interpret is our task. With regard to language, daily life furnishes plenty of examples of the discrepancy between positing meaning and inter-preting meaning in form of purely linguistic 'misunderstandings.'

p.79   These examples serve to make the problem visible and to bring into focus their parallelity in the relation between that which con-stitutes and that which is constituted, between noesis and noema, between the subjective (intended and to be posited) meaning and the objective (posited and to be interpreted) meaning. All these highly specialized applications can be reduced to one formula: the positing of meaning in another life form than that of meaning inter-pretation.

There exist meaning contexts which are not constituted by memory but originate in a higher life form. Such experiences enter meaningfully into our duration without passing through the medium of memory-endowed duration. However, the matter is not exhauste with meaningful integration into duration. The superstructure of symbol series, erected atop of every one of these life forms, has to reinterpret the symbol which had been constituted earlier. *That means, it has to integrate the already constituted symbol into the symbol series which have been explicitly created in the respective life form.* This is the actual difference between symbol positing and symbol interpretation. The former is satisfied with making meaningful quality experiences, which in themselves are meaningless, by integrating them into the course of duration. The latter returns to something which is already endowed with meaning; it merely integrates it into a new symbol system which actually contradicts the symbol system of the original meaning. Rules for the interpretation of symbols result here too; they are similar to those which, in the present chapter, we have formulated with regard to the positing of meaning. Only in the second, sociological, part will we find the occasion to formulate these propositions on the basis of the materials which will be offering themselves to us in the investigation of the individual life forms.[33]

Now a final proposition concerning symbol relations. It results,   p.80 as a matter of course, from our earlier investigations:

(5) *Turning from the symbolized to the symbol, and vice versa, occurs in a act of consciousness which is characteristic for the given life form.*

In the sphere of memory-endowed duration, this act is that of attention. By attention, we designate the specific attitude of consciousness which is directed upon quality experiences. Attention, or possibly clearer, the faculty of remembering, is that act in the life form of memory-endowed duration which is characteristic for the constituting of symbols.

(10) IMPLICATIONS OF SYMBOL THEORY

At this point, it may be appropriate to recapitulate the basic idea of the theory of symbols, as offered here, and to point out the implications of our conception of the symbol.

Much has been written about symbols and symbolic forms. But the problem has rarely been treated in general terms, focusing on cognition as such. More often, one of the special applications of the symbol relation was made the subject of a specific discipline – for instance in those sciences which are concerned with works of art. Practically always the concept of symbol has been treated as given and not in need of further explanation. Or else it has been considered unexplainable or as belonging to the logical category of representations. In the latter case, it was treated in analogy to the theory of judgments, that is, according to rigid logistic principles. Almost all investigations of symbol systems were concerned with the effects of symbol phenomena in individual cultural objectifications; the origin of these phenomena was not   p.81 pursued. Without doubt, this has its reasons. The investigations

were scientific and had to occupy themselves with the materials of
experience. At best, they considered pre-scientific materials as
presuppositions but not as objects of cognition. However, it seems
that the symbol phenomenon is actually situated in the realm of
the shunned pre-scientific materials. Seen from there, it appears
to condition all experiences and, still more, to govern their subsumption under categories.

This investigation is forced to deal mainly with 'pre-scientific
materials' because it plans to investigate the methods of a science,
that of the sociology of understanding. The subject matter of this
sociology - the Thou problem - certainly is situated in the pre-
scientific sphere. Therefore, we had to muster the courage to
recognize the symbol problem as such where it originally occurs.[34]
We did this in our investigation of the function of memory.

The pre-scientific sphere, in which this investigation operated,
is distinguished from the scientific sphere in this way: Its objects
are the phenomena of experience, not those of cognition. The
delimitation of the material occurs in the unity of consciousness,
which is not challenged by science and not refuted by any experience. Therefore, a science which occupies itself with the facts of
p.82   experience has no reason to be afraid of the spectre of the
syncretism of methods (the mixing of different methodological
systems, HRW) which is feared in every theoretical and empirical
discipline. The method of a science of experience can only consist
of acts of self-inspection.

However, a book must needs use language; more, it is forced
to resort to conceptual formulations. Therefore, such an investigation is always in conflict with its material, which is beyond
language and concept. We will never succeed in breaking through
the cover of language and concept. To try this would be meaningless. But, with the method of this work, we may be able to prove
that it is possible to irradiate this cover, as with X-rays, and to
show what is hidden behind it - even if only in outline. The nature
of the symbol is recognizable only in symbols. Why should this
fact be more astonishing than the famous self-reflection of cognition by returning to its preconditions, which is the character of
all epistemology?

These considerations had to use linguistic-conceptual means in
order to approach the phenomena of experience. Therefore, they
had to resort to an auxiliary device. They constructed a series of
ideal types - forms of consciousness or of life reaching from pure
simple duration to conceptual thinking in the world of space and
time (thus, in the actual realm of the experience 'science'); all
experiencing takes place in them. We constructed these ideal types
for mere practical reasons. The erection of such auxiliary construction is justified if it produces usable results. No science can
p.83   say more in justification of its method. But the auxiliary construction cannot be allowed to be in contrast with empirical reality. In
our case, it must take care that the unity of the experiencing I is
not disturbed. This, it seems, has not happened in the theory of
the life forms as offered.

What advantages inhere in such an auxiliary construction? Most of all, it allows us to investigate and order, according to their origin, the continuous flow of the most heterogeneous experiences. It indicates in what fashion the experience enters into our consciousness, how it is changed, which new experiences it initiates. It offers the possibility of seeing the experiencing I - affected by thousands and thousands of experiences - as if it were being fed from only one source of experience and as if it had to react only upon one specific group of experiences. Further, it shows us the relation in which such groups of experience stand to each other and to the experiencing I. More, it clarifies the way in which one group develops out of another one, which it has as its precondition. Finally, it teaches us the unity of the I within the manifoldness of conscious experience and spontaneous experiencing *(Erfahrung und Erleben)*. Thus, it connects Life and Thinking, Freedom and Form, Idea and Gestalt. As logistics, science can never achieve this.

Now, a curious and remarkable discrepancy occurs already in the primitive life form of memory-endowed duration and in the mere phenomenon of memory: the discrepancy between that which is experienced and that which is remembered. It must be rooted in the nature of memory. It occurs that the act of reflection on a former Now and Thus in our life brings about an arrest, and thereby a tension between the (formerly, HRW) experienced Now and Thus and the experiencing Now and Thus. This tension was object of our investigation. We ascertained the existence of a   p.84 symbol relation between memory image and quality experience. Further, we arrived at the assumption that special symbol relations correspond to every life form which we established. And more: the character of these symbol relations conditions the life form; it separates as well as connects them from and with each other. This will have to be tested further.

The recognition of the circumstance that the symbol with all its characteristics occurs already in the life form of memory-endowed duration is most important for the nature of the symbol. This, on one hand, explains why the sphere of pure, simple and symbol-free duration remains inaccessible to our symbol-conditioned thinking. On the other hand, it explains the fact that every experience of which we are conscious, even if we merely notice it, is symbol-conditioned and symbol-bound. We established five major propositions concerning the nature of the symbol relation; they will have to be amended. But we are now able to assert that all - even the most complicated - symbol systems must be reducible in their characteristics, respectively their functions, to these or analogous propositions - in so far as these theses prove themselves valid at all.

Here, it will be worthwhile to consider one circumstance: with every positing of a symbol, the I steps more out of pure duration and into an objective world. To symbolize an experience means to rob it of its belonging to a specific Now and Thus and, instead, to endow it with general validity. For instance: if I have meaningful integrated one of my quality experiences into the flow of my duration, I have lifted it out of the Now and Thus to which it belonged and in which it constituted itself while I experienced it as quality. I have objectified it, even though only for myself. Now, the memory image of this quality experience became determining for every Now and Thus which I experienced since then and which I will experience in the future. By an act of self-reflection, I can at any time make sure of this. *My life acquired a specific meaning only with the positing of meaning for the quality experience; but my quality experience became meaningful only through the meaning given to my life.*

In a way, the act of symbol positing detaches individual experiences from the string of my inner duration, in the manner in which one strips pearls from the string which united them, and restrings them on another thread, that of meaning relation. This event, too, belongs to my life. I do not merely go on, I go on *meaningfully.* This and nothing else is meant by our theory of life forms. All of them - including the spatially-temporally conditioned form of consciousness of conceptual thinking - belong to my duration. Experiences, which belong to this form of (conceptual, HRW) consciousness, are no less my experiences than those which belong to pure duration. But, for me, they are more meaningful experiences. They are not only connected with one another on the tape of my inner duration, which unwinds evenly; they are connected also through other manifold and special relations which nevertheless belong to me, to my flow of duration, to my life.

After all, what is 'meaning' if not the integration of an experience into the flow of duration, that is, its actual apprehension by the I? Bestowal of meaning, or positing of meaning, is the royal gesture with which memory seizes experience.

This distinguishes the theory of the symbol, offered here, from all others which were constructed about this subject matter. In the bestowal of meaning, it recognizes not merely a constituent of cognition but of every kind of experiencing. It accepts as meaningful not only thinking but every kind of experience; this, however, not in the sense of value accentuation, but exclusively as seen from the viewpoint of the experiencing I. Therefore, it asserts the strongest correlativity between individual experience and the course of life in general. Everything lying in the future will be influenced by the experience which, in itself, receives meaning and significance only from and through everything which went before.

Therewith, we arrived at an important conclusion from our symbol theory: *If every preceding experience influences the meaningful integration of a Now and Thus, the transformation of the symbolized into the symbol occurs simultaneously with an act of selection - or, to take a term from a highly complex meaning system, an act of evaluation.* In my opinion, it is this moment which Lask[35] subsumes under his theory of a 'meaning-evaluated (*sinnumgoltene*) reality.' We symbolize at every moment. Thereby,

p.85

p.86

we affirm the meaning of our life and the value of our experience. Would it serve any purpose, one could establish unconscious and most relative evaluations already in the most primitive sphere, finding there the existence of values and the fact of valuation. Maybe, with this (insight, HRW), the value problem will solve itself; the assumption of its universal validity renders it useless as principle of cognition. But, in reverse, it may become thereby the main problem of philosophy, and not only of philosophy.[36] This question cannot be decided in this investigation. But its consequences may be shown later. The importance of the problem of meaning remains in any case, whether one sees in everything which passes away merely an allegory, or in every allegory only that which passes away.[37]   p.87

(11) THE VIEW OF THE WORLD IN MEMORY-ENDOWED DURATION

Prior to the investigation of the second life form, that of the acting I, we will shortly look at the view of the world which emerged in memory-endowed duration.

Here, the world is not yet expanded. Nothing in it allows us to assume a contrast between outside and inside. All experience is quality experience, my experience. I-consciousness is limited to the continuity of duration. *In the symbol of language formation, 'I' means something entirely different. Most of all, the I would be linguistically meaningless without the opposite pole of the Thou (or an It). The necessity of singling out the I, as something special, from all subjects which (at first purely linguistically) can be combined with predicates - this necessity presupposes a manifold of such linguistic subjects: nouns.* However, this would mean to break through the succession of quality experiences and to assume a coexistence or at least a simultaneity which contradicts   p.88 the nature of duration. In addition, every pronoun, be it flexible or not, receives its significance through the possibility of entering into a relation with a verb. Every verb form, including auxiliary verbs, is capable of modification in tense, mode, and person; thus, it presupposes the Thou projected into space and time. Aside from this, we still lack any justification for positing an agent beyond all dimensions, especially since it would not be confronted by an act. If we speak of I-consciousness in memory-endowed duration, we mean nothing but a constant reference to the flow of duration.

Changing quality experiences flow inseparably and indivisibly into each other. A thing, something outside, is recognizable neither in spatial existence nor in name. Space, for instance, would be recognizable only as quality experience, such as a splash of color or a tactile impression. My memory, my faculty to remember, is the only regulator of the unregulated abundance of experiences. I know that my memory is the cause of the manifoldness of my duration. But this same memory unifies and separates the materials of experience; it lifts groups of quality experiences out

of the flow of pure duration and integrates them meaningfully
into the course of duration. It enables me to relive all experiences
again and again - not as quality which affects me immediately but
as symbol which, formed and transforming, makes every Now into
a Thus.

Thus, the I experiences its pure duration only with the help of
memory. Even though we started with sensory impressions as
materials of empirical observation, this I must be thought to be
essentially immaterial. That means: without body, without the
p.89   ability to carry out an action, without awareness of its bodily I.
It presents itself as one-dimensional, like a mathematical line moving in the direction of pure duration. Everything I know in
memory-endowed duration about my body is neither more nor less
than any quality experience. For me, my hand is quality experience as much as the pen which it uses, or the paper on which it
writes - maybe with the difference that 'my hand' belongs to
every Now and Thus of my duration, whether I am conscious of it
or not. It shares its duration with me.

But this is a very imprecise representation. When I write the
letter A on paper, the quality experience which I earlier called
'my hand' is not at all given. At best, I have a quality experience
of my-hand-which-writes the letter A, meaning this letter here
and thus. This, again, is an abbreviation for the quality experience of the muscular movements of my hand which, artfully complicated, are hardly interpretable in physiological and anatomical
terms. Just here and now and thus, it begins the first slanted
line of the letter A, draws it downward, interrupts, starts the
other line, draws it, interrupts, adds the cross line, etc.

With these considerations, I wish merely to show the gross inaccuracy of the earlier introduced theory that the quality experience of the body accompanies all other quality experiences. This
inaccuracy occurred because we put something which is conceptually unequivocally determined (*my* hand), something named, in
the place of muscular contractions and extensions.[38] The latter do
not reach language consciousness, not to mention conceptualization.
The expression 'my hand' was set down as abbreviation, as frozen
metaphor setting the effect for that which effected it.

p.90   And all this because I replaced all these movements, actions,
and quality experiences by one word, 'hand,' and by the individual
concept based on the word, 'my hand,' and thereby tied them together to a rigid unity of our spatial-temporal-conceptual consciousness. With this, we also supposed them to be a unitary
quality experience in pure or memory-endowed duration.

However, in memory-endowed duration we can in no way assert
that the quality experience 'my hand' is particularly privileged in
comparison to the quality experience 'paper' or 'pen.' Through
my memory function, I coordinate the quality experience 'hand'
to the experiences 'paper' and 'pen.' Yet, in actuality, the former
presents thousands and thousands of quality experiences, and
this in an entirely different sense than the quality experience
'pen.' Yet, the latter too is but an abbreviation of a long series

of quality experiences. The functional moment of naming aside, it is 'pen of this form,' of 'this colour,' in 'this light,' in 'this position'; it is 'posed now, here, and thus for drawing the first line of the A,' and so on.

What, then, is the difference between the group of quality experiences which I sum up under the name 'hand,' in particular the individual term 'my right hand,' and those which I sum up under the name 'pen' or - in order to also create a rather precise individual term, 'my black fountain pen "Diplomat Nr. 46212"?'

First, a negative answer: certainly, the difference does not issue from the fact that the experience 'pen' belongs only partially to consciousness, the experience 'hand,' however, constantly. One could say, when I close my eyes and put the pen down, it has disappeared from consciousness. Maybe, it no longer exists, is changed, has disappeared, etc. However, I am always aware of my hand, *my* right hand as belonging to me - regardless of whether I close or open my eyes, or move my hand from one position to a different one. I know that it did not disappear. The pen which is beyond my reach needs proof for its existence. The existence of my hand, which I do not see, is still immediately evident.   p.91

This (kind of, HRW) argument appears time and again in the history of philosophy. It may be correct or incorrect (it is not possible, at this stage of our study, to investigate this). In any case, it solely fits a world of concepts in which 'hand' and 'pen' are spatial 'bodies' of the 'outer world'; they have their exact location in space. It does not fit the investigation of the non-delimited and continuous quality experiences which we had agreed to call 'hand' and 'pen' - paradoxically and contrary to essence and possibility of memory-endowed duration. The pen, which I put aside and no longer see, is no longer a quality experience: no 'proof' will succeed in making it into one. Memory-endowed duration cannot say anything about this 'pen' beyond the preserved memory image of that pen which had entered a Now and Thus of my past as quality experience. I may pick up the pen again and, under otherwise equal circumstances, place it in the position which my memory has preserved and restart the first slanted line of a specific A. Yet, I am still not in a position to assert that it   p.92
is the same pen - not as thing (this is self-understood: there are no things) but also not as quality experience. In the meantime, my duration was flowing on; according to our conception of the character of inner duration, I can never experience two qualities as the 'same.' In addition, the memory image itself changes with duration; this deprives me of the third point of comparison. But does this not also apply to my hand? Is the quality experience of my hand in this or that position the same, when I close my eyes? Is it still the same when I open them again? Even if I leave my hand 'at rest,' is the quality experience 'my hand Now and Thus' still 'now and thus' in the next moment? To aver this would mean to deny everything we have said about the nature of duration. No 'memory image' entitles me to state that my hand, which draws a

cross line now, is the same (or the same quality experience) which drew a diagonal line earlier.

We inserted these lengthy considerations for several reasons. First, we wished to demonstrate that it is untenable to think that 'things of the outer world are quality experiences which have been abstracted by memory and, so to speak, have been bracketed' - even though such a notion seems obvious to our primary and primitive realm of ideas. Second, we wanted to demonstrate that the whole problem has its origin exclusively in an arbitrary transposition of the conceptual apparatus of the spatial-temporal world upon the phenomena of duration. In other words: within memory-endowed duration, such a problem does not and cannot exist. Naturally, there is no solution for this problem.

p.93

Two quality experiences are never comparable to one another. The faculty of memory to form symbols of quality experiences does not make possible the identification of a quality experience with a symbol or - worse - with a passed-away quality experience by means of a symbol. In inner duration, it is simply impossible to assume the existence of 'two' things, that is, of one object which is compared with another one, not to mention a 'third' one as standard for comparison. To posit 'two' means already juxtaposition, simultaneity, coexistence, which belong into discontinuous space but not into the continuum of duration.

Therefore, the solution of the problem of the privileged position of the body has to be banished from the realm of the investigation of memory-endowed duration. In the sphere of this life form, no quality experience acquires a privileged rank - not even that of the body. Only the unity of consciousness feigns such a circumstance. If one intentionally ignores the unity of consciousness, as we did in our theory of the forms of consciousness, one can investigate all phenomena separately. In this procedure, however, all phenomena have to be reducible to the unity of consciousness. Under this condition, the problem has no place in the life form of memory-endowed duration. We have to look for it in another form of consciousness: in the sphere of the acting I. We turn now to this sphere.[39]

p.94

(12) THE SOMATIC FEELING OF LIFE

Let us forget for a moment what we said earlier about duration and memory. Let us make an effort to divest ourselves of all sensory perceptions, quality experiences, memory images, and fantasy representations. Let us ignore all thinking and feeling, all willful movements of our body. Instead, let us turn our attention to the phenomenon of duration. This will be the easier as we have freed ourselves from all quality experiences. In spite of all this, the awareness of our 'I' will not abandon us; although not in the sense of pure duration. But every breath of my chest, every heartbeat is mine, belongs to me. It is *my* heart which beats, *my* chest which rises and falls. I completely feel the rhythm of my body, of the heartbeat, of breathing. We may call this I-consciousness of the body the feeling of life, the feeling of existing. *This essence of feeling (esse) does not result in knowledge (cogito).* Basically, I do not know anything about my existence. But I know that I breathe, that my heart beats, and that I live in immediate evidence. *That this being-alive (vivere) is in fact an essential mode (modus essendi), I indeed come to know only by detour through cognition.*

Let us compare this experience with the experience of pure and simple duration. For the latter we could establish the continuous   p.95 transfer of qualities. While contemplating our purely somatic feeling of life, we were unable to discover either differentiation or continuity. Systole and diastole, breathing in and breathing out follow each other rhythmically in our feeling of life, *in no way differentiated,* in nothing different from each other. Although rhythmically advancing, nothing passes into something else. I breathe deeply and distinguish exactly the moment at which my ribcage begins to expand: I feel how it takes in more and more air but then exhales it again, sinking down: two acts which can be clearly distinguished.

For the sake of testing, let us imagine that the act of breathing is a quality experience in the flow of duration. What has changed? The acts of breathing in and out became codeterminants of a series of 'Now and Thus' in our inner duration. Can I compare two breathings? Between two exchanges of air, I find in the continuum of pure duration a world, a world of experience of such fullness and manifoldness that I am unable to account even for a few of these quality experiences. The flow of inner duration is indivisible even between two breathings. Therefore, no exchange of air will resemble the next. Should I want to compare them, I could only resort to comparison with the memory image of my prior breath. But this image partook in the change which occurred in the whole world situated in our inner duration between two exchanges of breath. In pure duration, the quality experience of breathing in the Now and Thus is absolutely different from that which it was in the Now and Thus of the earlier act of breathing.

However, 'pure duration' as well as pure somatic feeling of life   p.96 are assumptions, artificial abstractions, which we made for specific heuristic purposes. It took specific and very difficult acts of self-reflection to limit ourselves to such a form of consciousness. The unity of the experiencing I contains both experiences as one: pure duration and pure somatic feeling of life; 'élan vital', to use Bergson's related term. We experience everything in duration as well as in the rhythm of somatic processes. Thanks to our awareness of their regularity, our breathing and our heartbeats create a division of the indivisible, a discrete arrangement in the manifold of duration. In the latter, everything somatic is quality experience. All awareness of duration is harnessed by the periodicalizing rhythm of the somatic feeling of life.

Let us turn back to the 'somatic feeling of life' and go beyond the 'spontaneous' movements of breathing and heartbeat. Some kind of 'stimulus' - its nature and provenance are not clear to us and cannot be so in the sphere of the somatic - hits a place of my body, say the eye: I make a movement, recoil, close the eye. What kind of consciousness, in our consciousness, lies at the bottom of such 'reflex movements'?

First, we may offer an interpretation from the viewpoint of the life form of memory-endowed duration. Here, the event presents itself as a series of quality experiences, independent of each other and not reducible to each other. They are merely strung together by the thread of my duration. The only thing they have in common is that they are *my* experiences. We know that it is

p. 97 impossible to capture this event in even remotely adequate words. But if I permit myself such an interpretation. I may say that the events - light ray, pain, feeling blinded, closing eyes, no pain, opening eyes - occur absolutely independent of, but run into, each other; and this next to thousands and thousands of other quality experiences which, together and intermingled, may constitute the respective Now and Thus. They all occur along the line of the quality experiences of duration, which flow ever manifoldly, streamingly, continuously and differentially. Separated from one another by nothing, they are by nothing set apart, or distinguished, from other quality experiences.

How do these events present themselves in the consciousness form of the pure feeling of life? I have assumed that my body is completely at rest; only the rhythm of heartbeat and breathing produces the awareness of the feeling of life. Before the stimulus hit my eye, I did not at all take notice of my eye. For the experiencing I (for instance, in pure duration) it is impossible to establish from where the quality experiences come. The statement, that I see with my eyes, demands a most complex cognitive apparatus. It presupposes *experience* - mostly scientific experience - in order to realize that I move these or those muscles which, in some fashion, change that part of my body which I called 'eye' by an act which I called 'closing the lid.' Thereby, I have conceptually presupposed 'sensory apperceptions' as label for a group of quality experiences. They suffer rather specific changes; for instance, disappear from consciousness, are forgotten, etc.

Our considerations are still far away from the sketched series

p. 98 of experiences. For these experiences, the 'eye' as such does not exist. Likewise, for this form of consciousness there exists no 'stimulus' hitting the eye. The muscular movement of the lid of my eye during its 'closing' and 'opening' is the one and only event which is evident in my feeling of life; it belongs to me as evidently as heartbeat and breathing.[40]

p. 99 Another example: I want to lift the little finger of my left hand, and do this. What does this mean for my consciousness?

Physiology teaches that an impulse issues from a certain point of my central nervous system, passes the spine, affects the motor nerves, enters ganglions, causes the contraction of this or that muscle.

In memory-endowed duration, most manifold quality experiences

take their course, even if I lift the little finger while keeping my
eyes closed. Bergson spoke of the 'cinematographical function'[41]
of memory which forms each of the 'states' of lifting the finger –
in reality, this act occurs in continuous motion. This function is
an essential ingredient of the corresponding Now and Thus.
Without it, the Now simply would not be a Thus. *Only, this quality
experience would not consist in 'lifting a finger.'* I could convince myself of the latter only if I opened my eyes and, in the
given Now and Thus, receive a group of visual experiences which,
by way of retrospective interpretation through conceptual and
linguistic symbols, we could comprehend as 'lifting a finger.' We
ignore here the 'act of will' which is involved. In the somatic
sphere of a pure feeling of life, I evidently know about this or
that muscle movement as belonging to me.

Let us remain, for another moment, with the example of the
'lifted finger.' In the sphere of memory-endowed duration, we
established two series of quality experiences which were evoked
by the event of 'lifting a finger': First, when at this moment I
look at my finger, the series of visual quality experiences enter
into my Now and Thus like any other quality experience. Second,
the series of sensual or somatic quality experiences of which I   p.100
got hold while having my eyes closed; they consist in the experience of the contraction of muscles. We said of the second series
that it belongs to the sphere of the evident feeling of life. Now,
we experience these events also as qualities in memory-endowed
duration.

The unitary I-consciousness does not execute a separation of
the life forms; it exists simultaneously in all of them. The series
of experiences mentioned offer to I-consciousness the guarantee
that the experiences concern the movement of *my* muscles, the
action of *my* finger. This is so because the experiences of my
muscle contractions are by my memory assigned to duration: yet,
they had already been executed in the form of somatic feelings of
life as belonging to me in absolute evidence. With regard to the first
series of quality experiences, namely, the visual experience of
the lifted finger, the following must be stated: within memory-
endowed duration exists no precondition whatsoever (to assume,
HRW) that it is just *my* finger whose movement I now apperceive
visually. The coincidence of both qualities experiences could
only be established through (the combination of, HRW) the
memory image of the visual movement and the memory image of the
muscle contraction. (This, however, would be necessary only,
HRW) if I had not already, in the sphere of the somatic feeling
of life, identified in full evidence this muscle contraction as belonging to me. In other words: quality experiences of my body,
perceived *only* in memory-endowed duration, do not suffice for
giving these quality experiences a privileged position above all
others. This privileging occurs exclusively because I experience
in immediate evidence this action as belonging to me in another
form of consciousness – which we called the sphere of the purely   p.101
somatic feeling of life. In mere – maybe visual – apperception in

memory-endowed duration, it is not possible immediately to recognize that the event issued from my body.

The lamp next to me throws a grotesquely distorted shadow
image of my head against the wall. It almost looks like a horned
devil. Is this horn the shadow of a lock of hair or of a finger?
I move one finger after the other and find that my middle finger
threw the shadow of the horn. In the same manner, the purely
visual quality experience is in need of control by the somatic
feeling of life. On the basis of visual impressions, I cannot
theoretically decide that the finger I saw in movement is in fact
the finger I *moved*. However, this series of experiences coincides
with a quality series issuing from the somatic sphere. It is only
thus that the experiencing I actually ascertains that the finger I
saw in movement is identical with the finger I moved. This leads
to important implications for the theory of the 'visual field' and
the 'tactile field.' It also justifies the dual conception of 'movement' as quality change within duration and as path travelled.
Both phenomena shall be treated more extensively later.

In our example of the 'lifted finger,' we have up to now intentionally neglected the factor of the act of will. Let us now investigate this aspect of the phenomenon. In order to gain a provisional
common starting point, we will mean here by 'will' what Schopenhauer[42] understood by it during his discussion of the concept of
p.102   will: that is, an act of consciousness which transforms itself
immediately into a bodily movement. Without being grossly inexact,
we may view the bodily movement as 'expression of an act of will'
- or, since this is a tautology, as the act of will in itself. Earlier,
we asserted that we 'know' our body also in the sphere of the
somatic feeling of life when it, respectively one of its organs,
starts to act. I know about my finger only if I want to lift it and
start doing so. The fact that I have a finger comes to the fore in
my somatic feeling of life only in the moment in which I move it.
Aside from 'sensations of pain' - which will be discussed later -
I actually do know nothing about the immovable parts of my body
in the sphere of my somatic feelings - for instance, of my hair,
my eyebrows, my eye lashes, my spine, my liver, my spleen.

I am able to 'locate' certain sensations of pain or experiences of
touch in certain organs merely on the basis of a more or less
exact knowledge which I borrow from the scientific-empirical
contexts of anatomy and physiology. By way of a very complicated
detour, which leads through several chains of symbols, I conclude that these organs are my organs. This phenomenon will be
extensively treated later. Here, it suffices to state that these
phenomena have nothing to do with what we called immediate
evidence in the sphere of the somatic feeling of life. In this
sphere, only the movable and the moving body exist in immediacy.

This does not mean that only the deliberately movable and moving parts of the body are objects or carriers of this 'life feeling.'
p.103   As our example of the blinded and reflexively closed eye shows,
spontaneous muscular contractions, of which we become aware,
also evoke the immediate evidence of life feeling (reflex movements

of any kind, heartbeat, breathing, etc.; but not, for instance, the movement of blood through my veins, or inner secretion).

These considerations may be summed up in the following proposition: *In the form of consciousness of the immediately evident feeling of life, the I experiences its body only in movement, that is, in functional context.*

What is the nature of this movement, and how is it linked to inner duration?

We said before that all somatic quality experience must occur in pure duration. The immediately evident feeling of life adds to this quality experience merely the sensation which issues from my body, that is, from part of my I. Therefore, it is practical to start with the experience of movement in duration when answering the above question.

We assume a regular and uniform movement and exclude, as well as we can manage, all external manifoldness. Perhaps I move my finger regularly and uniformly over a homogeneous surface, that is, a surface even in terms of temperature, structure, form, etc. I am closing my eyes; only the impressions of the moving fingers enter into my consciousness, not those of the finger seen in motion.

During the 'duration' of this movement, my inner duration also flows along. I can assert that, in my pure duration, a quality experience is coordinated to every moment in simultaneity. This experience corresponds to the image of the homogeneous object as mediated to me by my sense of touch. I cannot yet speak of movement and of the experience of movement; in the sphere of pure duration I cannot even assert the similarity of these quality experiences – not to mention the duration of this similarity or the evolvement of this quality experience, 'moved finger,' respectively, 'tactile impression,' at moment A (which precedes moment B of our experience, HRW). Pure simple duration as such is without cohesion aside from that of the flow of duration of the I in itself. I can only experience a touch impression at moment A and one at moment B; both belong to me. I do not know anything about the nature of the touch impression or about the relation between the two impressions: the one passed away before the other became – both as quality experiences without entering as symbols into my duration. p.104

The latter can happen only in memory-endowed duration; only here occurs the awareness of a continuity of the whole event. The quality image of the movement at moment A, which is turned into a symbol, has its after-effects at moment B. In itself, the quality experience at moment B is similar (to that at the earlier moment, HRW). But it turns into something completely different: it is not in itself experienced by me, but by my I who already experienced the earlier moment in a Now whose Thus constituted the preceding A. The meaning images of the passed experiences join the quality (apperceptive) images of the becoming experience. This means nothing else but that the movement occurs continuously in my consciousness.

This derivation is valid for every kind of movement but also other experiences. We have shown in the earlier example of
p.105   researcher and coin that the amassing or repetition of similar images never produces similarity but manifoldness. From this, we concluded that our memory is the cause for the manifoldness of our inner duration. As long as we deal with moving (but not with having-moved) in the sphere of memory-endowed duration, it cannot make any difference whether the experience movement-of-my-finger has been executed by me or another object. However, one difference remains: in this case, the sphere of evidence has to be sought in the somatic feeling of life, in the experience of my body as functional context. Yet, here, the identity of the I cannot come into evidence; it does not at all issue from the somatic sphere. Rather, it is limited to the succession of quality images which are merely mediated by sensory impressions.

Let us assume that it is not *I* who moves my finger along a homogeneous surface but that the surface is moved below my finger at rest.[43] If we ignore visual control, the quality experiences accepted in memory-endowed duration are in both cases similar: they are mediated by the sense of touch. However, if I myself move the finger, an entirely new and in principle different series of quality experiences is added: a series of quality experiences of my finger in a functional context. In other words: the experience of my body in the somatic sphere enters as quality experience into my duration; it joins the series of images which have been mediated by pure 'sensory impressions.' Not consider-
p.106   ing other experiences, the 'Thus' of the Now at moment B does not only establish the experience of the homogeneous mass at moment B and the earlier experience of this mass at moment A, continuing as meaning image. Mediated by the somatic feeling of life, it also constitutes the quality experience of *my finger* at moment B together with the memory image of my finger at moment A.

This formulation is only provisional. In our example, this becomes evident as soon as we open our eyes. Aside from other quality experiences, we then obtain the following constituents of the 'Thus' as moment B (imagined as immediately following moment A at which the movement started).

(1) Quality experience of the touched homogeneous surface at moment B, mediated by a 'sensory impression.'[44]

(2) Meaning image of the touched homogeneous surface at moment A, mediated by memory.

(3) Quality experience of the seen homogeneous surface at moment B, mediated by sensory impression.

(4) Memory image of the seen homogeneous surface at moment A, mediated by memory.

(5) Quality experience of the seen moving finger at moment B, mediated by sensory impression.

(6) Meaning image of the seen moving finger at moment A, mediated by memory.

(7) Quality experience of the finger, moved by me at moment

B, mediated by the somatic feeling of life, experienced as functional context.

(8) Meaning image of the finger which I moved at moment A (and experienced as functional context), mediated by memory.

With reference to this tabulation, we can state the following: p.107
the seventh and eighth experiences represent the 'Thus' at moment B of memory-endowed duration. They alone differentiate the movement executed by me from other movements which I may experience in memory-endowed duration. The fifth and sixth experiences, too, offer no criteria. As explained, I have no possibility whatsoever of experiencing the finger, which I see moving, as my finger, as the finger moved by me, as long as the seventh and eighth experiences do not penetrate into my consciousness.[45]

In this manner, the life form of the somatic feeling of life is linked to the life form of memory-endowed duration: on the one hand, memory in its function as awareness of the ongoing I; on the other hand, the somatic feeling of life as awareness of the acting I. Earlier, we have attempted to represent this acting I as quality experience of the ongoing I. If we want the I to be one, and if we claim validity for our theory of symbol and life form, we have to try the following: to interpret the acting I as a life form sui generis on the basis of the somatic feeling of life. We will have to answer the question of the specific symbol structure of this life form, and we have to demonstrate the linkage between both life forms - namely, that of memory-endowed duration and that of the acting I - on the basis of the 'somatic feeling of life' and of its symbol relations. If the hypothesis of life forms is to prove itself, it must be shown that the manifoldness of the world finds support in the lowest as well as the highest life forms - even if only imperfectly. The imperfection itself follows from the symbol relation of the higher life form. The unitary I, which exists, acts, and lives simultaneously in all these forms, becomes accessible to analysis only when we attempt a total synthesis of the living (*Lebendiges*).

(13) SOMATIC EXPERIENCE AND QUALITY EXPERIENCE   p.108

When considering the functions of our body, we found that the somatic feeling of life enters into our consciousness only as functional context and that the duration of the feeling of life is exclusively effected by the steady movement of our body in heartbeat and breathing. The exception is pain, whose phenomena have still to be clarified. I spoke of 'duration of the feeling of life', even though the difference between this feeling and inner duration is clearly recognizable in the characteristic periodification and rhythmification which distinguishes the somatic feeling of life.

We may imagine a deliberately executed movement of our body, for instance, of my right hand writing the letter A on this sheet. Thereby, I execute deliberately (what deliberately means will have

to be established later) certain muscular contractions in my body.
These are muscular contractions which, in case I had the necessary
anatomical and physiological knowledge, I would be able exactly
to describe and label. Unfortunately, I lack this knowledge. For
the moment, I also try to keep memory-endowed duration out of
my considerations. Thus, as actor, I have no reason whatsoever
to doubt that my hand, which draws the first diagonal line of the
letter A - respectively those muscular movements which I execute
in order to draw this line - belong to me. But this less or in
different fashion than those muscular movements which I make in
order to add the cross line. The doubt arose earlier because I
viewed 'my hand' at first as 'hand seen by me.' Thereby I considered it a quality image of memory-endowed duration. In this
context, it was indeed important to coordinate a specific Now and
Thus of inner duration to every one of the quality images in which
p.109   individual movements manifested themselves in consciousness. I
could say that the quality image of my hand at moment X concerns
only the muscular movements called hand: the hand which just
here, just now, and just thus draws the first diagonal line of this
A on this paper, at this moment, under this light, etc., now
starts, now draws, now ends.

For my somatic feeling of life, in which my hand muscles become
evident just through and in their functions, such doubt cannot
exist. Rather, I could assert that I become aware of *every* movement of the hand muscles in question, so-to-speak somatically,
whether I execute the first line of this A or of any other A (on
another sheet, at a different time). As long as I do not resort to
my memory, I would find no theoretical difference between a first
and a later line. However, I would also not be in a position to compare the two phenomena. Yet, it is impossible for me to think
away memory, whenever I am at all set to think. I cannot merely
appeal to the somatic sphere. Like pure duration, it does not
offer me the possibility of comparing two phenomena with one
another. By isolating the somatic feeling of life I merely arrive at
evidence for all bodily movements which belong to me. I was not
in a position to do this solely from memory. But, without resorting to the latter, I will never be in a position to establish the
similarity of, or the difference between, my muscular movements.
In order to do this, I have to appeal to memory. Yet, this appeal
too will remain effectual. Memory, as cause of the manifoldness of
inner duration, necessarily has to designate every one of these
muscular movements as different simply because each of them belongs to another Now and Thus of inner duration. In the sphere
p.110   of memory, nothing similar exists. Nevertheless, it seems to me
that the muscular movements of drawing a line for the letter A are
'the same' or 'similar' to the muscular movements of drawing any
other comparable line. Obviously, this probability issues not from
memory but from the somatic feeling of life. Only in the latter is
the similar, if not established, at least possible.

At this moment, it may be practically impossible to find a way
out of this dilemma. Obviously, we deal here with an equivocation

of the word 'similar,' that is, of a term which is meaningful and
valid only in the space-time world of concepts. But the fact that
the phenomenon of similarity has its origin in the sphere of the
somatic feeling of life calls for reflection. We did not even answer
the question *'what* is actually similar?' The muscular movement as
such? Or has one *inferred* similarity in a most complicated
conceptual-logical fashion, starting from the similarity of the
effect, that is, the visually perceived A-lines? My feeling of life
offers as evidence merely the execution of muscular movements.
My memory necessarily reveals the differentiation of the quality
images which have been coordinated to these muscular movements.
Here, we cannot say more.

The circumstance that the problem of similarity arose just here,
however, shows with absolute clarity that the investigation of the
acting I has to be carried further. We must pursue the effects of
this I beyond the sphere of the pure somatic feeling of life. Under
comparable circumstances, the recognition of the manifoldness of
our duration had forced us to investigate our memory-endowed
duration. The experience of similarity is not limited to muscular
contraction. It is not merely the movement of my body during the
execution of movement which appears 'similar' to me; the already
executed movement seems to produce a similar result.

Another example: I bent a little finger. What does my somatic
feeling convey to me? I feel the flexors of my finger in movement. p.111
. . . With the execution of the movement, in the functional moment,
the muscular movement enters into my experience of inner duration with the help of my somatic feeling of life. Uncounted quality
images offer themselves to my memory while I execute the movement; of them, I will select only two - two which I can establish
also when the movement has been concluded. For reasons still to
be explained, these two impress themselves especially upon my
memory: the beginning and the end of the movement: thus, the
memory image of the straight and the bent finger. With regard to
the consequences, I will stress once more that, in this case, it is
not a matter of the finger seen in movement but of the finger
moved. Primarily, it is experienced in the sphere of the somatic
feeling of life: it penetrates memory-endowed duration solely
through the somatic medium.

The comparison of these two quality images or of their symbol
relations can never be achieved in the sphere of memory-endowed
duration alone; it can only be accomplished by us as humans who
exist in space and time and think conceptually. If I make the
comparison, I first of all establish a being-different. According
to our theory, this is self-understood. . . . I have grown older
between the two quality experiences. Disregarding this for the
time being, I obtain only a partial cause of this being-different:
a purely somatic experience which is rooted in the state of tension
of my flexors. Physiologically speaking, it may manifest itself
sooner or later in a 'tiring' of the muscles in question.

At first glance, this vaguely posed assertion seems to contra- p.112
dict the postulate that I experience my body only in movement,

that is, as functional context. The fact of the origins of these experiences in the somatic feeling of life comes to light only when I refer to other quality experiences - experiences both which entered into my memory-endowed duration without having passed through the somatic sphere. So-to-speak, I mobilize them as means of control.

Let us assume that, eyes closed, I move my left hand along my stretched and then bent right finger. We may now set up a table of the experiences which, in this case, make up the constituting Now and Thus. For the sake of simplification, the movements of my left hand are not included.

(1) Quality image of the flexors of my right finger, mediated by the somatic feeling of life.

(2) Quality image of the right finger felt by my left hand. According to our earlier view, it enters pure duration as 'sensory impression' of touch sensations without mediation of the somatic feeling of life.

(3) Quality image of my left hand which moves along my right finger, likewise mediated by sensory impression.

The difference between (2) and (3) is obvious. If not I but Peter would move along my finger, (2) would disappear while (3) would be maintained. The same would be the case if I did not use my left hand but a piece of wood.

Thus, I have executed a control movement with closed eyes. For the moment, I shall limit myself to (2) and (3) in the analysis of the corresponding quality experiences. . . . Is it possible to
p.113   establish a relationship between these two experiences - that mediated by the somatic feeling of life and that accepted by way of sensory impressions - without interpolation of a series of experiential contexts and regular sequences (of quality experiences, HRW)? This question has to be answered with a categorical 'No.' Nothing instructs me that the finger, which I touched, is also the finger which I bent, unless it is the touch sensation of even this bent finger. But, this we have excluded. Maybe I did not glide with my left hand over my right finger but over a glove into which I slipped my finger. It follows that, in this case, only the sensory impression which my finger gained from the touch of the hand produced a quality image which is different from that of the stretched finger.

It turns out that we can, and must, generalize these results. It is not entirely irrelevant whether the touch impression (3) was evoked by my hand, the hand of Peter, a piece of wood, by a breath of air, by water, etc. If this is the case - no reason speaks against it - I can assert *that every somatic experience of the body as functional context is accompanied by a quality experience which is guided into my inner duration by the touch sense of the moved organ.* In other words: indeed, I somatically experience my body in a functional context. Yet, thanks to the quality experiences which reach me through my sense of touch, I am ever aware of the *boundaries of my body.* This awareness is truly constant: it is coordinated to every moment of my inner duration: it inhers in

the touch impression which I receive from the medium in which I
live. This recognition forces us to revise our whole theory of the
somatic feeling of life: we have to remove the inexactitudes which   p.114
we introduced earlier. . . .

(14)   THE ACTING I AND THE SOMATIC FEELING OF LIFE

We stated earlier that the I experiences his body only as functional
context. This assertion calls for a dual correction. It assumes
that the somatic feeling of life is mediated only through the movement of parts of the body, meaning thereby a tensing and relax-
ing of certain muscles. From this it could be concluded that,
aside from breathing, I am deprived of all 'somatic feeling of life'
and of all awareness of my body when it is in a state of absolute
rest. However, such an 'absolute rest' position for my body, or
even a part of it, can be imagined neither theoretically nor
practically. In fact - purely somatic - I am always aware of the
position of my body. Whether I stand, walk, lie down, sit;
whether my arms hang down or are akimbo: certain muscles are
always in 'action'; others are 'switched off.' In my somatic feeling
of life, I am ever aware of the state of tension of my muscles.
. . . This pure somatic feeling of life is subjected to correction
by the continual experience of the boundaries of the body through
the sense of touch. This includes the points of contact with
surrounding matter. Here is the true core of the idea that our
body, at every moment, is correlated to pure duration. This is
indeed so but not, as one may believe, in the mere somatic feeling of life. It is so by virtue of a quality experience which enters
directly into pure duration and is mediated through the sense
of touch. The quality experiences of the boundaries of the body
are common to pure duration and the somatic feeling of life. But
this too is imprecisely expressed. Actually, somatic feeling of life
and the quality experiences of the sense of touch are strongly
correlated, but not identical.
      The somatic feeling of life, as such, abandons me no less than   p.115
the experience of quality. What, then, means the proposition
that the acting I experiences his body only as functional context?
Here a second correction of the proposition is called for.
      The proposition is valid only for the acting I. With it, we in-
tended to break through the sphere of the pure somatic feeling of
life and to speak of an experience which goes beyond the mere
awareness of muscular tensions, which has as object the change
of the state of tension, the movement of our body. Thereby, we
deliberately ignored that this body always enters into our inner
duration as quality experience and into our somatic feeling of life
as awareness of muscular tension - the first, however, without
ascribing a privileged position to the body in contrast to all other
quality experiences.
      Through his acting, the acting I creates the synthesis between
quality experience and somatic feeling. For it, indeed, the body

may become experience only in movement. However, what is decisive is that the acting I experiences his body *in* functional context but not *as* functional context. Rather, he reinterprets this
context and puts a symbol in its place: the body as something expanded, extensive, as body in space. What is performed here is
the miracle of the inclusion of extension into the intensive world
of experience. The experience of this movement is not transformed
by the fact that I move, and not by experiencing this movement
simultaneously as somatic context and as change of quality images,
which are mediated through the sense of touch. Rather, the transformation takes place because this experience is necessarily and
exclusively reinterpreted, by and for the acting I, as an experience in space. This opens up access to the world of extension; it
alone mediates the experience of space and therewith of time and
p.116   of external objects. It will be shown forthwith that this alone
secures the privileged position of the body. Only as actor do I
execute this most significant step out of the non-dimensional
manifoldness of qualities and enter into the discontinuity of heterogeneous space, filled with quantities.

(15) THE ACTING I

The important symbol function of the acting I will be investigated
later. Its first precondition is the realization that this symbol
function is due to the acting I and not to memory-endowed duration. The latter, as stated, claims the sensory experience of the
'boundaries of the body.' This experience inhers in the respective
Now and Thus; like any memory-bound experience, it is differentiated. The experience of the 'boundaries of the body' at moment
A is basically different from that at moment B, whether my body
moved in the meantime or not. It is also basically different from
the experience of the body as extension. As purely sensual experience, it may be comparable to seeing our body. As object of
sensory apperception of touch and vision, the body assumes no
privileged position whatever. On the one hand, it merely occurs
as subject of my sensory apperceptions, as mediator of the images
of my inner duration, and as content of my somatic feeling of life
p.117   in functional context. On the other hand, the body - more exactly,
the image of my body - attains a position privileged above all
other images. Of the two constituents of the privileged position
of my body, only the second presents immediately evident experience: experience of the acting I. The first is cognitively obtained; it is context of observation, result of eminently scientific
speculation. That my body is mediator and carrier of my sensory
impressions, is a fact very much in need of proof which, to the
satisfaction of experience, can only be produced negatively
(visual images disappear with the loss of the eyes, etc.). By
contrast, the movement of the body, and most of all its deliberate
movement, is immediately evident experience of the acting I.
    The experience of that which is extended is rooted in the

immediately evident experience of the movement of my body. The experience of extension is nothing but the symbol of bodily move-ment, posited by the acting I. Only by transposition into language does there result an 'outside' which is given together with the sensory images of the boundaries of my body. Actually, this image is totally embedded in pure duration; it has no more claim to 'reality' in the sense of the materialization of extension than any other sensory experience. I can experience the existence of an 'outside' only when I succeed in changing the boundaries of the body, that is, when I move. I experience my body as something extended, something spatial, only in the shifting of its boundaries which brings the awareness of outside space. In other words: the symbol function of the acting I, which consists in the reinter-pretation of movement as spatial extension, does not stop at the   p.118
image of the moving body. He projects it into an outside sphere, experiencing it as something external.

Of what nature is the movement which is experienced somatically? Is this experience the same that the acting I transposes into spatiality?

I am holding a pen in my hand and intend to draw a line from one point to another on a sheet of paper.[46] (What happens? HRW)

[[I do this slowly and continuously. I move my hand through various points in succession, starting at M and finishing at N.[47] However, I did not have the intention to draw a line from one successive point to the next: there would be an infinite number of intermediary points. In fact, when I started drawing the line, I did not know anything about intermediate points.]]   p.119

At the time the movement was projected, at the time of positing this act of will, only start and final point of the movement were   p.120
given to me. I neither imagined that points between these two points existed, nor did I intend to touch them. For the (planned, HRW) direction of my movement, they were irrelevant. But does this not seem to be a paradox? When my hand executed the move-ment from M to N, did it not also execute, in partial movements, the move [[to and from every intermediate point in succession]]?

The answer is that, in the given case, we deal neither with a movement which has been executed and finished, nor with a move-ment in progress. We deal merely with an intended movement. . . .

For good reasons, the word movement can be interpreted in at least three ways. If these three connotations are confused, in-soluble paradoxes occur. In our example, the first major connotation was inspected: the *intended movement*: a movement which as yet does not presuppose anything moved or moving. It is the project, the design, the idea of an intended movement, in short, a willed movement. It may never be executed and become reality. This 'movement' asks only about the goal, the direction, the path – as would a hiker on an unknown road. He wants to reach the next village. The farms, the trees, the rocks left and right of the road are not the object of his inquiry, unless they are inexpendable points of orientation. In a similar fashion, definitely relevant intermediary goals exist for the intended movement. In such a

p.121   case, the purely intentional character of movement disappears; it
is planned on a rigid rational basis. That means, a context of experience is evoked which is adequate to conceptual thinking but
not to the sphere of the pure acting I. If I had been given or set
myself the *task* of moving in a *straight line* from M to N, I would
be dealing with such a *rationally* intended movement. Since I
know that points A and B are situated directly between M and N,
I will first try to reach A in order *correctly* to reach N. This concept of the *rational intention of acting* will gain great significance
for us. Thus, we will state what we mean by it: the intention of
an action which depends on intermediate goals known from experience.

Aside from rational intention, the type of intended movement is
characterized by the exclusive givenness of starting point and
goal of the movement but also in the circumstance that this movement belongs to the acting I. What function it fulfils in the symbol
system of the I will have to be shown.

(II) While my hand guides the pen from M to N, I co-experience
this movement in my memory-endowed duration - and this in a
dual manner, since I assume that I execute the movement with
eyes open: first as constant change of quality in the visual image
of the respective Now and Thus, as mediated by my eyes; second,
p.122   in the series of quality images which my somatic feeling of life
projects into my memory-endowed duration.

The flowing-along of these quality images amounts to an ongoing
intermingling, a continuum of manifoldness. In essence, it coincides with duration: therefore, it is absorbed by duration. While
I execute this movement, while it unfolds, there is nothing spatial
about it. [[When my hand begins the line, two experiences of my
inner duration begin: the visual quality image of the 'writing
hand' as well as the somatic experience of muscular tension. Both
are attached to the functional context of the 'hand moved' in a
certain direction. However, while my hand has moved part of the
intended way, I have grown older. Therefore, the experience of
the 'hand moved' has changed, even if there was no change, during the movement, in the 'muscular tension.' Movement, while
flowing along, is without residue dissolved in memory-endowed
p.123   duration. Yet the somatic feeling of life - if not dissolved in
quality images of duration - remains as residue.]]

What is the relationship between the *ongoing movement*, which
enters memory-endowed duration, and the intended movement?
In the search for an answer, we begin with a course of movement
which is not initiated by my body.

(1) I stand before the pendulum of a clock and follow its swings
with my eyes. It offers certain visual quality experiences which
are connected with one another because they belong to me.[48]

Without reference to my inner duration, I do not know whether
my experience of the pendulum at the start of the movement is
p.124   related to the experience at the next movement. . . . Only my
spatial-temporal and conceptual experience allows me to infer an
inner connection between the two experiences themselves. This is

supported by the circumstance that I speak and that I gave the name 'pendulum' to the group of experiences which I transposed into space. But this is an inference which does not have to occupy us here. At the moment, there remains a series of quality experiences of the seen swings of the pendulum which hang together because they belong to my inner duration.

(2) Now, I put my finger on the pendulum and allow it to swing with it. I assume that the pendulum is heavy enough to carry my finger along without my deliberate 'help.' What has changed?

The visual image, analyzed under point (1), has been addended by the quality experience of the somatic feeling of life. I experience part of my body - my finger, my hand, maybe my arm - as functional context, as specific muscular tension.[49]

Herewith, a new element is added to the pure visual experiences. p.125 Immediately, it subsumes all individually diffuse quality experiences under a unity which, in principle, is different from that related in the flow of my duration. It unitarily refers to the movement of a part of my body to which, thereby, are coordinated the visual quality experiences. The latter, up to now, had been independent. It follows that, by way of the somatic feeling of life, the unity of movement enters without residue and completely into pure duration.

(3) I now retract my finger from the pendulum; I intend to copy with my finger the movement of the pendulum, a whole swing, without touching it. . . .

First of all, I have here an 'act of will.' In the conception of the projected movement, I intended the movement of my finger from point of return to point of return. The rest of the actual movement occurs analogous to the event analyzed under (2): as a series of experiences of visual quality experiences, unified in reference to my inner duration and my somatic feeling of life. But a third moment of greatest importance has been added. Namely, the intended movement did not disappear: it continues to be opera-   p.126 tive in a dual sense. (a) In the realization of the planned movement, it transformed itself into a functional experience of my body. (b) It acts forth as meaning image in my memory, into which it entered, at the moment it was conceived, as quality experience of my inner duration. In cases (1) and (2), memory created symbols or meaning images of movement. It allowed the individual 'states' of the movement to enter into pure duration without dissolving them in traversed space and without impairing the continuity of the course of the movement. In the present case, we are facing a second series of symbol experiences:

[[My movement was intended at one moment of inner duration and started at a specific point. The important question, whether the moment of intentional decision is identical with the moment of the beginning of the movement, is here irrelevant. At the later moment, I have erected not only a meaning image of the start of the movement, but also of the movement intended at the earlier moment.]] The intended movement itself has been symbolized - and this at every moment of the flow of duration. This is so because

the intention of the movement (or the act of will), as any other
experience, enters as quality image into memory-endowed duration. There it is subjected to the same reinterpretation as any
other quality experience. This process again creates a connection
between the quality image offered by the ongoing flow of an intended movement in memory-endowed duration. In this case, we
obtain the following connections:

p.127   (a) Memory-bound unity relation by the appearance, in the
flow of my inner duration, of all individual quality experiences
of the course of movement.

   (b) Somatic unity relation between the course of movement and
the experience of my body as functional context. This again, as
quality experience, enters into memory-endowed duration.

   (c) Intentional unity relation established with the belonging
to ongoing duration of the intended movement as experience of a
Now and Thus of my inner duration.

   The third movement links the 'ongoing movement' to the 'intended movement.' It actually constitutes the specific experiences
which distinguish a movement of the acting I from every other
movement experienced: the execution of a movement, which was
intended by the acting I, belongs exclusively to him. Of the three
examples, only the third one has as object a movement of the
acting I. The other two are to be thought of either as mere
quality experiences of pure duration, or in the second case, as
affecting the somatic feeling of life. Both lack any intentional
relation to the acting I. However, in all three cases the nature of
the course of the movement becomes completely recognizable only
in the flow of duration even though they enter it by a detour
through several symbol processes which exclusively belong to the
sphere of memory-endowed duration.

p.128   (III) We now turn to the third meaning of the term movement:
passed-away movement. The distinction between ongoing and
passed-away movement is one of the deepest and most fruitful dis-
coveries of Bergson. As practically everywhere, the present expositions try to follow Bergson.

   [[We now return to the example of the hand drawing a line and
state that our hand moved along the line and finds itself now at
another point. Obviously, we thereby mean something basically
different from the assertion that our hand moves between two
points. The latter expression indicates a manifold continuum, an
event which occurs solely in inner duration and will never be projected into the external sphere. When I assert that my hand has
moved a certain distance, which I can do only at a later moment,
p.129   I definitely interrupt the flow of inner duration. I simply state
that my hand has travelled along a certain path. Thus, by 'passed-
away movement' I mean here nothing but the traversed path.
According to my assumptions, my hand directs a pen. Consequently
the 'passed-away movement' is identical with the distance I drew
on paper.]] This movement is completely different from the intended movement in the course of its execution. It is not a quality
experience in inner duration. It is nothing intensive at all; its

character is exclusively extensive. It is something expanded in expansion, something quantitatively measurable and homogeneous; it is the substratum of a formerly differentiated inner event which has been robbed of all differentiating manifoldness. In itself, the past movement is not reducible to the ongoing movement: it is the symbolic form into which the ongoing movement has been transformed by the acting I. Thus, the third connotation of the term movement is movement as traversed space, as travelled path. We know it well from physics, which counts among its con-   p.130 stituting categories just this kind of measurable movement in space and time.

An investigation of the relations among intended, ongoing and passed-away movement may serve a better understanding of the symbolic function of the acting I.

Again, I stand before the clock with the pendulum and, without touching it, try to follow its swing with my hand.[50]

[[I intend to traverse a path, to execute a movement, which matches the swing of the pendulum. However, at a certain point, my finger meets a solid object, preventing it from moving on. When I planned the movement, the obstacle was 'unknown' to me. I may say that I discovered the object when it stopped my movement. By being stopped, I became aware, in terms of passed-away movement, of the distance travelled thus far.]]

Up to this point, everything would be simple and obvious, were   p131 it not for the ongoing movement which occurred between intended and arrested movement. Let us look at the ongoing movement of the pendulum which our finger intended to follow. [[Since the object hampers only the movement of my finger but not that of the pendulum, I can visually follow the complete swing of the pendulum. I can experience it, in inner duration, as flowing-away quality experiences. The same would be the case if I would put my finger on the pendulum and let it be carried along with its swing. When my independently moving finger is stopped, what happens to the rest of the intended movement? I do not experience this rest in the same manner in which I experienced the intended and executed movement. The preconditions for the ongoing movement of the acting I, the memory-conditioned and the somatically given unity[51] in inner duration are totally absent. Yet, the intentionality of the movement of the acting I remains. The idea of the intended total movement continues to be effective in memory-endowed duration. The question is whether the intended movement would be experi-   p.132 enced, after the interruption, as ongoing or whether the intentional unity relation is not a suitable criterion for differentiating between movement and action.]]

As insoluble as it appears, this paradox springs from a tautology in terms, in the conceptions of 'action' and 'movement.' The case is highly remarkable; on it depend all theories of freedom and determination of the will. With the unmasking of this paradox as a false problem, the dispute between determinism and indeterminism - an abundant ingredient of the history of philosophy - is also characterized as a false conflict.[52]

The reason for the confusion is given in the treatment of the life form of memory-endowed duration as completely equal with the drastically different symbol structure of the life form of the acting I: The characteristic aspect of symbol formation by the acting I is ignored. Intended movement, ongoing, and finished movements in themselves are not comparable. Similarly, the flowing-away of duration and (the events in, HRW) the spatial-temporal world are incommensurable.

p.133   Indeed, the connection, established under (II) in terms of the ongoing movement, is merely a connection among quality images. The three unity relations which we established there apply only to memory-endowed duration. If we postulated under the (II) the existence of the intentional unity relation as criterion of 'action,' we did so only in order to distinguish the 'experience of action' from all other 'experiences of movement.' This investigation was necessary. Thanks to the unity of the I, reciprocal relations between individual life forms must allow their mutual reduction to one another. Our example showed most clearly that the acting I merely executes the symbolization of intentional movement into finished movement, and that the flowing-along of the movement belongs exclusively to duration. In so far as the 'acting I' participates in the ongoing movement, it does so only by executing it. In other words: *in ongoing action, the acting I symbolizes the intended movement in* (the form of, HRW) *traversed space. And this in the same manner in which memory, by 'remembering,' executes the symbolization of the quality experience of the apperceptive image in the meaning image.* The flow of the movement, the manifestation of life by the acting I pure and simple can be experienced only in memory-endowed duration.

We now turn to the symbol function of the acting I and the reinterpretation of the intended movement or the intended act of will in (the conceptions of, HRW) extended space.

(16)   THE SYMBOL FUNCTION OF THE ACTING I

p.134   Most of all: in the investigation of the symbol function of the acting I, we deal with a much more complicated symbol system than that of memory-endowed duration. In the latter, the symbol relation concerned merely apperceptive images and meaning images. In the sphere of the acting I, we have a dual relation. As in the case of memory-endowed duration and its neat separation from pure duration, an exact definition of the acting I is of greatest significance for establishing the appropriate symbol relations.

Our earlier investigation of the form of awareness of our body has shown that we 'experience' our body in most diverse ways. The following is an attempt at giving a short summary of these events of consciousness:

(I)   Forms of experience of the body which belong directly to memory-endowed duration:

(a) Body as experience of quality, or else of the apperception
of one sense, notably the sense of vision and touch: I look at my
hand. I touch my hair. Such experiences are not different from
other sensory quality experiences. They enter memory-endowed
duration, where they are symbolized yet do not give the experience
of the body a privileged position. Special case: pain as particular
sensory experience of touch.

(b) Body as 'constant' quality experience of the sense of
touch; actually, 'constant' experience of the 'medium' surrounding
my body: 'boundaries of my body.' This experience stands out   p.135
from other quality experience in that it is 'constant.' That means,
it belongs to every Now and Thus of memory-endowed duration.
However, on account of continual manifoldness, it is not experienced as constant. Thus, it too does not acquire a privileged
position.

(c) Sensual and visual experience of bodily movement: my
finger slides over a piece of paper. The finger, which I see in
movement, does not in itself entitle me to conclude that the finger
seen is my finger - the quality of experience of the somatic feeling of life does (see below under (II)). Therefore, this form of
experience, also, does not warrant a privileged position. In itself,
the experience of movement during its course is common to every
movement, not only that of my body. This is so because the ongoing movements belong exclusively to memory-endowed duration.
But, for this sphere, it is irrelevant whether I move my finger
across the paper or whether the paper is moved across my finger.

(II) The form of life belonging to the somatic feeling of life
which enters memory-endowed duration only mediately.
The body as functional context; namely:
(a) The body moved involuntarily:
    (A) Without parallel experience of an 'impulse': breathing,
    heartbeat.
    (B) With 'simultaneous,' that is parallel, experience of an
    impulse: reflection of light which blinds my eyes.
    (C) The body moved by an 'external' force: the finger on   p.136
    the pendulum.
(b) The body moved deliberately.

All forms of experience of the body, mentioned under (II),
enjoy a privileged position among all quality experiences. They,
and only they, own the somatic feeling of life in immediate experience. The 'moving' body alone conveys to me a specific awareness
of belonging-to-me; it is immediately 'given' in my experience. It
does not need proof; yet, it is as original as any apperceptional
image of inner duration.

Which of these forms of consciousness is characteristic for our
'acting' I?

Obviously, none mentioned under (I). They are not specific;
they were investigated only in order to demonstrate the effect of
the acting I upon memory-endowed duration.

Even a superficial glance at the experiences, which we named under (II), shows that, in the course of the investigation thus far, we have drawn two events together under the title, 'acting I.' First, the involuntary movement which nevertheless is accessible to the somatic feeling of life; second, the deliberate movement which alone constitutes the concept of 'action' in linguistic usage.

p.137   The difference between the two groups ought to be clear: both have in common the somatic experience of the given functional context; therefore, both share the symbolization of this functional context as something extended, expanded, as space or, what amounts to the same: not with regard to somatic feeling of life but in respect to the quality experience in memory-endowed duration, they share the symbolization of the ongoing movement into the passed-away movement.

In future, we shall designate by the term '*acting* I'[53] those experiences which language calls 'action' pure and simple (IIb) - in contrast to the first group of the 'moved I.' Beyond this, in these experiences inheres a specific characteristic: the act of will. Its content is the 'conception,' the 'project,' the 'plan' of the future movement. Its nature awaits investigation. As specific symbol relation, the 'intended movement' belongs exclusively to it. Therefore, this symbol relation must be connected both with the symbol function of the 'finished movement' common to the 'moved' as well as the 'acting' I and with expansion, with space.

First, we turn to the less-complicated experience, the moved I. What constitutes the symbol relation has been repeatedly stated and demonstrated. But we must again emphatically refer to the dual function of this relation. One or the other comes into play according to whether one focuses on that which is specific for the higher life form or for the primitive life form.

p.137a   (A) With regard to the specific mode of the moved 'I' (that form of consciousness which separates this I from memory-endowed duration) and thus with regard to the somatic feeling of life, the moved I symbolizes the experience of the functional context into an experience of extension, of space.

(B) With regard to the more primitive life form of memory-endowed duration, the moved I symbolizes as finished movement the ongoing movement, the movement going on exclusively in memory-endowed duration.[54]

(17)   INSERT: LIFE FORMS, METHODOLOGICAL A PRIORI, IDEAL TYPES

According to our theory of life forms and of the symbol relations which alone constitute the former, every life form - on the one hand -- must be reducible to the more primitive one. On the other hand, one specific characteristic must be added in order to change the more primitive into the higher life form. In our sphere, this specific characteristic is the somatic feeling of life. Our symbol theory is confirmed only if its five propositions fit the symbol structures of the moved and the acting I.

These major propositions, most of all, treat the relation between higher and lower life form. Nevertheless, they will have to be applied to the present context. In unchanged form, according to their essence, they apply only to the relation of the symbol to memory-endowed duration, that is, to the reinterpretation of the ongoing movement as passed-away movement. Should one feel compelled, for any reason whatever, to exclude memory-endowed duration from consideration, one would have to derive the validity of these propositions within the life form of the moved I as the more primitive one. It is easy to see that, here too, they could be deduced from the parallel position of somatic feeling of life and pure simple duration and of the parallel position of moving I and memory-endowed duration - both without reference to quality experiences. p.138

It should be possible to demonstrate that, in the more primitive life form (= somatic feeling of life), the symbol (= extension, space) is identical with that which it symbolizes (= functional context). In the higher life form (= the moved I), symbol and symbolized are discrepant. This results from a simple consideration.

However, we are not forced to exclude either pure or memory-endowed duration from our investigation. On the contrary, it is our problem to reduce all experiences of our being and our world to memory-endowed duration, to let them originate in it. Thus, we will attempt to prove that our major propositions pertain to the reinterpretation of the ongoing movement as finished movement. This completely suffices for the purpose of our investigation. According to our conception, the phenomenon of the somatic feeling of life can be introduced in the sphere of the moved I as constituting factor. This includes the positing of the ongoing movement as experience of my body in a functional context: a new fact which constitutes the sphere of the moved I.

Even in memory-endowed duration, I do not start from every ongoing movement whatever, but solely from the ongoing movement of *my body* as substratum of the symbol relation. My somatic feeling of life selects from among all ongoing movements which I experience. Due to this, the functional context is included in memory-endowed duration. It is easy to recognize that the 'finished' movement, if not *signifying, presupposes* extension and discontinuum, the quantifiable and the homogeneous: in short, *space*. When starting from memory-endowed duration and explaining the transformation of its experiences by the moved I (ongoing into finished movement), we will have explained the symbol relation. In the sphere of the somatic feeling of life, it will have to be shown as a specific characteristic of the moved I. However, not only for the sake of completeness but for reasons of principle, we had to point out that the asserted symbol function of the moved I can be formulated in dual fashion. This depends on whether the investigation reaches into the next lower form of life or whether it is executed immanently. On this occasion, I may be permitted to offer a short remark about the method of these investigations. p.139

From the above considerations result important consequences for the theory of the symbol; in every respect, they justify the tenets established so far. The relativity of all life forms manifests itself clearly; it is the primary starting point of any kind of considerations which have as their object the symbol or other structural analyses. This is sufficiently justified already by the pragmatic character which inheres in the 'life forms' as ideal-typical concepts formed for this purpose. Yet, serious consideration is warranted by a demand which can be derived from this methodological position: every Apriori must be viewed as relative as long as it does not penetrate into the most primitive life form in which symbols can be found at all and, thus, are accessible to our cognition. That means memory-endowed duration.

p.140

Otherwise, to assert an Apriori in any kind of context does not say anything but that the aprioristic form is not discoverable (that is symbolically not explainable or interpretable) in that life form which, in the given case, is investigated. In such factualities, when accepted as a priori, manifests itself most clearly the boundary at which philosophical, epistemological, or logical systems stop their investigations in order to fall into metaphysics, religion, or methodological syncretism. Of course, no objection can be raised against positing such an Apriori for practical reasons. More, it is absolutely necessary to do so when one does not want to or cannot continue certain investigations beyond a given sphere (we would say: beyond the actual life form). But one ought to realize that nothing more is stated with the assertion of the apriority or aposteriority of a phenomenon.

We deliberately decided to work with 'pre-scientific' materials and believe that we have avoided the main disadvantages of any Apriori because we accepted the world as experience, not as object of cognition. Yet, we too encounter certain phenomena which we have to recognize as given data, as fundamental presuppositions of our 'experiencing,' in short: as Apriori of experience. However, these Apriorities are found long before (much prior to, HRW) the Apriorities of cognition: they motivate the latter and make them deducible. It cannot be denied that our method, too, has forced us to accept at least apparently a-prioristically givens *(Tatbestaende)*, such as: 'inner duration,' 'memory,' 'somatic feeling of life,' 'consociate' (Thou). They remain as unexplainable residues. Nevertheless, it appears to me that these 'Apriori' are basically different from the cognitive 'Apriori.' The a priori of experience admits merely the incommunicability of everything lying before it, but not its non-immediacy.[55]

p.141

Further reduction is not communicable. This results from the fact that we cannot go beyond the sphere of memory-endowed duration: we are symbol-bound by our cognition, thinking, speaking, acting, remembering. Our ultimate possibility of communicatio exists in the ability to irradiate the symbol cover, not to break through it. Such a break-through can appear only in the most primitive, most original devotion to ones most personal, most primtive, most original life. Now, everyone may check whether it may

be just this devotion to his own life which makes evident that
memory, inner duration, somatic feeling of life, etc., are merely   p.142
mediacies *(Mittelbarkeiten)* of experience. Behind them is the
mystery, which is solved by every one of our changes of breath
but by none of our thoughts.

Maybe this leads really into that metaphysics of which the
general considerations of this book have already been accused
from many quarters.[56] One accusation, however, will have to be
accepted as justified without fear and perhaps with some pride –
provided one means by metaphysics that truly transcendental
method which finds the precondition of cognition not in cognition
but in experience, as far as the latter is recognizable. This
pride finds its justification in the self-liquidation of relativism.
The latter occurs here in a similar way as in Einstein's physics –
regardless of the great difference in the range and significance
(Tragweite) of the respective investigations.

The Apriori may be limited by this or that life form: the symbol
or meaning relations exist rightfully as derivations from that life
form which was selected as basis. The same goes for anything
which constitutes the typification of these relations. However, we
grant freely that we do not deal with categories when we deal
with life forms and derive apriorities from them; we simply deal
with ideal types. Certainly, these ideal types are cognitively and
therefore categorically defined. This, too, has to be freely ad-
mitted.

It follows that the limit of the ideal type, thus defined, is given
in its usefulness exclusively for cognition but not for experience.
Essentially, the latter is non-rational and beyond all typification,
as long as it is experienced and not considered in retrospective
reflection. Secondly, the limits of the ideal type result from the   p.143
self-imposed limitations of the characteristic realm of our thinking.
All this will have to be treated more thoroughly, at the end of the
first part, after the conclusion of the investigation of the theory
of the life forms.[57]

(18)   CONTINUATION: THE SYMBOL FUNCTION OF THE
       ACTING I

To (A): The conceptually thinking person lives in time and space;
he is accustomed to the process of reinterpretation which occurs
with the symbolization of life as the functional context of the body
seen as something extended, as object, as substance. This is
practically taken for granted. For our investigation, we have to
refer to such habituation because we deal with the origin of these
habits of thought. To the thinking person in the space-time world,
the relations between functional context and substance become
most of all evident on the grounds of a logical conclusion: with the
concept of function itself, a substance which functions is posited.[58]
However, no 'substance' exists for the somatic feeling of life as
datum, as something given. Substance, as something extensive,

as thing, as something prevailing, is solely the product of a
symbol transformation, executed in and through the somatic feeling of life.

Earlier, we demonstrated that the somatic feeling of life experiences the body in functional context. Within the feeling of life,
the body which does not function does not become evident. However, at best, the assumption of a body which does not function
is admissible for pedagogical reasons. For the living and conscious

p.144   person, a 'position of absolute rest' is always assumption, never
experience. An 'absolute state of rest' is reached only with the
disappearance of any consciousness and thus also of specifically
somatic experiences: that is, in death. As long as I breathe and
am aware of my breathing, as long as my heart beats, as long as
- beyond all memory-endowed quality experiences - I am aware of
the position of my sitting, standing, lying body, I cannot speak
of a 'position of absolute rest.' On account of this, the somatic
feeling of life obtains a character of perpetuity and continuity
which is closely related to inner duration and is often confused
with it.[59]

p.145   No moment of our life passes in which somatic feelings of life
would not be active; that is, in which our body does not function.
Therefore, we cannot speak of a rest position but only of perpetual change. In the sphere of the somatic feeling of life, this
change is experienced as change in muscle tension. But it is
interpreted as awareness of the extension of our body. In an
important respect this change is different from the change which
is the criterion of memory-endowed duration: although perpetual,
it does not change constantly; it is not manifold. In the act of
breathing, I always experience somatically the same muscles in
tension and relaxation. In principle, they are and have to be
different, for instance, from the movement of my hand (that is,
from changes in the states of tension of the muscles of my hand
or finger) or of my foot. The similarities (of somatic experiences
of muscular movements, HRW) disappear immediately when one
steps out of the sphere of pure somatic feeling of life into the
sphere of memory-endowed duration - even though the latter is
indirectly affected by somatic experiences.

Earlier, we posed the question as to how this 'sameness' of
somatic experiences can be recognized in the somatic, memory-free
sphere. The question is justified. The answer can and must be
that the 'sameness' is not experienced in the somatic sphere itself;

p.146   the moved I constitutes it symbolically in the somatic sphere. That
the pure somatic life form, in the experience of the functional
context of the body, admits of groups of similar experiences is an
inference from the experiences of the 'moved' I. The latter does
not solely belong to the somatic sphere; simultaneously, if flows
along *(dauert)*. Therefore, it symbolizes not only the functional
context into substance but also the ongoing movement into passed-
away movement.

If our hypothesis of the symbol function of the acting, or else th
moved, I is correct - at best, every symbol theory can only pro-

duce hypotheses – our body is experienced in the pure somatic sphere, although *in* a functional context but not as functional context. Rather, thanks to the moved I, it is experienced as something extended. For instance, somatically I experience my hand only when I move it. On the basis of my anatomical and physiological knowledge (saying that my hand is moved only by specific muscles and that such movement manifests itself in a certain state of tension and relaxation of these muscles), I have so far assumed that I experience, in pure somatic feeling of life, only the changes of the tensions in my hand. This is a complicated natural-scientific conclusion drawn from a context of experience. I am entitled to assert that I 'experience' my hand only when a change in the tension of my hand muscles occurs. But, then, I   p.147 do not experience it as change of muscle tension but as hand; that is, as (presently still unknown) organ of my body, which I can move: I can shift its 'position' in an extended medium *outside of me,* without thereby changing the 'self-awareness' of my hand, the awareness that it belongs to me. The positional change in an outside medium specifically constitutes the experience of my hand as an extended object, as thing. With reference to the sphere of the pure somatic feeling of life, the most important thing remains the unitary reference to something remaining unchangingly similar. I may lift, raise, move to left or right, and turn my hand; I may constantly change its 'position' in the outer medium. Nevertheless, for my somatic feeling of life, it is my *right* and not my left hand which I moved: it is a not-yet-named organ which, in the higher life form of the speaking I, I will give the name 'right hand.'

It seems to me that this somatic unity relation is the main proof for the statement that, purely somatically, the body becomes something extended just through movement which is reinterpreted by the functional context. Ultimately, the position of our body in space can be experienced only somatically. The terms 'right,' 'left,' 'before,' 'behind,' 'above,' 'below' are definitely of somatic origin. They explain themselves, in the pure feeling of life, through the experience of the 'position' of our body. This, however, becomes only possible through the discussed transformation   p.148 of something functioning into something extended.

It remains to investigate whether this transformation can indeed claim symbol character. Do the five major propositions of the symbol relation, as formulated, apply to this relation? As already explained,[60] this proof can easily be furnished if one parallels the relation of somatic feeling of life to the moved I with the relation of pure duration to the memory-endowed I. Here, we shall refrain from carrying out this comparison in greater detail in order to prevent a further swelling of these unavoidably inflated expositions of the acting I.

But we will shortly point to the reinforcement and self-clarification to which this experience is subjected in the somatic sphere of the moved I: experiences of a sensual, and especially of a visual and tactile nature. They issue from memory-endowed duration yet join the experiences of the moved I.

(1) The somatically experienced shift of the body in space is also sensually experienced through the stimulation of the sense of touch, which evokes an awareness of the 'boundaries of the body.'

(2) The somatic change of position is visible. That means, the initiated change of the tension of my hand muscles, which is somatically experienced as 'hand movement,' regularly evokes (through memory) certain changes in the given visual quality experience of the coordinated Now and Thus.

p.149   (3) The somatic change of position is ascertainable by touch. The initiated movement in the tension of the flexor of my little finger, which I experience as 'bending the little finger,' brings about a change in the quality experience in the given Now and Thus, which corresponds to the sense of touch. These experiences are of dual nature:

(a) Tactile experience of the touched hand.
(b) Tactile experience of the touching little finger.[61]

It may be noted that the experience under (1) constantly coincides with the somatic feeling of life of the moved I. Experiences (2) and (3) occur only when the 'movement' of my bodily organs actually falls, or is brought, within the 'field' of my sense of vision or touch. A still other experience partakes in the perpetuality of the 'touch sensation of my body,' namely,

(4) the experiences of the ongoing movement which symbolizes itself in finished movement through the moved or the acting I.

p.150   Of all these parallels between somatic and sensual experiences, as described above, only those mentioned under (1) and (4) are relevant for the moved I. (2) and (3) are not relevant for the reinterpretation of the symbol but attain highest significance for the coordination of the constructed symbol with the space-time world of the unitary I. They offer extremely important information for the theory of the fields of touch and vision.

Most of all, the fourth of these parallels between somatic and sensual experiencing demands greatest attention. In it manifests itself the symbol function of the moved I, offering the reinterpretation of the ongoing movement into finished movement. However, before we turn to this symbol function, a few explanations of the concept of the extended are in order; we recognized it, in the somatic sphere, as symbol of the bodily functional context.

(19) EXTENSION

Generally, common sense comprehends as extended that which can be touched. This issues from the preponderance of touch experiences. Before all other experiences, they are connected with the apperception of that which is expanded. This linguistic usage may appear to be philosophically justified. Indeed, as repeatedly stated, in the experience of space the sense of touch occupies an especially privileged position.

However, what, in the sense of our previous considerations, is   p.151
the extensive and what are its specific characteristics?

In preparation of the answer, let us recapitulate that, by
contrast, we understood by the intensive that which belongs to
all experiences in duration.

The major characteristic of the intensive was its purely qualitative feature. . . . It entered completely into pure duration.
Consequently, it was subjected to all rules of the flow of duration,
but only to these. Nothing in the flow of duration allows me to
infer an external from which I obtain my experiences or by which
I am affected. My experience is completely in me. As long as I
remain in the sphere of my duration, I cannot in the least establish
whether there exists something which releases or causes this experience. I am not even provoked to look for a cause of experience
or for an inducement of being-affected. I receive quality images
without as yet knowing from where they come or how I receive
them, or whether I produce them myself. They are well ordered
in themselves; and this already for the reason that they belong to
me, the I which experiences his duration. They enter residueless
into the given Now and Thus of my duration.

In memory-endowed duration, these experiences are grouped
differently. My memory, which directly constitutes the manifoldness of my duration, coordinates individually received quality
experiences into new symbol series. Now, they belong to me in   p.152
two respects: first as series of apperceptive images, second as
successions of meaning images. This arrangement is determined
by my given Now and Thus and the direction of the flow of my
duration. Otherwise, it occurs independent of me according to the
principles of symbol contexts. In this respect, my quality experiences have no life of their own. They are not constant; they lack
the features of similarity and closure, of homogeneity and independence. In reverse: the manifoldness and continuity of my
memory allows me to experience my experiences as continuous and
manifold. Further, their intensive character is connected with the
fact that experiences are not 'things,' that is, objects closed in
themselves; they are images, that is, apperceptions enclosed in
my experiences of duration.

By contrast, the world of the extensive is characterized by the
comprehension of qualities as quantities. Quality 'experiences,'
having been images in inner duration, are now considered characteristics of such substances *(Wesenheiten)*, seen as self-sufficient
(autark). Necessarily, the self-sufficiency of things presupposes
their removal from the flow of duration. They are transposed into
externality. Thereby, they lose most of all the character of manifoldness typical for the flow of duration. Individual quality experiences are no longer constituents of my Now and Thus. Rather,
they are qualities of things which are in themselves closed and   p.153
independent. They are chosen and put together according to
selective criteria of relative similarity. These objects - and this is
important - would be there and have their particular form of

existence even if I did not experience them.

What had been quality experience of my sense of touch becomes now a dimension of things which would exist and persist, even if I do not touch anything. What had been visual quality experience in my duration, becomes color and shape, existing independently of my eyes. And more: all those forms and colors belong to a single object, to an individual thing as such. It is divisible and measurable and characteristic for this particular object. No flowing-together-and-apart . . . exists in the realm of objects. Every object is delimited in itself and exists independently of me; it changes independently of my duration. Nay, it has its own duration, inaccessible and incomprehensible to me, and follows its own laws. The multitudinous appearance of objects, also, no longer obeys (the rules of, HRW) the contexts established by my I, which is affected by these objects. Scattered over the whole discontinuous yet homogeneous space, every one of these objects leads its own self-sufficient existence. As a thinking being who also lives in the sphere of concepts and Science, I know of re- lations between objects, for instance, cause and effect. Such re- lations must be thought of as primitive, as self-sufficient as the things themselves and without relation to me and to my duration. A relation to me may occur only when I, no longer acting, face objects in space cognitively. But, in this case, they are related to me not as subjects of experience of my acting I, but as subjects of cognition. The identity of such a subject of cognition with me cannot be recognized without ado.

This is a preliminary characterization of objects, still incomplete and in need of further elaboration. All these characteristics of objects can be reduced to the fact that things do not exist within me. Rather, because and while they are extended, they exist in space. All their other characteristics can be deduced from spatial- ity, from dimension as such. If I fill the conception or the experi- ence of space even with only one single object, it necessarily follows that the qualities, which are experience, are also objecti- fied and materialized in this newly created space. The latter, it will be shown, is unlimited. I have discovered a form of the exist- ence of things which is different and independent of my existence. For me, this space is no longer a confusing agglomeration of color patches or other visual apperceptions – which it was in the experi- ence of space in my memory-endowed duration. It now is filled space, filled with things which have (their independent, HRW) characteristics and dimensions. I can convince myself of their existence any time by stepping toward things or bring them close to me and allow my body, as carrier of my apperceptions, to be affected by them.

From this follows that, with the spatiality of *one* thing, the spatiality of all other things has been discovered and given. And more: with space itself – wherever this conception may have originated – a world is constituted which is basically different from non-dimensional inner duration.

Thereby, one question has been answered which may have force

itself upon the reader of this characterization of the extensive:
the experience of my own body, of something extensive, occurs in
my moved or acting I; how could it affect such a basic change in
the whole world?

The answer to this question results from the following considerations. In its effects, the discovery of space cannot be limited to
the object which led to it. When I observe the characteristics of
the spatial and the extended on my body, I have not only discovered the dimensions of my body but the dimensional world itself. When I discover an 'outside' in the sense of not-belonging-
to-me - and this discovery occurs with the somatic awareness of
my moving in what necessarily is an outside - it becomes possible
also to project quality experiences into a sphere outside-of-me.
An acting I, just by its acting, is in fact forced to establish a
coincidence between his somatic - better, his acting - experiences
with the flowing-along of certain quality experiences in his inner
duration. If I am permitted to say so, I act toward things. Formerly, they yielded only quality experiences; now, I pull them   p.156
into the realm of my sphere of action. And while I make them into
objectives or means of my own bodily movements, they become
corporeal things. They acquire object character through contact
with my body. I establish that they have in common with my body
a space-filling quality: extension.

This can be established only by my moved, by my acting or
else I. I alone can experience similarity in a homogeneous discontinuum instead of manifoldness in the continuum of duration. Nay,
more: the reinterpretation of ongoing into finished movement,
which occurs in and through the acting I, destroys inner duration.
It breaks through it and simultaneously renews it in a different
and higher sense. Thus, the acting I brings a dualism into the
world, which has not yet been overcome, and never will be. The
passed-away movement, as traversed road and travelled distance,
is conditioned spatially and temporarily. It is fundamentally different from ongoing movement; through its dimensionality, it constitutes space in the same manner as the body in its somatic
activity in itself.

Next, we will shortly investigate how this symbolization occurs.
More, too, will have to be said about the experience of space itself, about its consequences, and especially about its retroactive
effects on the formation of the world of qualities in the context of
duration.

(20) MOVEMENT INTO SYMBOL   p.157

To (B): We still remember the results of our earlier investigation
of various kinds of movement. For a start, our thesis says that
the moved I reinterprets the ongoing movement which, according
to our presupposition, belongs exclusively to memory-endowed
duration. It transforms it into a new form of movement by way of
the symbol relation. To prove this will be the easier as we already

have collected the necessary materials for it in earlier investigations. By way of a short reminder, we will reiterate what differentiates the ongoing movement in memory-endowed duration from
all other movement in progress: the somatic component entering
into my duration.

I am holding a pen in my hand and put it on this sheet of
paper. By an external force, the paper is drawn along under my
unmoving hand. A line . . . occurs on the paper. In my inner
duration, I can exactly follow the movement of the sheet. However,
this movement is not specific, not privileged before any other
movement apperceived by me, for instance, as the swings of the
pendulum of a clock which I see. Like any other movement, it
consists of a constant change of quality images. The line which
appeared on the sheet is merely another quality experience. I
conclude that it originated through movement, but I do not ex-
p.158   perience this. In itself, it has as yet nothing to do with the movement.

How different (is this experience, HRW), when the paper is not
pulled along under my hand but when, through an external force,
my hand is pulled across the sheet, or when I myself guide my
hand over it.[62]

Here, the somatic feeling of life, as quality experience, is included in the flow of duration. It constitutes the new life form of
the moved I.[63] The ongoing movement still exists, but only for the
subordinated life form of memory-endowed duration. Thanks to
the moved I, only the finished movement can be experienced in the
actual life form.

[[While my hand moves a certain distance, my inner duration
moves accordingly. At any given Now and Thus, my quality experiences in inner duration find an image of the hand at the corresponding point. Every Now and Thus simultaneously contains,
next to the specific apperceptive image of the hand, also the
memory or symbol images of previous moments. This effects a
p.159   steady continuity of quality experiences. The latter is evoked by
the constant reference of the given Now and Thus to the flow of
duration and the symbol structure of earlier moments.]]

*In accordance with the nature of duration, I experience the on-
going movement as continually becoming movement.* [[Extensive
mathematical expositions show that]] the movement will ever be
experienced as becoming, as flowing in the direction of duration.
p.160   [[Turning to the algebraic illustration of this flow in its significance for the moved I, the following must be realized:]] (. . . it
is no more possible to dress this event into words than any other
event in inner duration. The preceding exposition will have to be
accepted as an attempt at 'translating' the immediate experience of
duration into words.)

*For the moved I, experience is not the becoming movement but
movement as far as it has passed away.*[64]

p.161   [[In the sphere of memory-endowed duration, a quality image of
the hand had been coordinated with a series of meaning images of
the hand at earlier moments. Originally, these meaning images

were quality images of somatic quality sensations. Thus, they
were identical with the experience of the moved I passing through
points in space. – The original identity of quality image and meaning image and the fact of their subsequent separation may be
viewed as contradiction.]]

However, this is no objection but merely a confirmation of the
symbol character which must be ascribed to the passed-away
movement, in the life form of the acting (moved) I, in contrast to
the ongoing movement. In content, the apparent objection is nothing else but our *first major thesis about the symbol.* Applied to
our life forms, it says:

(1) *The nature of the replacement of the ongoing movement by*   p.162
the symbol of the passed-away movement is rooted in the identity
of the space traversed (as symbol) with the ongoing movement (as
that which is symbolized) in memory-endowed duration (as the
more primitive sphere of the I) on the one hand. On the other
hand, it is rooted in *the discrepancy between space traversed (as*
symbol) and ongoing movement (as that which is symbolized) in
the life form of the acting (moved) I (as actual life form).

By dividing this dual thesis, we obtain:

(1a) *Traversed space and ongoing movement are one in memory-*
endowed duration as form of consciousness which precedes the
acting I.

(b) *Traversed space and ongoing movement are discrepant*
already by virtue of the points which are coordinated to them in
the flow of duration and in the acting (moved) I. The ongoing
movement passes into traversed space in the same manner as
becoming passes into passing-away.

Possibly, this proposition is in need of a small correction. The
two experiences, points of which are coordinated either to the
symbolized or to the symbol, are actually not located in the flow
of duration but in the element of time which is characteristic and
specific to the moved (acting) I. This is to be understood only
in the following sense: the reinterpretation of duration as time
comes about only by interpolating the concept of space, by projecting the intensive givenness (Element) of duration into the homogeneous medium of space. We will demonstrate this later.[65] Proposition (1b) would have to be formulated differently, according to
whether one derives the symbol relation on the basis of memory-   p.163
endowed duration or whether one uses the relevance system of the
medium of time, as constituted by the moved (acting) I. The proposition is justified in both cases.

[[The distance covered by a movement becomes traversed space
not only when seen from the vantage point of the passed-away
movement; but also when seen from the perspective of a becoming
movement.]]

What has been said above leads effortlessly to the formulation of
the *second major proposition* of symbol relation, when applied to
our case:

(2) *The ongoing movement can be experienced as becoming and*
passing away only in memory-endowed duration. As present move-

*ment of the acting (moved) I, it is passed-away movement. Thus,
it can be experienced only as existent* (by itself, HRW). *Space
exists independent of our duration.*

The comparison of (the formulation of, HRW) this proposition
with that given on occasion (of the exposition, HRW) of the
analogous symbol relation of apperceptive image and meaning
image shows several deviations. They are rooted in the nature of
the two different life forms which are involved in each case. We
should remember here what we said about the earlier thesis concerning the positing of the symbol of the apperceptive image in
pure duration and its transposition into a 'meaning image' in
memory-endowed duration.

At that time, we confronted actual and potential experiences.
p.164 By actual experience of that which is symbolized, we meant that
it can be experienced as phenomenon which passes away. This
is clear with regard to the apperceptive image in pure duration.
. . . Only, one must remember that the relation of becoming and
passing away . . . represents a provisional auxiliary construction, made for didactic reasons. In the same life form exists nothing passed away in itself or (if it did, HRW) I would not know
about it. For this reason, we said that what becomes of that
which has passed-away becomes visible to us in the perspective
of the higher life form. That it is something passed away in a
lower life form I know only because I symbolized it in a higher
life form. Only what has passed away allows itself to be symbolized.
The relation between that which is symbolized and the symbol is
embodied in the tension which our experiencing suffers, on
account of the disparate points in inner duration (or else, as will
be shown, in time) to which the symbolized and the symbol are
coordinated. We called this tension between life forms 'meaning.'
The meaning character of memory-endowed duration, most of all,
manifests itself in (the fact, HRW) that the apperceptive image
did definitely pass away but, time and again, *becomes* anew as
meaning image. We called this constant becoming the potential
experienceability of the symbol.

While this form of consideration can claim much general significance, in derivation and form it is too much adapted to the re-
p.165 lation between pure and memory-endowed duration. For this
reason, we had to resort to the auxiliary construction of becoming
and passing-away. However, in the symbol sphere of the acting I
. . . pure duration with its - merely apparent - becoming and
passing away is pierced through. The acting I constitutes its own
adequate form of consciousness: the world of space and time.
Through 'attention,' through a change of the direction of our
view, duration has been 'arrested.' Duration is ever and ever
again suspended through the experience of anything extended -
be it derived from a passed-away movement and thus by way of
memory, or else from the functional context of the body and thus
somatically. It has no place in the world of the acting (moving)
I in which exists only space-time.[66]

It is necessary to clarify this circumstance sufficiently in order

to make understandable the meaning of our second major proposition. . . . Therefore, we feel obliged to insert here an intermediary consideration, concerning the nature of the experience
of time. (Yet, we remain aware that, HRW) this nature can be
completely determined only in the over-all description of that
world which offers itself to our acting (moving) I.

(21) THE EXPERIENCE OF TWO LIFE FORMS

Earlier, we attempted a characterization of the world of space. As p.166
discontinuum, space is filled with objects, that is, with exten-
sities *(Ausgedehntheiten)*. They are homogeneous, independent
of me, endowed with specific qualities, and self-sufficient. In the
concepts of the extended and the homogeneous, we have denied
everything which we established as essential for our image of
objects in pure duration, for our quality experiences. We did the
same when we stated that things are self-sufficient, that is, exist
in themselves without having been priorily related to me. At this
point, we are solely concerned with designing an articulated picture of the space-time world as such and contrast it to the world
of our memory-endowed duration. Thus, it cannot now be our
task to investigate the relations between the world of our duration
and the space-time world. This must be reserved for later - after
we have solved all questions concerning the symbol relation (obtaining, HRW) between duration and acting I.[67]
   For now, we ask permission to assume that our I does not live
simultaneously in all life forms - even though this is the case by
virtue of the oneness of our consciousness. Contrary to fact, we
will for the time being admit that an imaginary I, which never
existed, lives separately and successively, within the space-time
world, in the two life forms of memory-endowed duration and of
the acting I.
   This imaginary I, suddenly, would find itself torn out of the
world of memory-endowed duration and dropped into the world
of space and time.[68]

NOTES

Editor's note: Schutz provided more than thirty footnotes, which
were typed at the bottom of the corresponding pages of the manuscript. The editor added about forty of his own. They are identified in the proper fashion.

1 AS: This is an intentionally a-logical position but not therefore
   a psychological one. For the time being, we abstain from investigating the logical character of these 'images.' For now, we
   merely refer to the significance of this term by Bergson.
   'Images,' for him, are impressions of experiences of the non-
   speculating human, a human who is non-scientific in the real

sense. They are situated midway between representations (or appresentations, HRW) and objects.

2   AS: The particular means which the artist uses in order to make this manifoldness into an experience in each by us pre-constituted picture will be treated in a separate chapter.

3   AS: When I spoke of the simultaneity of these impressions, I meant nothing more than that they, together, make up the quality of my Now and Thus in the experience of my inner duration.

4   AS: We realize that the comparing function of our memory is in no way self-understood. For the time being, we replace a complicated unknown within the complicated formula of the whole process by another unknown. This is done for the sake of simplification. Already the next section will prove that it is necessary to analyze further this provisional formulation.

5   AS: It goes without saying that Plato's theory of anamnesis deals with another kind of memory. Nevertheless, it seems to me that the need for a metaphysical derivation of our memory issues from the mystical function which it has for our life.

6   AS: One should excuse this preliminary imposition of the 'similar.' The term, of course, can only be applied to the sphere of concepts and objects but not that of images. Here, we mean only that we deal with experiences which are similar to each other when removed from our duration and formulated in concepts.

7   AS: We beg to excuse this formulation, which is raw and inten-tionally exaggerated. Here, we aim only at working out the sharpest contrast possible.

8   HRW: At this point, Schutz inserted a line diagram called 'Figure 1.' Almost two pages of the MS. which follow are covered with the interpretation of the diagram in mathematical-algebraic symbols. In the paragraph set in double brackets, I have given the core of the exposition in ordinary terms. The reason for this has been given in the 'Editor's note' on p. 29.

9   AS: (In fact, our line . . . does not present inner duration (how could it do this!)) but the line of time which corres-ponds to it.

10   HRW: Here, Schutz introduced 'Figure 2,' a variation of Figure 1. The latter is enriched by the introduction of Greek-letter symbols for the designation of time elements. The illustrative discussion of the diagram covers also two pages of the original MS. I give the essential content of this ex-position, as far as possible, in the words of Schutz.

11   HRW: The typed German text says '*korrekt*,' a term which does not make sense in this context. I assumed that this was a typing error and replaced the term by 'Korrelat,' the term most likely meant.

12   AS: There is a good reason for our statement that the symbol function of *memory* can only occur with regard to quality experiences which passed away. The relation of *the I* to the becoming quality experience is not different from its relation-

ship to the quality experience of that which passed away.

13 HRW: I omitted here nine lines of the original MS in which Schutz pointed to the 'most arbitrarily assumed representation in Figure 2.' Its mathematical expressions symbolize relationships between experiences about which 'nothing can be said.'

14 HRW: At about this point, Schutz wrote on the margin: *'Besser Spracharbeit 2ff.'* Obviously, he meant that the thoughts expressed in the present paragraph had been better presented on pp. 2ff of the essay on 'The Meaning Structure of Language.' I refrain here from a comparison of these two versions. The reader may consult the text of this essay in the present volume.

15 AS: In no way can it be taken for granted that memory inheres in every ongoing I, even though human reason would not comprehend this. Of course, the duration of a memory-free I would lack the criterion of continuous quality change. But is the *plant* (cf. Richard Semon, *Mnementheorie*) not just such an ongoing I which, merely for the want of memory, is not accessible to our life form?

16 AS: Up to now, the difference between pure and memory-endowed duration played no role in our investigation. Therefore, we indiscriminately used the term 'pure duration' without any differentiation. Now, it will become necessary to clearly differentiate between these two life forms. . . .

17 AS: Needless to say, all these 'life forms' are constructed concepts. As auxiliary hypotheses, they serve to explain certain phenomena of life. But the (existence of, HRW) symbol relations shows that consciousness is aware of these differences.

18 HRW: Here, Schutz introduced 'Figure 3.' In this diagram, he corrected the impression created by the earlier diagrams that apperceptual and meaning images are situated on a single unidirectional line. Figure 3 shows tangential lines, representing memory-endowed duration, which separate the apperceptions of memory images from the meaning images which they evoke. The explanatory text runs over two and a half pages of the original MS. I have kept my summary to a bare minimum. Schutz's comments largely serve the purpose of undoing the erroneous impressions created by the linear form of the first two diagrams. He remarked that one objection could be raised with regard to the seeming contradiction between the assumption of the identity of event and symbol in pure duration and their presentation as separate features in the new diagram: 'For the larger part, this objection is justified by the simply grotesque distortion of the actual facts *(Sachverhalt)* which we were compelled to commit in our diagram for the sake of perspicuity.'

19 HRW: About nine lines of the original MS were omitted here; they repeated notions stated in the preceding paragraph.

20 HRW: Here follows a paragraph of twelve lines, repeating prior considerations in condensed form. It has been omitted

with the exception of one remark.

21   HRW: An algebraic illustration of the preceding statement,
      given in parentheses, has been omitted.

22   AS: This, however, does not touch the possibility of symbol-
      izing the symbol; we will discuss it later.

23   AS: We will show later that the meaning image of a former
      quality image, which became a quality image, is again trans-
      formed into the meaning image of a later quality image. In
      this manner, the first quality image continues to persist in
      untold meaning images.

24   AS: We allow ourselves only one presupposition: the assump-
      tion that lower forms of life can be thought (to exist, HRW)
      without the existence of higher ones. But higher life forms
      cannot be thought without the lower ones; according to our
      hypotheses, they issue from the latter.

25   AS: We will have to return to one characteristic circumstance:
      All memories of memory images tend to be stronger than the
      memories of the quality experiences themselves; they in part
      suppress them or even replace them totally.

26   HRW: This account is interspersed with algebraic symbols.
      They are omitted here; hopefully, without impairing the
      clarity of the exposition.

27   HRW: When writing this passage, Schutz was at least 26
      years old.

28   HRW: Here, Schutz inserted 'Figure 4.' It was a single uni-
      directional line diagram, starting with O and showing tran-
      sitional points N, G1, G2, etc., but also A, B, C, etc. The
      first indicate apperceptional or memory images, the latter
      time moments. The explanation of the diagram covers almost
      six pages of the original MS. Contrary to other presentations
      of the content of Schutz's diagram illustrations, the present
      one has not been set between double brackets. It follows
      Schutz's formulations closely with the omission of the algebraic-
      symbolic parts. Omission of such passages (part of one sen-
      tence or a whole sentence) have been marked by a row of
      dots (. . .).

29   AS: Let us assume that it was not me who was anaesthetized
      but Peter, and that I witnessed the event. If, at the time, I
      had never been anaesthetized and had never heard anything
      about anaesthesia, the scene would necessarily have been in-
      comprehensible to me. Nevertheless, I would have noticed
      the man in white who stepped close to Peter's table; I would
      have heard Peter counting. If I stood far enough from the
      table, I would not have smelled the ether; and I would not
      have felt anything of Peter's fears. Yet, my memory image of
      Peter's anaesthesia would be no less meaningful than that of
      my anaesthesia. What I noticed of this event has been brought
      into my memory sphere as *my* apperceptions. Therewith, it
      has been meaningfully integrated into my (memory-endowed)
      duration, even though the event was incomprehensible to me
      and I was unable to re-experience Peter's feelings. (These

considerations do not belong into the present context. They
have been written down only because the example of anaesthesia will again be referred to for purposes of explaining
the concept of the understandability in the sphere of the
Thou. Here, it suffices to maintain that positing a meaning,
in the sphere of memory-endowed duration, signifies nothing
but the inclusion of the experience into duration. This has
nothing to do with understanding.)

30   HRW: Points (1) and (4) as well as the last paragraph have
been slightly altered by the replacement of algebraic symbols
by qualifying adverbs.

31   HRW: At this point, this paragraph carries a vertical pencil
line and a large question mark on the left margin.

32   HRW: This formulation, too, is challenged by a question mark.

33   HRW: Since Schutz did not write the second part of this
study, the announced propositions have not been written.

34   AS: In a separate chapter, to be placed after the First Main
Part, we shall deal with the argument that the recognition of
a pre-scientific sphere is simply impossible. However, we will
have to have to refer already here to some methodological
points. (HRW: This chapter was not written.)

35   HRW: Emil Lask was a member of the Southern German school
of neo-Kantianism which, through Heinrich Rickert at
Heidelberg University, influenced Max Weber's methodological
thinking considerably.

36   AS: Of course, we speak here not of 'ethical' or other particular evaluations but only of the significance of the *principle*
for life and cognition.

37   HRW: The last sentence is an allusion of a famous quote by
Goethe: 'Alles Vergaengliche ist nur ein Gleichnis'.

38   AS: It bears mentioning that 'muscular contractions and
extensions,' too, indicate a 'frozen metaphor.' The first,
'my hand,' belongs to popular language; the second to the
language of the 'well-informed' layman.

39   AS: In his *Confessions,* Saint Augustine reflected: 'You, who
wish to know yourself, do you know who you are? I know.
How do you know? I do not know. Do you know whether you
are homogeneous or manifold? I do not know. Do you know
whether you are set in motion (motivated, HRW)? Do you
know whether you think? I know.' (HRW: Schutz quoted this
passage in Latin. I am obliged to Professor Ford Weisskittel
of the Department of Classics of Hobart and William Smith
Colleges for this translation.)

40   AS: To prevent basic misunderstandings, we stress that this
kind of investigation has nothing at all to do with empirical
psychology. One may refer to the 'movement of my digestive
organs' which occur unnoticed by consciousness, in order to
refute my theory that all that which is somatic becomes evident only as movement, as the functional factor in our feeling
of life. However, this is definitely no argument against my
theory. Actually, I know extremely little about some somatic

processes - for instance, inner secretion. But what I know about them, I have not evidenced in my feeling of life; I have learned it from strictly *scientific* empirical investigations of a physiological and biological nature. Likewise, we must refute the objection that, in certain pathological cases, this or that contraction of muscles occurs unconsciously even though, according to my conception of feeling of life, it should have become evident. The (concept of, HRW) consciousness of physiologists and psychologists is completely different from that evidenced by the feeling of life. By introducing the life forms, I make a deliberate abstraction which is justified by its usefulness. To the psychologist, consciousness may mean the totality of 'psychic facts.' In addition, he comprehends these facts empirically, that is, as being subsumed under a scientific-conceptual frame of reference.

41 HRW: On first sight, one may think that 'kinesthetic function' would be a better expression. However, Bergson's choice of 'cinematographic function' is as correct as any technical term could be. Attention is not paid to the physical process but to its experience in duration. The cinematographic analogy is introduced in order to describe a succession of apperceptive images appearing in duration; they are viewed as discretely and minutely changed from one 'moment' to the next, somewhat like the frames of a moving picture strip. In his correction of Bergson's idea of successive 'states' by speaking of 'continuous motion,' Schutz may have tried to lessen the mechanical implications of the analogy.

42 HRW: Arthur Schopenhauer: *Die Welt als Wille und Vorstellung* (The World as Will and Idea), Leipzig: 1819.

43 AS: That I say also, in this case (that the surface, HRW) 'is moved,' of course is knowledge which has been conveyed to me by my observational practical knowledge *(Erfahrungs-wissen)* of the world; it is not grounded in memory-endowed duration or the somatic sphere.

44 AS: If I guide my finger not over a 'homogeneous surface' but an area of my body, the touched finger replaces the touched surface!

45 AS: In view of the whole derivation given above, it must be maintained that we deal always with a movement during its duration; that is, with becoming movement but never with passed-away movement which is retrospectively reconstructed.

46 HRW: Here follows another line diagram. It would be 'Figure 5,' but any designation has been omitted. The diagram shows two parallel lines; one gives groups of points passed through by moving from left to right, the other gives the correspondent moments of time. Diagram and explanatory text cover about two pages of the original MS.

47 AS: It is irrelevant for the present investigation that . . . I draw a straight line. Even if I would draw an . . . undulating line, the phenomena described here could be observed.

48 HRW: Between this and the next sentence a space of four

double-spaced lines has been left open in the MS. Obviously,
this was done to keep space open for another diagram ('Figure
6'). - I have the vague impression that a diagram of a pendulum in motion was drawn either on the back of the preceding or the same sheet. If so, it was overlooked in the xerox-
ing or the photographing process.

49 AS: Here, it is in principle immaterial whether I intended the
movement and carry it out myself, or whether it is executed
on me. The only important thing for the somatic experience of
the body as functional configuration is that changes of the
'tension relations' of individual parts of my body occur. . . .
If this is not the case, my somatic feeling of life does *not*
enter 'action.' So I do not somatically experience the movement
to which my body is exposed by the rotation of the earth. I
recognize this movement in terms of already executed movement, as space traversed, for instance, in the change of day
and night (see point (3) below).

50 HRW: Here follows the heading, 'Figure 7.' Four double-
spaced lines have been left open in the text. No diagram has
been drawn. The explanatory comments take up almost two
pages of the typed MS.

51 HRW: Schutz's term was 'Einheitsbezug.' The second part of
this combined noun means reference as well as relation. I was
unable to form an adequate combined noun in English.

52 HRW: Schutz referred here parenthetically to an unnumbered
and untitled chapter of the second part of the study. It was
not written.

53 AS: Up to now, we have used the term 'acting I' for both
groups without further discrimination. This will have to be
justified.

54 HRW: Here follows a footnote by Schutz, numbered 28. It
covers about six pages of the original MS. I have converted it
into a regular section of the English version, marking it as
an insert.

55 HRW: In the German text, the two key terms ('incommunicability' and 'non-immediacy') present a word play:
'Nichtmitteilbarkeit' and *'Nichtmittelbarkeit.'*

56 HRW: This statement may be a hint at private discussions
with some of Schutz's friends who were members of the circles
of the Geistkreis and the Mises Seminar.

57 HRW: Schutz did not finish the first part of this project; the
announced continuation of this topical investigation was not
carried out.

58 AS: In this context, we refer to Ernst Cassirer's investigation of the 'concept of substance and function.' (HRW:
Cassirer published this study in 1910 under the title *Sub-
stanzbegriff und Funktionsbegriff. (Substance and Function*
(combined with Einstein's Theory of Relativity) Chicago: Open
Court, 1923.)

59 AS: This assertion is not at all contradicted by the phenomenon of sleep. It even seems that, exactly in sleep, the

somatic feeling of life remains in invariable awareness. By contrast, the experience of memory-endowed duration suffers a certain change; mostly because the apperceptive images – which offer themselves to consciousness in the state of awakeness as 'main cause' of continual manifoldness – yield to memory or meaning images. The meaning images, stored in memory, therefore come to the fore in the world of dreams. Every interpretation of dreams, psychoanalytical or not, will have to put its main emphasis on the interpretation of these symbols.

60   HRW: Here, Schutz referred to his footnote 28, which I integrated into the text under the title: (17) Insert: life forms, methodological a priori, ideal types.

61   AS: We remark at this occasion that touching a body organ at rest, which thus is not somatically activated, leads to a dual touch experience. Only in this case the touch experience of the touched organ belongs exclusively to duration; the experience of the touching hand, as organ moved, is also somatically experienced. For this reason, the 'touchability of the body' – in the sense of being touched – cannot be viewed as 'proof' of the extension of the body, but only in the sense of an active possibility of touch inhering in each of my organs. Anything else is implication, based on the proposition, 'what is extended is touchable.' However, in this form, the proposition does not apply to our investigation.

62   HRW: Here follows the heading 'Figure 8.' Six double-spaced lines have been left open for the planned diagram. It has not been drawn into the MS. The next four pages of the original MS contain numerous algebraic notations which refer to the missing diagram.

63   HRW: Schutz's term is *'bewegtes Ich.'* My translation, moved I, sounds contrived, but was the best I could do. In German language, the term suggests emotion (as in: I am moved to tears) rather than bodily movement. Schutz used the term in the unusual second sense in order to express the notion of a given person (a living body of which an ego is aware as his 'own') which, as a whole or in parts of its external organs, is in motion without deliberate decision to move.

64   HRW: The subsequent text brings further elaborate algebraic illustrations for this statement. They lead to the formulation of several equations. Refering to 'travelled distance,' they display 'an exact geometrical character' and 'state that travelled distance can be added up.'

65   HRW: The demonstration of this statement was reannounced in the first paragraph of the next section of this MS. The latter came to an end half a page later. The constitution of time by interpolation of space, then, belongs to the themes of the first part of the project of the life forms, which Schutz did not treat.

66   AS: Language created two words for this – here still unitary – concept. This is explained by the fact that language finds

a given substratum for its symbol relations in form of the world constructed by the symbol-forming medium of the Thou-relation. In it, a clean separation of time and space obtains.

67 HRW: This is the last of a number of announcements of additional themes which were to be treated in the sections of the MS which Schutz did not execute.

68 HRW: The text continues with the words, 'It would most of all. . .' They complete the last page of the MS. The left margin of the first page bears the handwritten title and a note: '166 pages. Last page or pages missing.' It is unlikely that Schutz carried the investigation for the first part of this project much beyond the point at which the available MS ends.

PART II
Theory of the Structure of the Objectification of Meaning

Editor's note

The second part of Schutz's project of 1925-7 remained unexecuted. In his 'main overview,' Schutz gave a four-point outline for this part. Its translation is offered as the first item of this part. As indicated in the 'Editor's Introduction,' the manuscripts UM 1925 (on language), UM 1925-6 (on literary art forms), and UM 1924-5 (on drama and opera) will be presented as independent pieces which, by virtue of their topics and their theoretical contents, belong in the thematic realm of the second main part of the Bergson project.

The three contributions to this part are preceded by a short outline. Although the substantive topics of the three manuscripts appear to be incidental to the overall theme of Part II, they are very much concerned with the 'objectification of meaning.' Language is the extreme form of such an objectification. Literary art forms play a pronounced role in the linguistic mediation between the meaning meant by speaker, writer, author and the meaning understood by the listener or reader. The performance of a drama draws the spectator, as witness and vicarious participant, into dialogue and action on the stage, that is, into a stream of intersubjective communication in which objective language becomes a vehicle of an optimal mediation between the meaning meant by the author, the meanings expressed by the actors, and the meaning understood by the spectator. Finally, in the form of the opera, where drama is projected into the additional dimension of a musical performance, the chance for intersubjective understanding reaches its maximum. This chance results from the basically quandrangular but further differentiated relationship between composer, orchestra (director and musicians), actor/singer or actress/singer with his or her counterpart, and the listener and spectator who is in turn indirectly involved with other members of the audience. This is brought about by the unique combination of the medium of an interactive dramatic language with the medium of intersubjective musical expression: the emotional fringes of the meaning of the dramatic dialogue surrounded and enveloped by the emotional fringes of meaning of the music-in-performance.

Schutz announced the second part of his planned study as an exposition of 'meaning contexts without visible Thou.' This, indeed, applies significantly to the treatment of language as means of communication and carrier and evoker of meanings. It also applies to the literary means of expression in so far as they are read in silence: the poem or the tale and novel read. But, already on this level, Schutz's exclusion of the 'visible Thou' cannot be completely maintained. Poetry readings are not at all uncommon, and sometimes an author reads from his prose pieces or another person assumes the role of the oral narrator of a literary creation which, after all, originated in oral narration; the latter has remained the form of artistic narration: the tale written cannot be kept separated from the tale told.

But, at least the separation remains a possibility. This is not the case as far as the dramatic or the operatic art forms are concerned. Their 'consummation' occurs in their 'enactment'; they are interactional and intersubjective art forms by definition. To read a drama or an operatic score - if one has the gift to do the latter - means to reduce them to something they are not meant to be, to change them from forms of collective experience to forms of solitary absorption.

As the first main part of Schutz's project shows, his decision to confine himself analytically to the treatment of strictly individualistic aspects of consciousness and experience broke down ever so often. In the same manner, only more so, his decision to treat the 'objectification of meaning' consistently 'without visible Thou' could not be maintained. Indications of his entering the spheres of interaction and intersubjectivity can be found already in his study of linguistic forms; they become central features of his expositions about several forms of the literal and musical arts.

Yet, there is one sense in which objectified meaning can be viewed without its interactive framework. Its strictly analytical treatment becomes possible - as preliminary operation or as a limited objective - in the service of the attempt of creating a purely formal theory of the media and styles or modes of the fixation of meaning: the grammatical and syntactical rules of language, formal theories of narration, of the dramatic dialogue, of the forms and variations of composition, etc. But, in his outline for Part II, Schutz expressly provided for an effective correction of the main flaw of such formalism: the temptation - to which many 'experts' had yielded - of converting the rules distilled in such theories of expressive and communicative forms into 'meaning-immanent laws.' He intended to devote the whole second chapter to the refutation of this error which beset almost the whole of the corresponding literature on language, literature, and other forms of art.

By contrast, the first chapter was to deal with the 'positing of meaning' on the part of the speaker, writer, author, and the 'interpretation of meaning' by his or her counterpart: the listener and reader. The formalism involved, here, is somewhat similar to that which governed Simmel's earlier treatment of forms of human interaction, notably the dyad and triad. It is offering a scheme within it becomes possible to offer interpretations of individual cases of interaction and theoretically generalize about some of their recurrent features.

The third chapter was to deal with 'Origin and analysis of "values".' It would take a particular scrutiny of the existent texts for this as well as the first parts of the project in order to find out whether a tentative line for the treatment of this topic

could be ascertained. At face value, it seems to be completely open.
   The title of the fourth and last projected chapter, finally, aims
at 'Origin and analysis of "collectives."' It makes clear that the
reference to meaning contexts 'without visible Thou,' expressed
in the subtitle of Part II, does not exclude the treatment of meaning contexts of indirect social or collective connotations. The
whole part, then, is not based on a preliminary solipsism as, for
instance, much of Husserl's 'Ideas' I. It was to move toward the
forms of social relations of an indirect nature, as implied by, or
hidden behind, all concepts which refer to a multiplicity of persons, ranging from family and group to association and society.
Hints which can be found at various points of the manuscripts
presented in this book leave no doubt that this, too, would have
been a partially critical chapter, refuting the hypostatization of
concepts standing for collectives, that is, their treatment as if
they were denoting individuals instead of serving as convenient
abbreviations for complex interactional wholes - quite useful and
necessary in their place and, indeed, achievements of abstraction
which tremendously facilitate communication and transfer of meanings under the proper situational conditions. But, as Schutz indicated occasionally here and would stress emphatically in his
later writings, their acceptance into his own theoretical framework
hinged crucially on the condition of their being at any time reducible to the concrete interactional networks of relationships
among concrete persons which they socially present. It suggests,
then, that this fourth chapter of the second part would have
become a prominently sociological chapter.

Outline for Main Part II

Theory of the structure of the objectification of Meaning: meaning contexts without visible Thou

1 Formal laws of the interpretation of meaning: reflections about the positing of meaning
2 Apparent meaning-immanent laws: grammatical, esthetic, juridical, theory of harmony, etc.; the Refutation of these laws
3 Origin and analysis of 'values'
4 Origin and analysis of 'collectives.' The achievement and the necessity of this concept

Meaning Structures of Language

EDITOR'S NOTE

There are two reasons why the present fragment has been chosen
as the opening piece of Part II. First of all, its topic is everyday
language, the ordinary and universal means of communication.
As such, it is the foundation of all other uses of language, be
they scientific or philosophical, or else - as in the case of the
other two pieces of this part - artistically expressive, narrative,
and dramatic. The second reason is that of continuity. Speaking
roughly, it picks up the discussion of the life forms at about the
point it broke off in the unfinished first part. After a few general
considerations about his approach, Schutz gave initially a repetition and continuity of his considerations of the acting I. Next,
he introduces the Thou within the framework of the life form of
the speaking I -; the first of the last two life forms not treated
in the first part. Finally, he introduces the other and last one:
the life form of conceptual thinking. In this fashion, then, the
theory of the life forms is finished at least in its basic outlines.

These considerations fill nearly one quarter of the manuscript.
The rest is taken up by the consideration of the basic structural
elements of language. However, of the main forms noun, adjective,
verb, only the first two are treated. Even so, the development of
Schutz's ideas about grammar catch our attention for the way in
which he links grammatical forms to experience and intercommuni-
cative requirements, laying the groundwork for what had the
making of a phenomenology of grammatical forms.

Subdivisions and subtitles have been provided by the editor.

LIFE FORMS AND THOU

Any consideration [of any spiritual complex, of social man] can
be undertaken from two completely different points of view. Most
of all, one can carry out a conceptual inspection and establish a
methodological order of the objects which are encountered and
arrange them into a system. This leads to the formulation of a
series of empirical propositions. The sum of these propositions
concerning a given subject matter (Objekt) forms the body of a
given science. This procedure, considered the only proper one
for the natural sciences, was up to recent times also respected by
the so-called Geisteswissenschaften.[1] But another way, which is
completely opposite to this method, allows a series of phenomena

to be brought into a context of understanding yet can justifiably claim to be scientific. It is an approach which grasps the world neither as a concept nor as an idea which only has to be systematically ordered with the help of experience. Rather, it accepts experience itself as understandable and capable of being integrated in the course of life as a whole according to the same laws which govern the latter. Such a philosophy will be transcendent in the truest sense. Of course, it does not claim to postulate propositions beyond all experience; yet, it will deliberately go beyond experience by way of the intuitive inclusion of metaphysical elements into the sphere of experience.

However, this approach will not apply to all 'objects of cognition,' but only to those phenomena which can be experienced and thus are understandable. In particular, it concerns a comprehension of the meaning of the world which is unapproachable by, and different from, the ordinary empirical facts which are unquestionably accepted as [already] endowed with meaning, as given. [Presupposing such a meaning within the context of their data,] (empirical sciences, HRW) never can, nor intend to, come closer (to the investigation of the positing of meaning, HRW).

p.2   After putting aside the conceptual temporal-spatial notions, which have become usage and necessity for our thinking in the social world, one may attempt *to accept the world as experience.* If one makes the effort to investigate the spheres of experience of the I in their strata and the relations among them, one discovers a curious structure of these experiences. They reciprocally relate to one another in a very complicated manner; linguistically and conceptually, the latter is very difficult to comprehend. I have tried elsewhere[2] to order and integrate these experiences of the indivisible I through the construction of a series of auxiliary hypotheses, which I called 'life forms.' This yielded a very peculiar result.

It turned out that the last possible life form which can be grasped in our thinking is *pure duration.* In it, all experiences follow each other; they are connected with one another by nothing but the insight of the experiencing I and they are separated from each other by nothing but the discrepancies between each particular Now and Thus which is coordinated with each particular experience (and each other Now and Thus, HRW). Only *memory* brings some order into the abundance of the contents of experience: it preserves them, reshapes them; for instance, by adding to preserved memory images apparently similar or completely new actual experiences. Thereby, it secures the manifoldness of duration which, up to now, was experienced as mere continuity in the sphere of pure duration.

The phenomenon of *memory-endowed duration,* upon close inspection, turns out to be symbol relation, mediating between apperceived perceptional experience and the apperceived image *(Vorstellungsbild)* of the individual experience, which is stored in memory. Still, up to this point, the experiences of memory-
p.3   endowed duration lack extensity. They are timeless and spaceless.

they unroll internally, and they are continuous and manifold. Nothing exists; everything merely becomes and fades away without *being*. There is no thing, nothing delimited, since both time and space are missing. I am unable to say whether there is something external to, or within, this sphere. What is given to me is solely a series of intensities, of qualities into which enter extensive qualities only as intensive qualities.

I arrive at knowledge of the world outside of my duration only through a new symbolization; it is executed by the *acting I.* The latter doubly realizes itself: both as imagery of meaning-endowed duration and as seat of somatic feelings. It experiences itself as extensive-spatial. Only the movement of the body, through action, reshapes the acting I's intensive magnitudes into extensive quantities, and experiences space by projecting its duration into time. It dissolves the ongoing succession, which had been continuous and manifold, into a discontinuous and homogeneous side-by-side. The symbol interpretation, which occurs here, occurs on two levels. On the one hand, it exists in experiencing the ongoing body movement, which belongs exclusively to memory-endowed duration, as traversed space and thus something located 'outside.' On the other hand, the body itself was originally conceived in memory-endowed duration as something extended in movement, in short, as thing. Now, by fiat of action, it enters into a relation to other delimited things. Only here the world begins to be filled out with things in time and space which are sharply separated from each other. They relate to parts of my experiences which I project as *characteristics* of things.

Among the things thus created, a series distinguish themselves p. 4 which are related to my body in still another manner than merely by superficial and external similarity – that is, by extension in space and time. In outline and movement these objects are similar to my body and thus awaken special attention. Most of all, they stand out because they can be compared to the memory images of my own past I. Toward them, I assume the same most specific stance which I assume toward my own past I. In one word, they are *consociates* about whom I possess a quite primary knowledge. And now, a new *symbol relation* realizes itself, *the third.* I experience the Thou as if it too experiences a duration which in course and direction is similar to, nay, simultaneous with, mine; as if it possesses a memory which executes similar or maybe the same functions as mine. (I witness, HRW) its movement as if it is not merely movement like that of any other similar thing aside from me, but action – that is, movement which is accompanied by the characteristic phenomena of will and imagination which occur together with my specific bodily movements. Still more: I interpret the symbol which I impute to this object called 'Thou' as if its and my duration display a kind of parallelity, nay, as if the contents of experience in its duration enter into mine. The Thou stands at the intersection of two durations, two memories, two courses of action: mine, of which I have primary knowledge, and those which I interpret as my experiences of him.[3]

p.5   This symbol relation leads me to presuppose that the same experience which I have of the Thou the Thou has of me. I accept
the Thou as being understandable by me and as being able to
understand me and my life. Thus, I assume that I can posit actions
which have a chance not only to be observed but also interpreted
by the Thou. And I assume that I am able to comprehend movements of the Thou as his actions which, in turn, I can interpret
in the manner in which I interpret my own actions. In this way,
the space-time world, apparently created by my acting I, has
been significantly changed and animated.
         Up to now, I myself have imposed order upon the chaos of the
'images'; I have established the meaning-context of the phenomena.
Now, from the outside I am offered not only experience but experience already related to meaning which it is necessary to interpret. The act of positing meaning by the Thou - the meaning
interprétation by my I - this is the final enrichment of my world.
Yet, it is merely the starting point for all my relations with Thou
and thing, with world and surrounding. Up to now, the I has
accepted the things of the outer world indifferently *(leiden-
schaftslos)* as given or as objects of action. Now, the I has gained
access to the inclusion of the Thou into duration, and most of all
to the rich world of feelings *(Affekte)* which are immediately
released by the Thou or indirectly ascribed to him. Through this,
the I and eventually also the things receive a new meaning context: a context which is alien to my loneliness. This, however,
p.6   compels me to inform your Thou about all events in my life: first,
in order to posit the meanings of an action which is deliberately
oriented upon a Thou, which is left to him to interpret; second,
in order to check the 'correctness' of an executed interpretation
of a meaning posited by the Thou; finally, due to affectual conditions, to refrain from acting against the Thou or through him.
(However, for this purpose, my world has to undergo another
alteration.)

SPEAKING I, THINKING I, AND LANGUAGE

I have created the Thou in space and time already in the life form
of the acting I. However, it will not exist as long as I confirm its
existence only out (of the perspective, HRW) of my own life and
not also out of the course of the life of the Thou. Therefore, I
will have to delineate and determine it unambiguously in the intersection of both durations - unambiguously for the I as well as the
Thou - in that I establish its existence, through the witness of
my gesture or my glance, or because I name it by the word. It
seems that there is only a difference of degree between gesture
and word. However, I think that I have to assign the gesture
completely to the sphere of the acting I in the Thou relation; with
the word, a new life form begins: the *life form of the speaking I.*
         The world, again and considerably, changes with name-giving
and, further, with verbal communication. Up to now, only my

consciousness was open to experiences from the outside, be they things, actions, or Thou. Now, I am facing the pre-given word as something which corresponds to neither of these three categories yet comprises all of them. In principle, it does not make a difference whether the word which penetrates my consciousness is spoken, read, or written. These are differences of degree.[4] It is more than amazing to find that almost all philosophers of language saw their main problem in the coordination of acoustical or optical phenomena with conceptual characteristics. I am convinced that, in this the *fourth positing of symbol experiences,* one is exclusively concerned with a relation which no longer occurs within the unity of the I, which is indestructible throughout all life forms. It occurs just in the intersection of the courses of two lives. Basically, these intersecting lives determine, after the birth of the word, that there is no experience which simply belongs to me and not also to you and you and you: this already through the power of the word – if only potentially, only imagined and not experienced, not actually heard. The miracle is not that visual or acoustic experiences are brought in relation to experiences of another kind. Rather, it is that, through the symbol of the word, the symbolized experience is basically changed; that is, it is necessarily placed into the Thou relationship. The power of this change is so strong that the word effects a re-formation of the world. Behind its principles disappear all other experiences as if covered by veils. Now, the word governs the world by schematizing and re-forming it in a manner which is inaccessible to all other life forms.

p.7

The thing and its character, the affects and its intensity, the action and its course – all are given names and thereby completely removed from the sphere of my specific experiences. Since the word belongs immediately to the Thou sphere, it can designate what is common to me and you. I find my personal experiences only in that sphere into which the word does not descend. The word cannot grasp that this world belongs to me; it has distributed it to all. It does not know how to preserve anything unique, particular, unrepeatable. From now on, I do no longer live in a world of *my* experiences but in the language world which is filled with plain experiences, with the experiences of everybody. The word places itself before that which is experienced and removes it from experience. Now, there are only things named, only groups of things which are subsumed under one and the same word.

p.8

Language allows the comparison of experiences, the grouping-together of the most heterogeneous phenomena. The latter are necessarily heterogeneous already for the reason that, what the word – one word – designates, becomes real experience for different egos. This is the first [and most incisive] de-divinization of the world, the [most penetrating even though most primary] occasion of the disenchantment of life. In language, I do not encounter experiences but solely formulae, patterns which, in their manner, can make my experiences communicable. Instead of the abundance of images, which my life forms offered me thus far, I find a world composed of words *(Vokabeln)*. Each of them is for me simultaneously suitable and unsuitable; alas, all must remain far apart from everything alive. For the first time, the word has brought death into my world of the experiencing I. But it has also actually filled this world - which belongs not only to me but also to the Thou - with life; however, a strange and terrible life. Its ghostliness demonstrates itself in this: the language-endowed world is the world neither of mine nor of thine nor of anybody's experiences; it is a truly unreal world.

p.9

The tragical in the experience of language [- every poet is witness to this with all his work -] rests in the impossibility of catching the world of inner experience in the net of language. [The nature of fantasy is limitation, prudent selection of the mediate from the infinity of the I: Pious belief that the listener could reach his own most original experience through complete surrender to the word.] This aim of (poetic, HRW) language, however, is and remains unrealizable. The yield of every literary work is a value approximating a purely formal and schematic world.

THE LIFE FORM OF CONCEPTUAL THINKING

If the word separates Man from his experience, it also connects things, in a truly miraculous manner, and creates a new world out of the ruins of experience. It is illuminated by the light of *cognition;* it is the world of *concepts*: the highest *life form* accessible to us, that of *linguistic-conceptual thinking*. It is not necessary here to investigate closely its symbolic relation to the sphere of speech. [Since the onset of philosophy,] since the discovery of the concept by Socrates, all of formal logic represents nothing but the attempt to seize this symbol relation with no residue. The theories of conceptual content and concept delineation, of the logical relation between subject and predicate, of judgment and conclusion, the invention of the concept of experience, the subjugation of empirical propositions under categories, the deduction of categories from the transcendental schematism; all these, in mere appearance, are the attempt at linking sensory impressions and perceptions to rationality and reason, or whatever name shall be given to the mechanism of the cognitive apparatus. In reality, the struggle concerns not experience but the word. For 2000 years, the problem of Philosophy has been not 'How do I know the things of the outer world?' but 'what is the relation of the concept to that which I have designated with and also apperceived in a word?' And further 'what word-bound propositions can be deduced from this concept?' And finally 'what means are used by my consciousness in order to carry out this deduction?'

p.10

One should openly admit that this problem formulation of all modern philosophy has no longer anything to do with *experience*. Here the case is exclusively this: cognition is possible in spite of the world of words, yet just through it. This precondition is

definitely necessary but not at all self-understood. On it rests
the colossal structure of the Platonic-Kantian system, the New-
tonian physics and, in general, anything which up to now has
been understood as science. Our question was completely different: we looked for the experience behind the word, and we found
our limitations in language. The validity of the conceptual sciences
remains uncontested. But, possibly, the attempted contemplation
of the world of experience by circumventing language can yield
results of some evidence.

Language separates experience from the concept and thus from
Science. Therefore [in its own element] it must itself participate
in both. It must make possible, for each of the aforementioned
subjective life forms, a transformation into the objective realm of
the conceptual sphere. How this takes place thanks to its own
character, is to be shown in the investigations which follow.

LANGUAGE AND LIFE FORMS

On the following pages, we will attempt to establish the relation   p. 11
of language to the other life forms and their symbols on hand of
basic considerations concerning the theory of the (basic grammatical, HRW) form of European languages. This is done in recognition of the most problematic value of such an undertaking. In no
way do we intend to offer here either a methodological philosophy
of language, like Cassirer recently in his beautiful book, 'Philosophy of Symbolic Forms,'[5] or a general grammar, a task to which
Husserl devoted one his 'Logical Investigations.'[6] Furthermore,
the following investigations should in no way be construed as
being directed to the forming of historical types of grammar in
spite of the mode of representation which may unavoidably and
often invite such a misunderstanding.

The principle of the theory of life forms states that real man
necessarily lives in all life forms simultaneously and that the
establishment of individual life forms merely constitutes auxiliary
hypotheses of ideal-typical character; their purpose is merely
heuristic. In a similar manner, it is a principle of the following
considerations that language is given to us in its totality. It is
only in the symbol sphere of the word that we may risk establishing relations between a theory of grammatical forms and the ideal
types of life forms, interpreting the latter by the former. Of
course, in this undertaking we do not abandon the hope that, by
way of such a reciprocal reference, some light may fall upon the
logical and metaphysical preconditions of the forms of language.[7]

[If it were possible at all meaningfully to imagine language in
memory-endowed duration, it would solely consist of words which
designate a quality which is object of my present experience. In
this sphere exists neither body nor thing, be it internally or externally; there are only perceptual images and memory images of
qualitative experiences - and, moreover, of experiences which
are linked to one another through the continuum of duration.

They either remain undistinguishable or flow manifoldly into each other only with the help of my memory. I could not even assert that I am able to form words for individual states of my experience. There is not yet a 'state' which would be a mode of being in my memory-endowed duration; there is only a becoming and passing away of images which are strung along in my inner duration. The assumption, however, that an imagined language of memory-endowed duration would consist of adjectives is also completely wrong. There is not yet a substance, a thing, whose characteristics could be stated. There is no 'substantive' which would need an 'adjective.' Further, the assumption that individual quality images could be presented as qualities of my ego, too, contradicts the basic assertion that I-consciousness is already given thanks to the immediate evidence of the unrepeatable stream of duration, but that the quality images of this stream will be interpreted as independent qualities only through our linguistic and space-time conceptual thinking. These considerations lead us to conclude that the initially formulated hypothesis is of inherently contradictory character. It is not 'possible to imagine . . . a language in memory-endowed duration' which 'would consist only of words designating a quality.' Only a single experience is evident in this sphere: the self-experience of the I. Therefore, only one single word would be thinkable in this sphere; namely, the personal pronoun of the first person singular, the word 'I.']

p.13 Above, we sketched briefly the changes to which the world is subjected through the acting I. Suddenly, it becomes temporal-spatial and is filled with objects which exist independent of me and my duration. I interpret the quality experiences, which are connected with them, as their characteristics. By acting, I myself bring about changes in this space-time world. Everything, however, is related to me; I am still the only living being in this realm of dead objects. Yet, objects are situated in discontinuous space and are distinguishable from each other. In these objects inhere various characteristics; they can be counted, measured, weighted; they become simultaneously visible and touchable. In one word, they *fill* space and *exist* independently of the becoming and passing-away of the flow of my own life. This accounts for the fact that I can give names to these objects. They become nomina attached to which is the character of a noun, of objectness. Now, I can interpret my quality images of objects as their characteristics; however, I am also able to consider these characteristics, by way of the now possible comparison of objects, as being independent of any concrete thing and to compare them among themselves. This allows me to impute to the nouns of objects specific characteristics, which can be named (adjectives). Finally, I move and act, and act in particular toward objects: I change my body in a specific way which affects my somatic feeling of life and which is accompanied by a very characteristic inner experience, the phenomenon of will. These bodily movements are typical; their having-happened is also comparable in terms of traversed space. Eventually, as consequences, there are changes not only within

the boundaries of my ego but in the whole world of things within
my reach. All this makes it possible for me to give names to these   p.14
movements, these actions of my ego (verbs).

The three main elements of every language - noun, adjective,
verb - have their theoretical place in the sphere of the acting I.
The sphere of the Thou relation, in grammatical forms, adds only
the pronouns of the second and third persons. Yet, what changes
this circumstance entails is not revealed at first glance. One has
to consider that, in this life form too, a language would suffice
completely if it consisted only of 'roots,' that is, without declen-
sions and forms of conjugation. With the help of examples, which
are to follow, it will be demonstrated for each word category that
the development of variations of the roots can be interpreted in
terms of their relations to the space-time sphere and to the Thou.

SUBSTANTIVES (NOMINA)[8]

(a) *Numerus*
As mentioned before, the origin of the substantive is tied to giving names to things which are grasped in time-space. What, up
to now, was changing experience of quality in my duration is now
moved outside; it is formed, expanded, endowed with characteristics. But it is exclusively one object which is sensed *(affiziert)*
by my consciousness. A plurality of things, too, would be unrecognizable as plurality. The totality of quality experiences,
which issue from these things, would still be unitarily apperceived
and interpreted. To single out the individual, the unit, as segment of the total visual field of my experience is one of the most
complicated functions of the faculty of experiencing. This function
depends only partly on the fact that my sensory perceptions and
my actions establish the spatial continuity between a number of
objects which are experienced and apperceived as unity - so of a
number of trees - and to establish the autonomy of each individuality called 'tree.'

I do not believe I am guilty of an inadmissible psychologism   p.15
when I assert that the *experience* of a group of trees which, for
instance, offers itself at first visually to me from some distance,
is thoroughly different from the experience of a single tree under
similar conditions. The experience, 'tree group,' is not at all an
addition of individually experienced trees. I walk toward this tree
group, which looks like a unity, and walk into it. Moving around
each single tree, I discover to my astonishment that the tree
group, (from afar, HRW) experienced as completely homogeneous,
is not at all spatially autonomous. It shows clear differentiations,
it is discontinuous. As far as my sensory experiences go, it falls
apart into separate spatial continua, into 'things.' If I had microscopic eyes, I would not even be satisfied with the individual
tree as a spatially limited continuum. Yet, I am also not satisfied
with my sensory experience which results from moving around

this spatially limited thing. *Originally and under all circumstances, the experience is that of a singularity.* If, for the purposes of speaking, I had at my service no other means of interpretation than my experiences, language would still consist of nothing but singular words - so of the singulars 'tree' and 'tree group.' The relationship (of the two terms) to the same root should not mislead us to ignore the completely heterogeneous factualities (which they designate, HRW).

Indeed, language stops often at the formation of such singular subjectives which, actually, designate a sum of singulars. This
p.16   occurs in spite of all experience (to the contrary, HRW) because the primary unity experience cannot be dissolved into the addition of singular experiences. The singularity of the experienced 'thing' has to be linguistically expressed in the singular. Here, I think of nouns which designate a collective, so 'forest.'[9] The singular, 'forest,' is in no way dissolvable into a plurality of 'Tree,' even though doubtlessly the forest consists of trees. 'Forest,' likewise, is not at all a specific arrangement of trees, like a 'nursery.'[10] Further, the nature of the forest is not determined by the addition of certain characteristics, for instance, a floor of moss, or low thicket. Simply, the experience, 'forest,' is an experience sui generis; it is not dissolvable. Correctly, a German proverb alludes to a person without fantasy and of narrow-mindedness as to someone 'who does not see the forest for the trees.' I believe that the only possible explanation of this phenomenon is the reduction of the collective noun to an unitarily apperceived basic experience. This will be stated here in the face of the great difficulties which the collective concept has created for formal logic. Here we have one of the cases in which the formation of concepts follows the linguistic example of 'naming.' 'Naming' can be grouped with the delineation and constitution of the individual concept - even if the latter, as demonstrated by our example, is a collective combination. The step leading from a unitary experience to a unitary (singularized) word is smaller than that leading from a singular word to an individual concept. The latter, in any case, can be nothing else but a sum total *(Inbegriff)* of certain individual concepts which have been established long ago.
p.17   Many other examples could be mentioned in support of our assertion that the language of pure experience can only consist of singular concepts. However, we should not deny that the constitution of that which is spatially limited in the word, which names the former and lends it permanence, occurs through the stance of the *attention* which we devote to a segment of our field of vision. This stance will be conditioned by two factors: first by the degree of significance which the thing to be interpreted, the complex of experiences, has or may have for our lives, and, second, by the degree of significance it has, or may have, for the lives of other minds *(Intelligenzen)* who are related to us in the Thou relation. From this originates the purposiveness of any 'terminology.'

However, one should in no way assume that this terminological

differentiation (by attentional relevance, HRW), in spite of its
teleological character, could be traced back to a purposive-
genetical formation of concepts. That would mean that it would
occur in a sphere which already rests upon the linguistic world
of symbols. Above, I indicated that the so-called naming, which
occurs in the linguistic sphere, already determines content and
scope of the concept. The fact that both content and scope of
concepts are ambiguous stems from entirely different reasons,
namely, the discrepancy between the subjective meaning of the
speaker and the objective meaning of the listener. Here, this
is of no concern for us.

   Logic determines a concept, according to content and scope, by   p.18
definition. Thereby, it in no way continues the work of language
itself. On the contrary, it acts against Language. Logic is forced
to its activity only because language, in the act of naming, has
already unambiguously and in great consistency fixed the 'thing'
as a substratum of the concept. The theory of the formation of
concepts, in logic, is completely different from naming in language.
In formal logic this is consistently overlooked; thus, it has led
to a great confusion in the theory of definition. The terminological
difference, as described by us, is not of a logical nature. Most
of all, it is of linguistic nature and can be reduced to most elementary (primitive) experiences. According to its importance for my
or your life (at the moment, HRW), the attention directed at the
'tree' will emphasize the 'trunk,' the 'branch,' 'the leaf,' in order
to constitute it as a 'thing,' as something 'existing in itself,'
'complete in itself.'[11] It does this simply by giving it its own
name.[12]

   One still would not have to speak of 'branches' or 'leaves.' If
need be, however, specific names would have to be sought for
these experiences. Thus, new singularized substantives would
follow, so 'branch tangle' *(Astgewirr)*, 'foliage.' At first, then,
language consists only of nouns in the singular. One may wish to
think theoretically of a language in which there actually exists
no plural because the needed plurals are formed through singulars   p.19
of other roots.

   What are the preconditions for the origin of the plural? Most of
all, (the plural stems from the need for, HRW) comparability and
countability of specific singulars. However, only in the spacetime
world is it possible to compare multiple things. There, it is
possible through concept formation and (practical, HRW) experience. Mere experience, always tied to duration, cannot establish
that one thing is like the other. This is so because duration is
necessarily manifold and thus, in its own stream, perceives two
successive spontaneous experiences as different. Only conscious
experience, that is, conceptually typifying experience, measures,
counts, and weighs. It alone can construct 'sameness' which, for
the experience itself, must remain an approximate value. That
there can and does exist a multiplicity of objects is a product of
conscious experience, a statement belonging to the conceptual-
logical sphere.

However, this is tied to certain preconditions which have their roots in more elementary life forms: (1) the first is the existence of the Thou, since conscious experience can only be meaningful when your experience can be fully equated to mine. Conscious experience is not merely the sum of my logically processed experiences but the sum of the logically processed experiences of all minds who are equidirected with me - provided that conscious experience intends to claim general validity. (2) Establishing the

p.20   manifoldedness of like objects is tied to the constitution of the individual object, that is, to its naming and delimiting in the language sphere. As stated, the establishment of the plurality of singular (objects and names for them, HRW) belongs exclusively to the logical-conceptual sphere. But it would be wrong to conclude from this fact that the plural formations of language are solely practical forms for the use of conceptually thinking Man, and that here a process occurs which is the opposite of that of the forming of collective nouns. In the latter case, we found that only the unity of the *language*-experience leads to the invention of the collective *concept*.

As it turns out, the establishment of a multiplicity of individual things, undertaken in conceptual experience, brings the introduction of numerals (definite or indefinite). But it does not at all necessitate the forming of specific plural forms, as known to us through all those European languages which we have chosen as examples. By way of (practical, HRW) experience, one may establish that several experiences inhere in my experience 'tree group.' Each of them has 'tree' as its object. Should language wish to express this empirical factuality, it can be imagined that it does this through expressions like 'five tree,' 'many tree.'

p.21   Nothing would demand the forming of the plural 'trees.' According to our theory, it would occur only when the *experience* 'tree' suffers a change by comparison with, or adding of, another *experience* 'tree.'

This is indeed the case. One should not forget that our life forms are ideal-typical auxiliary hypotheses; in reality, we live simultaneously in all life forms. If we claim that these auxiliary hypotheses are valid and serve their heuristic purpose, we cannot merely offer an interpretation of phenomena of the more elementary life forms through the higher ones. It must also be concluded that every experience of higher life forms effects a thorough change of experiences in the more elementary ones. Otherwise, the ideal-typical precondition of the whole theory of life forms would be contradictory in itself; it would negate its own precondition, the indivisible unity of the experiencing I.

This is the case with our problem. We recognize here that there is a content of experience (tree) which is equal to another content of experience (tree). The experiences of both contents may be apperceived (separately, HRW). But this makes not yet for the additivity of both contents ('two tree'). On the contrary, the new experience which comprises the contents of the two experiences which formerly had been isolated, changes each of these. Formerly

I had experienced 'tree' (a) and 'tree' (b). If I preliminarily designate the new experience (c) as 'two tree,' experiences (a) as well as (b) transform themselves, in my retrospective memory, at the moment at which the new experience (c), 'two tree,' enters my life by way of my conceptual-logical sphere. What I had experienced as experience (a) (tree) changes now in my memory into the experience a' ('one of two tree') and the experience (b) into the experience b' ('one of two tree,' maybe also 'second of two tree'). The tree, experienced as (a), is no longer the same when I know that it is part of another experience. Therefore, I feel compelled to look for a specific linguistic expression for the old as well as the new experiences. With this expression, I say linguistically that the original experience has been altered. This is the secret of plural formation. Of course, the expression, 'two tree,' was only a theoretical assumption which we adduced from the pure sphere of experience. For the cognitive scheme, 'two *trees*' is the only correct and adequate expression. Seen from the perspective of the cognitive sphere, too, the original experience, 'a tree,' is no longer completely adequate. The correct linguistic expressions would be 'one of two trees' and 'second of two trees.'

Here results a most paradoxical fact: for immediate experience, only the forming of singulars is possible; however, for the experience which has passed through cognition, only plurals can be   p.23 formed.

The paradox dissolves itself in the miracle of language. Language remains ever close to experience. Whenever the grammatical form does not satisfy a cognitive proposition, one can assume that the contents of experience and of cognition are not congruent. With the security of a sleepwalker, a poet knows whether he means as content of experience 'a tree' or 'one of the trees,' 'one human' or 'one of the humans.' Both expressions are linguistically and programmatically possible; both designate concretely the same 'object': the same tree, the same human. Yet, both experiences are separated by a world – a language world as well as a cognitive world. 'A tree' is the content of the experience of one tree, without residue, which stands in front of me and delimits my horizon. There exists nothing else except me and the tree; it fills my duration and thus exhausts my word. 'One of the trees' is the content of my experience comprising not only the tree about which I intend to say something; it comprises also other trees which I see and to which it is similar in some if not in all respects. Maybe (the expression, HRW) comprises not only the trees which I see but also others of which I have only heard, which have long since disappeared or which will grow in the future: trees which exist somewhere, someplace, which existed, which will or may exist.

Here comes to light how close the singular is to experience, and how concept-bound the plural. But, thanks to the mystery of   p.24 language, concept and experience enter into the unity of plural formation, which cannot be dissolved: Idem – sed non hodem modo (the same itself at present not alone). Thus, the language world separates itself from the world of concepts as well as that of ex-

perience and forms its own curious and miraculous realm: a truly
third realm in which all contradictions are dissolved, because
they all originated in it.[13]

The considerations of the meaning of the linguistic formation of
plurals will be concluded with two short remarks.

One concerns the casualness of the representation offered. It
was chosen so as to avoid further complications of an already
complicated and cumbersome exposition. (As a consequence, some
considerations were oversimplified, HRW.) Thus, it was imprecise
to characterize naming in the sphere of experience as a language
of experience consisting of 'singulars of nomina.' Correctly, we
should have stated that, here, such a language consists exclusively of pronouns. Every experience is unique; the same expression for the 'same' experience occurred only on basis of the
postulation of sameness. So, for instance, in geography we have
nothing but proper names: every village, simply, is non-comparable
to all others. However, one should not forget that the nature of
the world exists in the possible application of the same singular
term upon several individualities. It is explained by the fact that
p.25   our experience in the language world is just not the experience
in duration but in time-space and in Thou relations. This problem,
too, belongs to the theory of the symbolic function of language
and the sphere of concepts; here, both flow here imperceivably
into each other. But this has not much to do with the question
which occupies us here.

A more interesting question is posed with our second remark.
However, it will be solved only partially in this study.

So far, we have discussed the constitution of the object and
its naming by a substantive only from the view points of the I
and of space. Should a discrepancy of time not also lead to forming the plural? And why does one assume that the concrete, tree,
X, which I see, is the same concrete tree, X, which is seen by
you and not a tree X' whose appearance in my experience would
lead to a plurality?

The relation of the substantive to time will occupy us later in
these investigations. The question can only be mentioned here; it
can only be answered after the study of the verb forms.[14]

Why, in my experience, does the tree seen by you become
identical with the tree seen by me, and can thus be linguistically
designated as the same tree? This - very important - problem goes
far beyond the framework of this study. It belongs to a structural
analysis of the Thou relation. Here, we will only mention that the
Thou stands at the intersection of two durations and that, there-
p.26   fore, the parallelity if not identity of the contents of both experiences represents the precondition of the symbol relation which is
basic for the Thou relation.[15]

(b) *Casus*

The substantive, whose formation we have pursued in the last
section, is first of all the cause of certain experiences of quality
which we are ready to interpret as characteristics of the object
and of which we can postulate a certain state comparable to our

duration. Namely, things *are,* they exist. This is the first and
main statement which we can make about every object and substance. That we can do this results from the character of our experience of time and space, in which alone can be constituted the
concept of the thing.

Linguistically, this experience is expressed by the grammatical
subject-predicate relation. These two main ingredients are connected by the 'conjunction' (copula). Von Lask[16] clearly demonstrated that this grammatical form does not fall together with the
logical form of the sentence. In linguistic form, we would say,
'subject is predicate.' The logical form suggests, 'subject-predicate
is,' 'subject-predicate is in the modus essendi.' Therefore, logically the predicate presents itself as attribute of the subject. The
subject, closer described by the merely attributive predicate, is
integrated into the mode of existence.

Example: the proposition, 'the rose is red,' would become in
logical formulation, 'rose red *is*' or maybe more precisely, 'red-
rose is.' What is said about the rose concerns primarily its existence, not at all its being *red.* This being *red* is contained already
in the rose perceived as subject; it is therefore attributively included in the idea of the 'red-rose.' (From a strictly logical point p.27
of view, Lask's theory seems uncontestable; and this the more
since it has proved itself thoroughly in his system.) But what
creates here the - not only by Lask - established discrepancy
between language and concept? What forces language to establish
a symbolization which does not correspond to the higher conceptual
life form? Or, in reverse, is it a reduction from the conceptual
sphere, as we encountered it in the character of the formation of
the plural?

Possibly this problem is the most difficult and most decisive for
the kind of consideration of language which we attempt here. It
forces me to a longer digression about the adjectival predicate.
To treat it, at this point, can only be justified by (the results of,
HRW) its application.

In the life forms which precede the language sphere, the thing
is simply and concretely given without any conceptual general-
ization. The latter, as shown, necessarily begins with naming.
Doubtlessly, the content of my experience is primarily not rose
with the characteristic of being red, perceived only in a second
and later experience. Rather, it is 'this rose there' now before
me. The formulation, 'this *rose* there,' while using a name, is
already drawn into the language sphere. Thereby, it turned
abstract. In exactly the same fashion, I could experience merely
a 'this there' which I have seized through the specific experiences
of my visual, auditory, and tactile senses. Nay, in inner duration
as such, it would not be possible to execute the concretization of
a 'this there.' In this life form, there exist only images of qualitative experiences which hang together merely through the stream
of my inner duration. However (pretending that, HRW) I could
express my experiences here, I could speak of 'smelling this-   p.28
there,' a 'soft this-there,' a 'red this-there.' But I would not at

all be in a position to state that each of these experiences is grounded in the existence of one and the same object. At the least, the experience of one and the same sub-stratum of all these perceived images of qualities is a space-time matter. It originates only in the movement of the acting I who gets acquainted with the 'object' as spatially autonomous and observes that, with a corresponding movement away or toward the object, all these quality experiences disappear or return. So far, we have believed that these experiences belong exclusively to our inner duration. It is thus that we interpret these quality experiences as 'characteristics' of the object, co-given with the existence and co-postulated with its concrete apperception. By positing a substantive, we are already co-positing a series of adjectives - at first in experience. This experience is that of qualities in the concretization of the thing; giving it a name is an apparently accidental act: one of the many miracles of language. At times, the incomprehensibility of these miracles makes us shudder and leaves us astonished. As a poem of Rainer Maria Rilke says:

> I fear myself the word of humans;
> they say everything so clear.
> This is called dog and this house,
> and the good is here and the bad is there.[17]

When Juliet faces the inconceivable and incomprehensible evidence of the erotic experience of the Thou, Shakespeare lets her realize that 'name is empty noise and smoke'[18]: 'That which we call a rose by any other name would smell as sweet.'[19] To 'smell as lovely' is the primary knowledge about the thing; it is incomparably closer to the experience whose name, more or less accidental, is 'rose.'[20]

Now, one has to realize that language has a place in a life form which already contains the Thou. (Here, it cannot be explained in detail how) the life form of the I in Thou relation produces in two ways the foundations of every experience. First, as a structural analysis of the I-relationship shows, the thing (already interpreted in an earlier life form and spatially-temporally constituted with specific characteristics for my acting I) is grasped not only by my own I but also by a Thou; in the same manner as by my I, that is, in the same temporal-spatial delimitation and by the same adjectival qualities. For the first time, the thing here acquires an 'objective meaning.' Now, the subjective formations and positions of meaning, issuing from my ego, are separated from my personal acts of endowing and positing meaning. They are valid not only for me but, at least according to my assumption, also for you. (This objectification of subjective meaning, which alone definitely separates the thing from my durational experiences, carries extremely far-reaching consequences. Most of all, it makes experience possible: through and in the Thou relation, it creates the objective chance of the apperception by a Thou. On the one hand, through it my apperceptions can be interpreted as

p.29

accessible to your experience; on the other hand, that which is apperceived by you can be accepted by me as something I at any time can re-experience. Due to the first reason, I am able to convey my experiences to you as being real also for you and can hope that you will understand me. Due to the second reason, I can limit myself *(begnügen)*, after the fulfilment of certain technical conditions, to learn *(erfahren)* about all of your experiences; I am sure to experience the same as you.)

At the least, my real experiences had become possible experiences for you in the same fashion in which, at the least, your real experiences are possible for me. Only this context creates the foundations of trans-personal experience. It alone makes possible (the integration of a meaning context into) the objective chance of experiencing by the Thou. Therewith, the final separation of the thing from I and actual experience in duration has been executed.

Since the object, no longer experienced by me, can neverthe- p.30 less be experienced by you, it and all its qualities must lead an independent existence, separate from my duration. It must persist in a form which in its continuity is similar to my duration; but it is also different from it due to the lack of manifoldness and the consciousness of the thing which is not accessible to me. This form of the existence of the object, for which I cannot imagine a becoming and passing away, I call the existence of the object, its *being*. This being, while resembling my duration through persistence and continuity, belongs completely to the space-time world, in which it also undergoes changes. Thus, we can say that the objective chance of experience is given only with the *being* of the thing. This being is always being-in-itself; every being-in-itself of the thing signifies inclusion in mine as well as your duration. Paradoxical as this may sound, only with this inclusion does there occur the complete separation of the object from any kind of duration and its integration into time. This is the first fundamental fact created by the Thou relation as precondition of all experience.

The second elementary effect of the integration of the word into the Thou problem seems to present exactly the opposite of the first thesis, as set down above.[21] The same object will be experienced by the Thou unchanged and in the same way as by the I; this is nothing else but a symbol function of the Thou relation. This assumption may be taken for granted. It states nothing but that this function, like all others, must actually dissolve itself in the tensions between the individual life forms, that means, in the psychophysical I which lives and acts simultaneously in all life forms. Actually, however, the experience of the same object by the Thou is in no way identical with experience of the object by the I. This assumption, conditioned by the structure of the Thou relation, applies solely to the pure relation, imagined in isolation. (Applicable and here also necessary is the symbolization of the world.)

We demonstrated above that this symbol function of the Thou p.31 creates the actual objectivity and autarchy of the thing. But, be-

cause it is merely a matter of symbolization, the tension between
symbol and symbolized (object, HRW) remains. The thing, now,
exists independently of me and you; it is now separated from
your and my experience in time. As soon as it is experienced by
me, it can also be experienced by you. However, up to now, nothing has been or could have been said about the identity of this
experience.

Because: at the same moment at which it turns from a possible
experience of the Thou to its actual experience, the object will be
integrated into life and continuous duration of the Thou. Within
this Thou, it will be subjected to a similar symbolization as within
the I. Now, the investigation of this process has shown to what
degree the construction of this symbol is conditioned by the
actually given Now and Thus of the I. The life of the Thou took a
completely different course than that of the I. Otherwise the Thou
would be identical with the I; this, however, is not the case.
Rather, the course of the life of the Thou and the course of the
life of the I 'intersect,' in order to use an image repeatedly in-
voked.[22] The occurring construction of the symbol of a possibly
similar experience takes place in a Now and a Thus which is different from the Now and Thus of the experience of the I. It follows
that the (subjective) meaning of my experience (which I, as objective meaning, hypostatize as the subjective meaning of your experience) is always the meaning meant by me but never the meaning as understood by you. Thus, a discrepancy results between
meaning intended and meaning understood, meaning posited and
meaning interpreted. Or, as one says since Max Weber's basic
investigations, between objective and subjective meaning - a
formulation which unfortunately has been often misunderstood.

p.32

By subjective meaning, we understand here the meaning posited
by the I which confronts the Thou as objective meaning, already
posited and now in need of interpretation. This tension between
subjective and objective is the second main proposition of experience as trans-personal experience as such. It alone yields the
criterion for the logical-conceptual validity of a sentence because,
here, the problem of truth is posed and decided for the first time.
Now, without the assumption of an objective positing of meaning,
the question of truth and validity of a sentence is logically meaningless. To assume an objective meaning content means to presuppose its positing by a subject and its interpretability by a
Thou.

To summarize, things gain existence, their being-separated
from all duration, in the life form of the Thou. But just this objective being must be meaningfully re-interpreted by the Thou and
from (the view-point of, HRW) every life. The first proposition
is a further development of the experience of the acting I; the
second belongs to the sphere of the Thou relation. Both are transformed by conceptual experience, which constitutes them in the
first place, and anew experienced in this life form. But between
the Thou and the concept stands the word. (It has to participate in
both, and both functions of the Thou must find their solution in it.)

As I have said repeatedly, thanks to the act of naming, the word - we think here at first about the noun - belongs to both life forms. It gives the object its own existence; it separates it from the duration of the speaker and hands it over to the duration of the listener for interpretation. Therefore, the word as such, namely, as objective meaning content, is always logically inexact. As imaginary object, it leads its own life in the twilight of the subjective positing of meaning and the - again subjective - meaning interpretation. It is surrounded by a penumbra which the concept penetrates only with great effort. In this context, James coined the brilliant term, 'fringes of the word.' Such fringes re-   p.33 sult from every formation of concepts. No word exists which would be unambiguous, and no word which is only ambiguous. Word and concept are discrepant just for this reason; it takes the whole complicated apparatus of the activity of reason in order to distil the concept from the word and to force the concept thus gained into a formula of convenience, the technical term. The technical term is nothing but the formula of the chemist, the exact designation of a point in a system of coordinates, the fixation of a tone, a musical notation according to height, strength, duration, timbre. (However, our considerations have nothing to do with these artificial constructions, these 'formulae' which become meaningful only when they are integrated into a prescribed scheme of meaning-positing and interpretation.)

The word, not yet turned into a concept, has through naming not only pinned down the thing but also its characteristics - even though the latter exist primarily in experience.[23] To formulate these characteristics, especially to impute them to those substantives which originated from the naming of objects, would not be at all necessary if the substantive were always a proper noun which designates only a single individual thing. However, this is not the case. The giving of a name already amounts to a comparison with other similar objects. Thanks to the conceptual-symbolic function of language, the experience is typified and generalized. And this in a dual manner: on the one hand because the experience of the I is necessarily coordinated to the experience of the Thou and thereby with that of everybody; on the other   p.34 hand because - within my duration as well as within the duration of everyone else - it can be coordinated with the same thing-experience, which it means objectively. Thereby, the word gains trans-temporality, trans-spatiality, trans-individuality. It remains the same even though the symbolized time-and-space-bound object changes.

What is actually persisting in a word? *Rose:* the rose which stands before me; the rose which I saw this morning; the rose of which you spoke; the rose which he gave to her; the rose in my garden; the rose in the park of Shirah; the rose which will bloom on the stock next year. What is common to all these experiences of the I and the Thou: actual, potential, past, present, future experiences? What is common to the things whose experiences are symbolized (by the word, rose, HRW)? What entitles language to

use one word for all these series of experiences and things? One
rose is red, the other yellow; one I have seen, of the other I
have been told. This one was here, the other is there, this third
one is not yet. This one smells, that one does not; this I can
touch, that one not. What are the *characteristics* which make all
these things into roses? What are the essential qualities of the
rose? When does the thing start to be a rose, when can one no
longer call it so?

It is not essential to answer this group of questions but it is
essential to investigate whether this group of questions belongs
to the life form of conceptual thinking or that of the Thou relation. By posing these questions, we are like a man who passes
through a gallery of parallel mirrors. He perceives all objects in
great manifoldness; one wall throws the mirror image of the other
back into itself with its own image. There seems to be no doubt
that our questions aim at the purely conceptual-logical function
of the word. They are questions of definition, appeal to conscious
p.35   experience. Indeed, they could all be answered by Linnée's system
or any definition of botany. This goes far beyond the act of mere
naming or the elementary experience of Juliet: 'That which we call
a rose by any other name would smell as sweet.' But it does not
excuse us from asking about what actually makes the definition
meaningful, and through what auxiliary means may one establish
such a definition. A hint is given by the old rule: definition determined by the proper genus and specific differentiations (definitio
fiat per genus proximum et differentias specificas). Logic asks for
characteristics, constructs a scheme of essentials; it determines
according to qualities. But, are these qualities identical with the
characteristics which are co-posited by naming? This is not at all
the case. Without ado, language allows the possibility of placing
contradictions together (contradictio in adjecto, sideroxylon).
Propositions, which logically connect what falls into 'spheres of
incompatibility,' are linguistically correct and grammatically
possible. In the language world, Liechtenberg's 'knife without
handle but with a missing blade'[24] has its place and existence.
Which, then, are those 'qualities' which are fixated by the word;
and what distinguishes them from the 'characteristics' of logic?

Obviously, the qualities which are labelled by naming are in no
way logical characteristics. On the contrary, they designate
primary qualities of experience. One may guess that, with naming,
only those qualities are pinned down which logicians are inclined
to call *essential* qualities: for instance, in the case of the word
'triangle,' the three sides, the three angles, the closed figure on
one plane, the 180° sum of the angles. If one of these qualities is
missing, the designation 'triangle' is false. To apply this obvious
assumption to the language sphere would be a fundamental error.
These qualities are not co-posited with the designation of a flat
p.36   figure as 'triangle.' They are not essential to the word 'triangle'
and also not to the concrete experience which I name thus; they
are essential for the concept, triangle. Kant, who saw in geometric
propositions synthetic judgments a priori, has shown better than

anyone that this concept, as such, is not yet endowed with those
essential characteristics named above. Their deduction, their
realization is already an act of aprioristic synthesis. That means,
the necessary 'characteristics,' which have resulted from a general
definition of the *concept* 'triangle,' are not basic for the *word*
triangle or the concrete experience (it designates, HRW). I can
very well imagine the experience of a spatial figure, which is not
determined by straight lines but by three curves and to which,
consequently, the essential characteristics of the concept 'triangle'
cannot apply. Only logicians or mathematicians could assert that
such a figure is no 'triangle.' Language itself would wrong them;
it feels justified in calling a triangle anything which has three
corners. The essential qualities, eminently necessary for definition
and concept formation, are in no way the same as those which
have already been posited by naming.

On the contrary, our example of the rose leads us to assume
that, just in the qualities which are constituted by naming, the
essential characteristics of the future concept are preformed; like
the future plant in the seed. Naming co-posits, even if only
potentially, all those qualities which, in future, can be said or
not be said about the thing named and about its meaning. Translated into the linguistic sphere, this in principle does not mean
that all adjectives could be imputed to every substantive. The
formulation chosen above will only demonstrate that that which is   p.37
logically and linguistically meaningful is thoroughly heterogeneous.
In other words: the 'spheres of incompatibility' in the language
world are completely different from those in the concept world.

In linguistic-historical sight, the word 'rose' means a rose of a
specific, namely, a reddish, color. Were this meaning accepted
today by us, a 'yellow rose' would linguistically be felt to be non-
sense. How could this meaning get lost, even though it (originally,
HRW) inhered in the word 'rose'? What makes possible the 'change
of significance' of a word? What changed: the linguistic meaning,
the relation of the word to the experience, or the logical sense,
which alters the relation of the word to the concept?

In my opinion, this question is identical with that posed above.

FROM QUALITIES TO ADJECTIVES

*In the language sphere, everything depends exclusively on what
qualities are meaningfully connected with the experience as such
- but meaningful with regard to the integration into their own
stream of duration without falling into contradiction with the
series of actual images of perception, of experienced images of
memory, of imagined images of fantasy.* This means in no way that
the incompatibility of logical conceptions is grounded in the
language sphere. The recognition of this incompatibility calls for
the total conceptual experience, and sometimes even for the sum
total of all scientific propositions. What is a linguistic metaphor,
in its essence, if not a possibility of uniting in the language world

what is logically disparate? Could one logically meaningfully assert of a theory that it is grey? Logically, this is as nonsensical as the statement that a triangle is virtuous. Nevertheless, to state that 'Grey, dear friend, is all theory,'[125] is linguistically meaningful. Nay, miracle on top of a miracle, it is meaningful not only linguistically but also in the deepest sense of experience. This 'word phrase' contains a content of truth for which an example is produced by any 'logical proposition.'

p.38   To repeat: earlier, I have asserted that all qualities are co-posited with naming and, in all future, can be said to be linked with the thing - whether this is logically meaningful or not. This does mean not that, in the language world, all adjectives can be imputed to every substantive. The unity of meaning *(Sinneinheit)* does not rest in the subsumption under concepts but in the inclusion into the sphere of experience. This also explains a phenomenon which is logically and psychologically almost unexplainable: that certain concepts of daily life refuse to fit into any definition, for example, the word 'table' with the exception of a purely teleological definition.[26] When I pronounce the word, 'table,' I think about a four-cornered table with four wooden legs, but you think about a round stone table with a support in the center. Starting from the piece of furniture, imagined by the enunciation of the word 'table,' it takes a certain act of reflection to comprehend that the 'table' imagined and described by you too is a table. Anybody who learns a foreign language, and also the child who learns originally to speak, will find that he or she uses one and the same word for heterogeneous objects. Only later does he or she recognize that each of these objects has been equipped with another name and *therefore* with other co-intended qualities.

p.39   The justification[27] of the difference between logical and linguistic meaning relevances rests mostly on the completely different character of qualities as experienced and as conceptual features. As soon as the adjective is lifted out of the language sphere and is brought into a relation to the logical concept, it loses its dependence and is no longer relying on the existence of a thing: a substantive. By contrast, in the sphere of logic, every adjective in principle is convertible into a substantive.

Within the Thou relation, the act of naming effects nothing but the separation of the thing experience, with all its corresponding actual and potential characteristics, from the duration of the speaker and its integration into the duration of the listener. By contrast, the conceptual formulation of that which has been *named* offers the latter for interpretation as something completely objective without reference to the act of positing meaning and to that which is subjectively meant. The named object, in its individual delimitation in space and time, is here transformed into a class while the qualities of the object, which are accessible to experience, become criteria of the concept. In this sphere of absolute being, not only things but also their qualities become comparable with one another. It takes only a small step to grant substance character to conceptual attributes and to sever their ties to sub-

stantives. Such substantified qualities lack the criterion of perspicuity *(Anschaulichkeit)*. With this expression, logic means   p.40
hardly more than being capable of being experienced in a lower
life form. However, substantified qualities do not lack the ability
to be thought of as existing, like things, in the modus essendi.
Duration will treat such criteria as if they were things.

As seen, in the mere realm of language, the origin of the
adjective occurs differently. The incompatibility spheres of logic
are valid in the linguistic sphere. All actual and potential qualities,
in so far as they can be experienced at all, are co-posited in the
act of naming. Thus, the generation of the adjective has two
roots of completely different origin.

1 *The adjective as attribute*

One can speak of mere experiences of the qualities of things,
which are placed in the Thou relation and which have been named,
solely, either in regard to the speaker or the listener. The intended, unexplained, meaning of the experience of the speaker
transforms itself, through the symbolic structure of the word,
into the meaning of the experience of the listener - set externally,
understandably, and now to be interpreted. To bring the word
closer to experience, to lessen the difference between intended
and posited meaning, to offer a scheme for the interpretation by
the listener which is as adequate as possible to the actual object-
experience - this leads to the origin of the attributive adjective.

This assertion will be explained with an example.

Peter says to Paul[28]: 'In my garden is a rose'. Paul, however,   p.41
has seen many roses. He also knows the meaning of the word
'rose' and Peter does not doubt that Paul will understand him.
The readiness of Paul to understand Peter rests exclusively in
the circumstance that Paul lives in the symbol sphere of the word.
He accepts Peter's experience as if he had experienced it himself.
Therefore, he does not doubt that, if entering Peter's garden,
he, Paul, would have the same experience as Peter. Therefore, he
could assert that there is a rose in Peter's garden. Now, Paul
has not only seen many roses, he also has a specific idea of 'rose'
as such. This is so, because he simultaneously thinks, that is
lives, in conceptual schemes. He has a specific idea of 'rose'
as such. He knows that there are red and yellow roses, some
which smell and some which don't. He has also seen roses with
many and with few petals and knows, from his own experience,
that no one rose is like the other. This experience may be completely trans-personal; for instance, it may be based on his read-
ing of several logical investigations about the nature of sameness.
But it will do when Paul establishes discrepancies when comparing
his memory images of his experiences of roses. [As shown above,]
when the word 'rose' is mentioned, Paul will recall *(vorstellen)* a
very specific rose, that is, one which was especially important to
him. (A specific intensity of a quality experience, an especially
pregnant memory image, an object of an intended or executed
action, an integration into an affectually motivated complex.)

p.42   Paul has the task of understanding Peter, that is, to reconstruct
the latter's experience of himself by interpreting Peter's experience. Therefore, it will be of highest importance for him to recheck
whether the ideal type 'rose,' which he, Paul, constructed for his
life, agrees with the experience of Peter (or what the deviations
of this type are from the experience of Peter). Thus, he will
appreciate learning what characteristics are displayed by the rose,
seen by Peter, in contrast to that imagined by him, Paul. For
instance, he will ask: 'What is the color of the rose in your garden?'
Peter can give two answers: 'The rose in my garden is red'; or:
'In my garden is a red rose.' Is there a difference between the
two statements of Peter and, if so, what?

With Paul, the reader will feel that Peter's answer, 'In my
garden is a red rose,' is not an adequate answer to Paul's question. The only adequate answer to his question would be: 'The
rose in my garden is red.' However, with Paul one would feel it
agreeable if Peter had originally formulated his experience in the
words: 'In my garden is a red rose.' In this case, Paul would not
have had to pose his question about the color of the rose. What,
now, is the difference between Peter's speaking immediately of
the red rose in his garden, and the apparently inadequate answer
p.43   to Paul's question? In other words: when will Peter speak of a
quality experience 'red rose,' and when will he make the assertion
about the quality experience 'rose' which displays the characteristics of 'redness.'

Let us first investigate the case of the statement: 'In my garden
is a red rose.'[29] The question as to what caused Peter to speak
just about a red rose is the more difficult to answer as Peter
alone may give information about it. He could render it only with
the help of a conceptual analysis of all those 'motives' which in-
duced him to speak just of a red rose and not of a smelling or a
long-stemmed rose. Possibly, he would be uncertain why he spoke,
from the start, of a red rose and thereby stressed its 'redness.'
It stands to reason that he did it because his ideal type of rose
does not contain redness but only other characteristics of rose.[30]
In this case, Peter used his statement already as one to be interpreted, actually as objective meaning. He proceeded in the manner
which he expected from Paul. This does not mean that Peter's
ideal type of rose would be, for instance, a yellow rose, or else
that this type would comprise all elements (that is, elements of
experience, not conceptual criteria) of rose except color. *It means
nothing else but that he considers it desirable, for some reason,*
p.44   *to accentuate redness also for the Thou whom he addresses.*

The experience, which is at the bottom of the word, is completely
unitary. Adding the adjective 'red' to the substantive 'rose' constitutes no enrichment whatsoever of the original subjective experience. It changes nothing on the given factuality of the rose
seen, which happened to be red. It is merely a concession to
language if two words, namely 'red' and 'rose,' are used to designate a unitary experience: a concession which is [exclusively]
occasioned by the circumstance that [the word adheres not only to

the Thou relation but also to every other life form or sphere; so
that, therefore,] language is not merely for speaking but also
for repeating.[31] Peter finds given word materials and formulae for
(describing, HRW) his experiences; he must use them in order to
express his experience as long as he hopes to be understood by
someone listening to him. (Unless he is a poet,) he is not allowed
to find a new word for his experience, lest he sacrifices his
chance to be understood. If Peter did not encounter language as
already existing material which he now has to draw into his own
scheme of interpretation, he would look for an expression which,
in the unity of the word, would be adequate to the unitary experience. For example, he would say: 'In my garden is a "red-
rose."' With this statement, he would have said nothing more than
with the sentence: 'In my garden is a red rose.'

Here,[32] the act of meaning depositing is completely unitary. The
addition of the attributive adjective does not occur in order to
complement the act of meaning positing; it occurs only in order
to anticipate a question of Paul; that is, in order to complement
the scheme of interpretation.

Paul, the listener of Peter, would also ascribe an objective uni-   p. 45
tary meaning content to the word, 'redrose,' if he hears it. He
may only ask himself what may have caused Peter to stress just
the 'redness' of the seen rose, of which he could say thousands
and thousands of things. He will arrive at the answer: either
'redness' is of special significance for Peter's ideal experience, or
Peter knows that Paul's ideal type is in need of contemplation by
stressing color.[33]

If Peter spoke only of a rose . . . , and if Paul's ideal type . . .
in fact needs complementation by color, . . . Paul must indeed
feel the need for an (additional, HRW) statement of Peter, ex-
panding the meaning he meant. Paul faces an incomplete act of
meaning positing by Peter; with the question about color, he asks
for complementation. Factually and linguistically, Peter can no
longer answer Paul's question correctly by the attributive statement: a red rose or redrose; but only by the predicative statement: 'The rose in my garden is red.' In contrast to the statement,
'in my garden is a red rose,' this sentence represents a new statement - not a new statement about his - Peter's - experience,
which remains unitary and undivided, but a new statement about
the meaning of the experience: a new act of meaning positing.

Herewith, we believe to have arrived at the main difference be-   p. 46
tween attributive and predicative adjectives. The attributive adjective signifies a complementation of the act of positing meaning.
The speaker desires to prevent an incomplete interpretation of
the meaning which he fears would be fostered by the mere naming
of the substantive. By contrast, the predicative adjective signifies
a complementation of the act of positing meaning.[34]

2 The predicative adjective

On occasion of the theory of the substantive, we said that, most
of all, it calls for an act of our attention in order to make the

selection of that which is named out of the indivisible Now and
Thus of the experiencing I. We have demonstrated that this
selective activity of our attention is already at work in the act of
naming. Thus, we call one and the same visual factuality now tree,
now bundle of branches, now leaves. And, as said above, we
would have to invent new names, if we had microscopic eyes and
were able to experience perceptually the unity and delimitation
of things in space on the level of cells.

p.47　　When stating this example, we realized that we had already trans-
gressed the boundary of the pure language sphere: the apparent
act of attention represents itself as a result of all experiences of
conceptually thinking Man. In this aspect of the language world,
which is turned toward the concept, selectivity occurs no longer
according to determinants of experience, but according to valuation, most of all logical valuation. Relevant for naming is no
longer suitability for my life, no longer the inclusion into the
stream of my duration, but the suitability not of the experienced
but of the recognized object for the totality of my empirical propositions *(Erfahrungssaetze)*.[35] Bergson asserts that even memory
seizes only those experiences of qualities which some time later
become important for the acting I. The truer is the assertion that
the word, subjugated under the primacy of the concept, merely
cuts out of the world of experience such factual complexes which
are relevant for the (given, HRW) conceptual-logical context and
which have logical or cognitive value (within this context, HRW).[36]

If we apply this theory of the substantive to the formation of
adjectives, we find that the accentuation of specific qualities of
the substance is not at all necessitated by the phenomenon of experience but only by logical necessity. Thereby, they become
criteria of the object but not of quality experiences. Because, in
the sphere of conceptual thinking, the thing leads its own life:
it neither belongs to my nor to your durations; it simply exists.
Its qualities can be established neither through my nor through
your experiences. In the dead and unanimated world of things,
quantities accrue to substance. They assume the same form of
the essential mode as the thing itself. Taking this logically, they
are essential not for the concept but for the word.

p.48　　Here start the theories of definition and of formalistic logic with
their specification the similarity of genus and differentiation by
specifics, with the theories of essential and accidental qualities.
Only here begin, in a true sense, those incompatibility spheres of
concepts which - as stressed above - are basically different from
the incomparability spheres of the pure world of language; they
originate in the incongruence between the spoken (word, HRW)
and the I as experience in the stream of duration.

The word, which became concept, has a scope and content which
can be unequivocally established; it knows very specific and
essential criteria. The omission of even one of these criteria would
render it logically meaningless. Through addition of another word,
its scope would be restricted, its content enlarged. This reciproca
relation between content and scope of the concept shows clearly

that we deal here not with one and the same factual complex of
experience. Rather, we deal with a phenomenon which has been
included in the world of objective meaning. The latter, necessarily,
will be altered by the addition of another concept (accentuation
of a specific criterion). This is the essential meaning of the predicative adjective. It changes the conceptual content and scope
of the substantive. It was never one with its substantive; it is
not connected with it through experience but merely through the
intentional inclusion of both into the essential mode. This imper-
sonality, which necessarily inheres in every predicative adjective,
makes it unsuitable for completing the act of meaning information.
Yet, it enables the predicative adjective to contribute to the   p.49
sharpening of the act of positing meaning. Since the predicate
has the power to withhold from duration the thing-turned-concept,
it reinforces the objective character of the posited meaning. By
removing the experience of the speaker from duration, the predicative adjective limits, for the interpreting listener, the meaning; it offers him a complex of interpretation which, for the most
part, contains objective elements which are independent of the
positing of meaning.

The attributive adjective is rooted in that aspect of the word   p.50
which is turned toward the pure Thou relation; it anticipates the
interpretation of the positive meaning by the Thou. It has nothing
to do with the experience of the thing, which ever remains unitary, but only with the listener to whom the word is offered for
interpretation. It has something to say to him but not to the
speaker. Most of all, therefore, it has its place in those literary
works which serve communication and in particular narration. So
in the epos, but not in lyrical poetry which, as solitary art of
expression, shuns the attributive adjective as artistic means. It
is also missing in the purest form of strictly logical-conceptual
structures of language, in propositions containing conclusions
which ever - at the risk of fallacy - are forced to convert attributive into predicative adjectives. It is capable of being connected
with every form of the substantive, even the oblique one, without thereby changing its function in any way. It belongs to duration and, as anticipated meaning *interpretation,* is never purely
objective meaning. It is ever mixed up with subjective meaning -
not that of the speaker, but with the subjective meaning expected
by the listener.

By contrast, the predicative adjective is a pure act of positing
meaning; it rises from the need of the speaker, not that of the
listener. It does not participate in the thing experienced but in the
concept. As completed act of positing meaning, it is purely objective meaning. It is reality. Therefore, it demands the copulative
conjunction as expression of the essential mode. It does not form
a unity with the substantive; it is freely movable and can itself
be made into a substantive. But just for this reason does it presuppose the accomplished act of naming. It can be related only to
an infinitive and to a nominative. More, the 'case forms' of the   p.51
substantive obtain their first distinction by the capability of

governing a predicate; every case - including the oblique one - may receive an attribute.

How is this result related to the metagrammatical theory of the sentence?[37] Does there not exist here too an unsolvable paradox? Our investigation has shown that the logical function is carried by the predicative adjective. Yet, the metagrammatical theory of the sentence assigns this role to the attributive adjective; it tends to ascribe to the copula[38] alone the character of a logical predicate. But the paradox dissolves itself if one compares the opposite aspects of both investigations with one another. The logician, just from his standpoint, considers the adjective inessential because it qualitatively belongs to the *concept* of subject. For him, the essential of each sentence - not the *spoken* sentence but the logical proposition - is the mode, the existential form, the validity. Everything else - quality, time, form, numeral - finds its place in the concept which is diametrically opposed to experience. By definition, and in order to be *correct*, the concept must comprise all possible logically meaningful statements.

We did not start with the thinking I but the I who speaks, who expresses his *experiences* or communicates them. Thus, for us, subject matter of consideration is not the proposition which has been developed out of concepts but the spoken sentence, bound to experience and Thou. It is impossible for us to accept the content of experience as existent without simultaneously to establish by what means this existence manifests itself. We posit the meaning into which, in deeper spheres, we have formed our experiences Thus, we see the essential form of the appearance of reality not in logical correctness but in adequacy with the stream of our duration. However, in the mystery of language, concept and experience enter into an insoluble unity. Language is carried in the stream of the real duration of the world of experience; and it is carrier of the world of concepts. It forms its own curious *(seltsam)* realm, a truly third realm, in which all contradictions dissolve themselves because they all originate in it.[39]

NOTE[40]

Concerning the theory of logical and linguistic qualities (characteristics - theory of marks *(Kennzeichen)* by Husserl):

But most of all: synthetic, analytic judgments. There Kant's error. Linguistic signification of the adjective; still more an intermixture of a priori and a posteriori. Every analytical judgment necessarily and simultaneously a priori and a posteriori.

Synthetic a priori not *possible* but *judgments necessary* as *experiences* - this permeates the whole of Kant.

Even antinomies of pure reason are reducible to phenomena of time and duration.

NOTES

1 HRW: Literally, the term *Geisteswissenschaften* means sciences of the spirit - a choice only explainable in terms of the German philosophical-idealist tradition. It is, by the way, hardly stranger than the classical British choice of 'moral science' as designation of social-science fields in accordance with the pragmatic-religious tradition of Scottish Protestantism. Interestingly, in both cases political economists played a conspicuous role if not in introducing then in propagating and popularizing the respective labels. The German term has been variously translated, for example as cultural sciences: a term occasionally used by Schutz. Basically, it resists translation; I prefer to render it in its German form. The *Geisteswissenschaften* comprise fields of inquiry other than those of the natural sciences but only in so far as they are treated not in natural-science fashion but take cognizance of the human uniqueness of their subject matter and consider both human cognition and human volition as essential factors in their inquiries.
2 HRW: In the first major part of the project of 1924-7, published above under the title, 'Life Forms and Meaning Structure.'
3 HRW: This passage (and its continuation in the following paragraphs) is remarkable because it is a first extensive formulation of the conception of intersubjectivity which Schutz, in 1932, should express in his 'General Thesis of the Alter Ego' (in 'Der sinnhafte Aufbau der sozialen Welt,' Wien: Springer, 1932: 106ff.
4 HRW: In his American period, Schutz spoke of the 'relative irrelevance of the vehicle.' The stress, here, is on the reservations: 'differences of degree' in the present text and 'relative' in the later formulation. For purposes of intersubjective communication, as Schutz emphasized already in the present study, gestures and facial expressions may be more important for conveying meaning than the words which are spoken.
5 HRW: See Ernst Cassirer: 'Philosophie der Symbolishen Formen: Die Sprache'. Berlin: Cassirer, 1921.
6 HRW: See Edmund Husserl: 'Logische Untersuchungen'. 2 vols. Halle: Niemeyer, 1900-1.
7 HRW: Here follows a whole page of text which was set in brackets and crossed out. I maintained it in this translation, placing it in square brackets.
8 HRW: This sectional title, like all those which follow and are marked by Roman or Arabic numerals, and subsection headings marked by letters, has been provided by Schutz. Next to the present title, he pencilled the mark '*S 26.' An asterisk without any further reference is found on p. 26 of the handwritten MS, clearly referring to the subsection labelled 'b. Kasus.' I concluded that the mark after 'I. Substantives' does not refer to this heading but to that of the subheading on the next line: 'a. Numerus.' This may be interpreted as a note Schutz wrote to himself, expressing the intention to switch the position of

the two subsections, taking 'Kasus' first and 'Numerus' second. Since this (a) is not certain and (b) could not be done without textual changes, I have maintained the original order of these subsections.

9 HRW: German = *Wald*. On occasions, the English language expresses a collective in the plural. So, the proper translation of *Wald* would be 'woods.' I had to choose 'forest,' the equivalent of the German word, *Forst*, that is, woods which are carefully planted and kept. In addition, English contains singular nouns which stand for pluralities in which the pronouns assigned to them are singular if a plurality of objects, but plural if a plurality of people are to be designated (the forest = it, the crowd = they).

10 HRW: But the German word, *Forst*, would be.

11 As it stands, the sentence about attention to parts of the tree as attention to the tree is misleading; at the least, it would demand explanation. At face value, attention to the 'trunk' would lead to the term 'trunk.' I doubt that Schutz would have introduced the idea of attention to specific parts of an object if, at the time, the incipient work of the Gestalt psychologists had been available to him and which made clear later that, at least in perception, attention moves from the whole to details and not from details to the whole.

12 HRW: The next passage in the original text is marked at its beginning and its end by an inverted T, preceded by the abbreviation, 'Anm.' *(Anmerkung)*. I take this as an instruction to separate it from the text and bring it as footnote.
AS: Note. For instance, with the introduction of the microscopic technique in the natural sciences, it became necessary to formulate a series of names for things which, up to then, were sufficiently characterized by a common name.

13 AS: Note. Certain words in certain languages have the same form in plural and singular. It is self-understood that this is no objection to these basic considerations; (the occasional identity of plural and singular, HRW) merely points to (accidental, HRW) phenomena in the histories of these languages.

14 HRW: Schutz abandoned this MS before he turned to the study of this topic.

15 HRW: Schutz inserted here the following remark.
AS: (To add: Note about the dial). (I assume 'dial' stands for dialect, HRW.)

16 HRW: It is a safe assumption that Schutz referred to the neo-Kantian philosopher Emil Lask.

17 HRW: I apologize for this poetically poor translation of Rilke's poem. Schutz rendered the original text as follows:
Ich fuerchte mich so vor der Menschen Wort,
Sie sprechen alles so deutlich aus.
Dieses heisst Hund und dieses heisst Haus
und das Gute liegt hier und das boese dort.

18 HRW: 'Name ist Schall und Rauch' - a popular expression taken from Goethe's *Faust*.

19 HRW: 'Romeo and Juliet,' Act II, scene ii.

20 On top of the next paragraph, Schutz wrote in pencil: * S 34. A line links it to the second sentence of this paragraph, which starts with a square bracket. An asterisk is found on p. 34 of the original MS, followed by a short remark which was crossed out and is not readable on my xerox copy of the MS. Another lone asterisk is found near the bottom of p. 37. It is possible that Schutz intended to place the first passage marked (on p. 28) to p. 34 and then to p. 37. The whole paragraph on p. 28 begins with a double square bracket. However, various shorter passages in this long paragraph are also set in square brackets. It is practically impossible to ascertain how much of the paragraph Schutz intended to transfer to a later place. Omitting the initial dual square bracket, I maintained the whole paragraph as originally written, converting the other square brackets into parentheses, in agreement with the here adopted method of indicating passages set off by Schutz.

21 HRW: After this sentence, Schutz inserted a closing square bracket and an asterisk. Possibly, this marked the end of the whole segment (covering almost two MS pages) which he wanted to transfer to a later place.

22 HRW: It is of interest to see that Schutz already here expressed the idea which he should later discuss as the 'biographically determined situation' of the individual (see, for instance, Common Sense and Scientific Interpretation of Human Action. 'Philosophy and Phenomenological Research', 14, 1953: 6).

23 HRW: Here follows an unfinished sentence, heavily crossed-out: 'Conceptually, of course, results an unbridgeable difference between substance and quality - so that all concepts are synthetical . . . '

24 HRW: I assume that the name was inadvertently misspelled and that Schutz referred to Georg Christoph Lichtenberg (1742-99), the German essayist who is best known for his aphorisms.

25 HRW: In his 'Faust,' Goethe lets Mephistopheles give this as advice to a student, crowning it with the mixed metaphor, 'Green is the golden tree of life.'

26 HRW: Lacking expertise in theory and history of logic, I am at a loss to pinpoint meaning and origin of the term, teleological definition. According to the comments Schutz wrote after mentioning this term, it seems that he had in mind identification by description; the latter cannot serve as definition because it makes it impossible to separate accidental from essential features (so, a square or round shape of the surface of a table). In the back of his mind may have been the overcoming of this hindrance to defining 'table' by resorting to the collection of purposes for which tables - of all shapes, materials, and sizes - have been built. This, again, fails to satisfy the rigid requirements of logicians, although there is no question that such a purposive-teleological 'definition' is quite useful in practical life and, in fact, typical of it.

27 HRW: The first sentences of the paragraph repeat the formulations of a slightly differently worded and unfinished paragraph which was crossed out in the original text. With this
reformulation, the MS switches from handwritten to typed
pages. The latter run from MS page 39 to 49. The last two text
pages (50 and 51) are again handwritten.

28 HRW: Peter and Paul are figures populating some of Bergson's
writings. Schutz met them there. However, they seem to be of
long ancestry in western philosophy of the Christian era.

29 HRW: This sentence was written by hand on the left margin.

30 AS: If, as before, we speak here of ideal types of an experience, we mean thereby no conceptual type at all but exclusively
the sum of several elements of those memory images which - in
spite of all manifoldness and determination by duration - display an invariable character. Just they make it possible for
Peter to reinterpret, as names, quality experiences in the
sphere of the acting I and in the sphere of the speaking I.

31 HRW: Schutz wrote on the margin of the passage which he
crossed out (given here in square brackets): *Vorwelt!* (world
of predecessors). The meaning of this note, which Schutz
addressed to himself, becomes clear in the next sentence. He
obviously intended here to write more explicitly about the
historical fact of formation and structuring of any language, its
historical givenness, its creation as achievement of untold
generations of linguistic ancestors.

32 HRW: This paragraph was handwritten on the lower margin of
the MS. A line on the left margin linked it to the middle of the
preceding paragraph. This indicates that he intended to integrate it into this paragraph. However, he made a question
mark next to the connecting line. Thus, he had second thoughts
about the transfer. Its integration in the earlier paragraph, in
addition, would have demanded a reformulation of parts of both
paragraphs.

33 HRW: In the original MS, this paragraph is followed by another
one which covers two-thirds of the page (45). It is crossed
out. In the midst of it is a mark referring to the marginal note,
Zettel (separate sheet). This indicates that the content of the
handwritten sheet is to be inserted at the point marked. However, its content is a reformulation of the original paragraph;
it has been placed here in its stead.

34 HRW: An incomplete sentence followed, crossed out by Schutz:
AS: [As can be clearly seen in the example above and will become still clearer when we now occupy ourselves with the
analyses of the predicative adjective]

35 HRW: That means, their suitability for comparison with, evaluation by, integration in, and correction or rejection by the
ensemble of ideas about the realities of a person's spheres of
life by way of commonsense conclusions rather than (scientific)
empirical propositions.

36 HRW: The central part of this paragraph has been emphasized
by a vertical pencil line on the left margin, and its last line by

a triple-lined cross. The meaning of these marks remains un-
clear.

37 HRW: Abbreviated to 'mgr Sth' in the original.

38 HRW: A verb form connecting subject and predicate in a 'weak'
manner, such as 'seem,' 'appear.'

39 HRW: The last three sentences (two in the original) consist of
a partially changed rendering of the passages which fill the
first six lines of p. 24 of the handwritten MS. They are the
conclusion of the existing text of Schutz's Language MS. This
MS is obviously incomplete. A consideration of the 'basic
grammatical forms' of European languages, at a minimum, would
comprise not only noun and adjective but also the verb forms.
But their treatment is missing.

40 HRW: This note was written on a separate sheet. It was not
numbered; it was found at the end of the Language MS. The
page itself carries one word of text *('Morphismus')* on its top
line. A comparison with the extant pages of the MS shows that
this word is not a continuation of the text of any of them. A
date given at the end of the note (29/VII 25) is identical with
the last date occurring in the written part of the MS. Thus,
it can be assumed that Schutz jotted the note down at the very
end of the vacation period in which he drafted the Language
MS, thus indicating the topic for a continuation of the work he
had to interrupt. The stray word at the top of the page indicates that Schutz had written at least one other page which he
either discarded or which did get lost. The note itself abounds
in word abbreviations. In the translation, I have of course
restored these words to their full lengths.

Meaning Structures of Literary Art Forms

EDITOR'S NOTE

The original title of this unfinished manuscript is 'Goethe: Novella'. However, Schutz abandoned it before he reached this topic. What he wrote was to serve as an extensive introduction, offering general considerations of the three major art forms which share the medium of language with one another: literary narration, drama, and poetry. For this reason, I have changed the title of this piece to the wording given above; in its changed form, it reflects the actual content of the unfinished text.

The German overall term for the literary art forms is *'Dichtung'*. A *Dichter* is the writer of stories and novels, plays, and poems, and possibly all three. Yet, in the narrow sense, *Dichtung* stands for poetry. It was thus necessary to vary the translation of these terms according to the actual connotation they gain in the context in which they appear.

The novella mentioned in the title is a designation for a narrative story which is inserted into a novel. It is self-contained yet related to the novel for which it has allegorical significance. Goethe used such inserted stories in his novel, 'Wilhelm Meister's Years of Roaming'. The present manuscript breaks off before the central topic of the novella was reached. However, it contains one reference to it; it shows that Schutz had planned to concern himself with only one of these novellas, the story of a travelling animal show. Schutz returned to the topic of Goethe's novella in the context of an unpublished manuscript of 1948, dealing with Wilhelm Meister's Wanderjahre.

The Novella is a specific form of the narrative tale. When Schutz spoke of the latter in general, he referred back to the Greek epos, the poetic account of the exploits of ancient Greek heroes, and to its analysis by Aristotle. Within Western Culture, the epos is the archetype of the narrative tale, and Schutz saw it as such. In my translation, I have maintained its Greek label in order to underline the archetypical significance of the term.

Likewise, I have maintained the Greek term, mythos, in its original form. Here, the reason is technical. While the term, myth, is reserved for any specific mythical tale, mythos designates the treasure of mythical accounts, the ensemble of the myths of a specific age and culture, and the common spirit which pervades all of them.

This manuscript, like the preceding one, is linked to the manuscript of the first main part by another reiteration of the life form of the speaking I. Thus, it deals once more – in clear fashion – with the positing and the interpretation of meaning, that is, with the speaker and the listener. These considerations, in turn, serve to characterize the three literary art forms: the differences among them, basically, are differences in the relationship between speaker and listener governed by the kind of intention the literary artist carries out, the kind of meaning he posits, when writing poetry, narrating a story or novel, and authoring a play. The draft of this essay was written without sub-divisions. I have divided it into major sub-themes and added the corresponding subtitles.

DIFFICULTIES OF LITERARY ANALYSIS

In these considerations, I will try to trace the transformation and meaning interpretation of primary facts of experience in the art form of the prose tale *(Erzaehlung)*. The attempt will be made dealing with the example of Goethe's 'Novella.' For various reasons, it has to be limited to mere hints. This is so because, first, every work of art is essentially irrational. Thanks to its specific symbolic characteristics, it can never be completely reduced to other systems of symbols – in this case logical ones. Second and most of all, a work of the literary arts can never be interpreted by means which themselves are language-bound. Language analysis itself has to use the linguistic symbol system. Thereby, it begs the question.[1] Third, in language, the purely technical means of representation form symbol systems which in themselves are so highly complex that they plainly prevent the reduction of the meaning of the spiritual world – as given in a literary work of art – to the original facts of experience.

Such difficulties occur in the investigation of any literary work; p.2 in the case of scrutiny of narrative prose, its unique relations to the word make for additional confusion. Since Aristotle, many attempts have been made to differentiate the individual kinds of literary form *(Dichtungsarten)* from each other. But all these attempts addressed themselves either to the suitability of specific themes *(Sujets)* for presentation in epos or drama, or to the characteristic technical preconditions of these art forms. Yet, the difference seems to be much deeper and more essential: it consists of a basic difference in the representative materials. The latter belong to language here as well as there; in epos, as well as drama, they consist of 'words.' But, due to the chracteristics of the meaning contexts into which the different literary creations are placed (they are the same only when seen from the viewpoint of grammar) lead to differences in 'materials' which are as great as those prevailing between, say, tone and color.

A more detailed elaboration of this idea leads to the center of the present investigation.

THE LIFE FORM OF THE SPEAKING I: SPEAKER AND LISTENER

The sphere of language is a life form of Man who lives in space, time, and Thou-relation. In it occurs the highest transformation and symbolization of that which is experienced in pure duration. The world of the speaking I has already passed through the life forms of memory and of the acting I, which constructed ever new symbol series, and through the meaning positing and meaning interpretation of the I in the Thou relation. Thus, it is quite remote from the original experience of pure duration.[2] It has become a space-time world, a world filled with consociates, with things named, with actions which can be expressed (linguistically, HRW). Language itself is a precipitate form of all these changing formations. It no longer solely belongs to me or to you, it is common to all of us. It comprises all objects which you and I can apperceive simply by naming them. For every of our present, past, or future actions, it contains a sign, a symbol. In short, within the language-permeated reality there is no event which language would not be able to seize - more, which could have been preformed in the word. In this sense, language and word themselves, being objectively endowed with meaning, have become an experience which is *interpreted* according to the same laws and symbol systems as any other experience seized by the word. They become *an objective meaning context* which it is necessary to subjectivize, positing a new meaning, a new meaning interpretation, through that complicated event which contains both elements and occurs in every conversation - and thus in the social sphere - or in every piece of writing - thus in an apparently solitary sphere. There is a difference between the just-mentioned stances of the individual I to the given objective meaning sphere of the context of language. This difference becomes completely clear when one follows some of the transformations to which an only apparently identical word element is subjected in the consciousness of the speaking, the listening, and the thinking I. The speaker selects from the given meaning content of language - which, he presupposes, is also given for the person addressed - those elements which he considers adequate to the conception of meaning which he intends to express and which he assumes will induce the person addressed to reproduce them.[3] He posits a new meaning context among the elements selected from the general context of the language as well as between these elements and the total context of the language itself.

For the speaker, the act of positing meaning is typical.[4] Through it, he executes the subjectivation of the word. He appropriates it in order to communicate it to others. However, with this appropriation, the word acquires a special, unique, a new meaning for the speaker. It is the intention of every 'communication' to convey, to the person addressed, this new meaning of the word. (This meaning results from (1) the relationship to the existing objectively meaning-endowed material of the language as such, and (2) its integration into the subjectively meaning-endowed context of speech.)

p.3

p.4

p.5

It is different with the listener.[5] First of all, he relates to the
objective material of the language what has been communicated to
him. This means that, first, he executes a process of meaning
interpretation according to the scheme of language which he has
attitudinally adopted and which is familiar to him. This is the same
process as that followed by the speaker, only in reverse. The
speaker selects and thereby posits a subjective meaning. The
listener integrates that which has been communicated to him and,
therefore, interprets it in terms of the objective meaning context
of the given language material. From here, he pursues the context
of the speech he has heard; that is, he tries to understand the
meaning which the speaker meant. However, he can do this merely
by means of integration (of the words heard, HRW) into the objective context of the language; that means only in so far as the
speaker was successful in establishing the 'right' connection between the objective meaning context of the language and the elements which he selected on the one hand, and between these
'appropriated' and 'communicated' elements on the other. Therefore: only when the speaker spoke 'correctly' (and posited the   p.6
correct meaning context) and the listener heard correctly (and
correctly interpreted the meaning context which was set by the
speaker), there exists a chance that that which was meant will
be subjectively interpreted by the listener as thus and nothing
else.

   Of what kind is the assumed subjectification of the objective
meaning context of the (understanding) listener? No doubt: The
positing of meaning on the part of the listener which occurs in
the act of meaning interpretation, is completely different from
the positing of meaning by the speaker which occurs in the act
positing meaning. The listener does mean nothing; he does not
want to provide a new meaning. Thus, he is not aware that his
meaning interpretation implicitly comprises subjectification, because only from the point of view of the third observer – this is
essential for the whole investigation which follows – is the act of
listening a subjectification of the objective meaning context of
language. For the listener himself, the word heard is and remains
an objective meaning which is integrated into the objective meaning
context of language, and vice versa. Not the listener, only the
speaker *means* something with the word; not the speaker, only the
listener interprets it. However, the listener interprets it at first
as he would interpret it if it had not been spoken by the speaker,
namely, the speaker in this context. For the third observer, this
kind of understanding may also represent a subjective positing of
meaning on the part of the listener. For him, the listener, the
word keeps its objective meaning, that is: a meaning not to be
posited but to be interpreted by him.

   In the following exposition, 'subjective meaning' shall always be p.6a
taken as the intended meaning (thus of the speaker) and 'objective
meaning' as the meaning to be interpreted (thus by the listener).
In order to simplify both terminology and investigation, the subjective positing of meaning, which inheres in all understanding,

will be neglected; so the act of meaning interpretation which must precede every act of meaning positing - because it is part of the character of language as objective meaning context that every word had to be heard and understood in the past before it could be meant and enunciated in the present.[6]

Yet, it should not be forgotten that, for everyone in any kind of language, each word is colored differently and surrounded by a specific aura of significance and meaning content. Simply, this aura is unique; for instance, it makes for the characteristics of style. The cause of this phenomenon is simple: the speaker is never only speaker but also listener. Therefore, it can be asserted that, in the linguistic sphere alone, a complete understanding of a meaning context posited by the speaker (subjective meaning) cannot be established in the meaning interpretation carried out by the listener (objective meaning). Within language alone, understanding remains an approximation between subjective and objective meaning, between intended and interpreted meaning. This approximation is asymptotic (that is, the two kinds of meaning, even in the most favorable case, cannot become identical, HRW).

The many misunderstandings of daily life aside, sufficient proof
p.7   for this exists in the unending possibilities of interpretation of every literary work, for instance, a single verse. The reduction of the distance between subjective and objective meaning is enhanced by elements which, in themselves, have nothing to do with the linguistic sphere; so through the logical context in which words are put, through the tone in which they are spoken, through facial expressions and gestures which accompany them. All are means of expression which help to divest language as expression (subjective meaning) of its mere 'character of communication.'

It follows that the character of words is very variable, according to whether it is spoken or heard. The form of the word is the same, the word meaning necessarily a different one. (Approximately, this corresponds to the deep distinction between word as communication and word as expression, which is postulated by the phenomenological school.)[7]

POETRY, DRAMA AND NARRATIVE PROSE

The material of a literary work of art presents itself, formally uniform, as objective linguistic meaning context. This circumstance tempts us to assume the essential identity of the word in lyrical poetry, drama, and narrative prose. However, according to meaning context and structure, there exists that deep-reaching basic difference between posited and interpreted meaning which just has been considered.
p.8   In the lyrical work of art, the word is expression as such. It springs from the subjective stance which the poet assumes toward language, and it exhausts itself in this function. In its essence, the word of the lyricist does not direct itself to the listener, except the author himself. The Lyrical does not want to communi-

cate; it wants merely to express. It 'means' no meaning contexts which could gain their full meaning only in the interpretation of the listener. It posits contexts as such; they are meaningful already because they have been posited, and they are not in need of consideration in the form of meaning interpretation. Therefore, poetry is a solitary art. It does not depend on the Thou, on the listener, as interpreter and completer of meaning. In this, most of all, it is related to music, the most solitary of all arts. In no other work of art is language allowed as much leeway as in the lyrical poem. Here, the word alone follows its own law. *The individual I stands face-to-face with language, forming himself out of it.* The listener is not essential for the existence of the lyrical work of art; but he has two ways for gaining access to the meaning of the lyrical poem: the path over the person of the poet or over the linguistic configuration. The poet can be understood by pure integration into the Thou relationship. Here, the listener, so to speak, reproduces the literary work of art as one which is still to be created. Thus, he repeats the subjective positing of meaning by the author. It is this co-experience of the creative forming of the medium of language, of the transformation p.9 of the experience through the symbol series of all life forms up to the word which renders original and close-to-life all true poetry.

The other path leads over the configuration of language as already posited and given. But, here too, the attempt is not made to transform the subjective meaning context of language as such into a subjective interpretation of meaning by the listener. In this kind of linguistic consideration, too, the listener stops short of the exploration of the objective language formation - provided that he knows how to listen to poetry, that is, provided that he is aware of the irrelevance of his own person for the existence of the poem. He will attempt to interpret the outer and inner regularities of this linguistic form out of its immanent meaning. Never does the listener to the poem feel that he has been addressed. He has been permitted to witness the self-presentation of an I in language. He may approach the literary work of art by way of the language configuration or through the act of its creation. But the subjective interpretation of the word, by necessity, is denied him because the word, in poetry, lives only in and through the positing of meaning. Every attempt at interpreting its meaning, on the part of the listener, would rob it of its most essential character; it would transform it into prose, something it can never become as long as poetry remains true to its essential character.

This also explains why poetry knows rhythm in the sense of the time-beat of the tones of language (metrical foot) and rhyme. The p.10 rhythm of the lyrical poem is an element of linguistic creation. It is related to musical rhythm in so far as it represents the purest projection of inner duration into time: the most noble and primary positing of meaning which is granted to the creating I. The rhyme is an element of the creation of language-art. It is enclosed in that realm of language which blocks any meaning interpretation by the listener. It is accessible solely to meaning positing by the speaker; for the rest, it is subjected to its own idiosyncratic and irrational law.

(Exponents of, HRW) a philosophy of the rhyme arrive at a mystique of language in which they try to decypher contexts in the unfathomable independent life of language - independent of speaker and listener - as a hypostasis of its immanent meaning. Or else they establish an exclusive relation between the positing and the configuration of language forms, but never between linguistic-art configuration and interpretation. To hear a rhyme can never become object of a meaning interpretation; it even never can be object of a solely esthetic evaluation. To form a rhyme is highest fulfilment of the self-representation of the I through and in language.

The word of the poet is only posited meaning. It does not need a listener; nay, it does not let him come close. It is pure spoken word.

p.11   (Here, it has to be inserted that, according to the whole orientation of these considerations, the differentiation between the art forms within language can be nothing but completely super-ficial characterizations of their essentials. They claim neither completeness nor classificatory significance. Here, too, one speaks only about the lyrical, the epic, the dramatic. Of course, a 'novel' may be purely lyrical; a tragedy purely epic, a poem (ballad) purely dramatic.)

The word of the dramatist is completely different: the dramatic dialogue consists of communications; the word is spoken, and that means spoken to another person. It is intended to be heard, understood, and interpreted. And this not only by the audience as the ideal observer but also by the co-player: the consociate, or better, the actor as symbol of the consociate who finds himself on stage simultaneously with the speaker. Thus, as communication, the word of the dramatist depends on a listener, if not already on the audience as listener, so on the antagonist (on the stage, HRW). The audience participates in the acts of positing and inter-preting meanings. But only when they identify themselves with the acting persons on the stage can they grasp the word, which now they have to interpret, as expression of the author beyond the mere communication between protagonist and antagonist.

p.12   Here, we must refrain from investigating the complicated manner in which these derivated acts of positing and integrating meanings occur. However, from the hints given it follows clearly enough that the word has a very different function in the tragedy and yields a totally different material for creative expression than it does in the lyrical poem.

p.13   On this occasion, we may look at the difference in the relations of the poet and of the dramatist to their respective works. The lyrical work of art disappears completely behind the personality of the poet; the reader is always dominated by the feeling that he is in the presence of the subjective expression of an individual personality. By contrast, to be successful, the work of the dramatist demands the complete retreat of the personality of the author behind his work. The meaning of the drama is to bring the tragical action before the eyes of the spectator as if he would really co-experience it from beginning to end. An interpretation of the dramatic action by the dramatist is completely unimaginable, in so far as it would be directed at the spectator – that is, to speak with Nietzsche, at Dionysian man.[8] The spectator can conclude that the dramatist equipped this or that figure with these or those traits only in contemplative considerations, that is, only after the curtain came down.

What is the position of the representing prose writer in comparison with these relations between playwright and work? It may be easier to answer this question if we consider first the role of the reader or listener of a tale. There is no art form in which so little   p.14 is left to the fantasy of the reader as in the tale. The listener of the drama enjoys the fascination of following the dialogue and, therefore, of simultaneously interpreting the subjective meaning of the speaker and the objective meaning of the addressed hero. Thus, under all conditions, he is better than any of the acting figures on the stage informed about all circumstances of the fate which this meaning undergoes in the dialogue. This state of tension is eliminated, let's say, in a dialogue which is reproduced in narrative form, since the narrator always offers it in the form of a meaning interpretation. What the spectator in the theatre has himself to deduce from gesture and tone, the reader receives from the narrator in form of directoral annotations. The audience is free to imagine the arena of the actions, according to their own fantasy, on the basis of the hints given with the scenery. But the prose author predesigns the arena of events for the reader – down to the smallest detail. The spectator of a drama can treat time in the auditorium at will during a change of scenes on the stage or with the lowering of the curtain. He is able, without transition, to step at any moment into the midst of the presently most important event. The reader of a narrative is forced to accept the course of time as imposed by the writer. In its way, this time represents a kind of continuum which can be interrupted only on the basis of specific reasons or with the help of specific technical tricks. In one word, the reader of a narration is completely dependent on the author; the spectator of the drama stands free in juxtaposition to the action and its exponents.

It follows that, in narration, the author plays the role of the   p.15 audience in the theatre or, more exactly, pretends to see what is played. It is not the reader but the author who is omniscient. Goethe's definition of the novella as an unprecedented event which took place, is in need of the complementation, 'which the narrator claims to have witnessed.'[9]

If the comparison is admissible, the ideal of a narrator is the theatrical spectator who went home and reported the course of the dramatic action. He will never occur in the tale of his visit to the theater; he wants to relate solely the events on the stage but not his appraisal of them. However, it is a presupposition for his account that he saw the drama to the end. Only seen from the last act does the first one become so understandable to the narrator that his account can create a clear picture of the course of action (presented in the drama, HRW).

Both the poet and the dramatist receive the raw materials for their artistic creations from the sphere of real experiences. The poet does not presuppose a reader when he forms his material. By contrast, the narrator receives the precipitate of his creative activity, so to speak, in an already preformed state. The narration, as presented to the reader, is a practically finished product; nothing in it changes during its presentation. The reader has one single task: to listen. He is excluded from artistic collaboration and participation, as far as the forming of the material is concerned. However, since the narration is a work of art, he has the task to interpret this work of art as presented in its inner meaning and symbol (content, HRW).

p.16

EXPRESSION AND COMMUNICATION

The conception presented finds support in the purely temporal relation of the reader to the work of art. As pure expression, poetry is apperceived by the always accidental reader in a sphere which transcends all time; it belongs solely to pure duration. For the spectator in the theater, the time conception of the event on the stage is necessarily that of the present. With good reasons, the author of a narrative work directs the reader to accept the content of the story as something (which happened in the, HRW) past. This alone makes it impossible for the reader to interfere with the course of the tale even empathetically. What is told has been, is finished and unchangeable. Therefore, it does not reach the present of the reader. This is the main reason for the fact that narration, in all languages, normally assumes the form of the past tense.[10] This form may be abandoned, in certain passages, only for very specific reasons. About these technical tricks, more will have to be said later.[11]

p.17   The need to make sure that the action has taken place and is finished and to exclude the reader from any direct participation leads to extraordinary precautions: A narrated dialogue is offered as being quoted by the narrator: 'He said . . . ,' 'He answered. . . .'

To summarize, it must be said that the bridge between narrator and reader is indirect.[12] The narrator remains hidden behind his work only for the reader. In reality, he stands above the action; he knows its complete course before the reader learns about it. As said before, the role of the reader is reduced to the sole task of listening.

As listener, the reader receives the word of the narrator. Thus, he faces an objective language context which he has to interpret. The connection with the subjective meaning of the narrator has almost completely been lost by him. For the reader, the narrator is always anonymous. The word in a tale, so to speak, shows the reverse of the word in poetry. In poetry, it belongs to the speaker as pure expression; the word of narration is necessarily directed at the listener. Through the word, the poet forms his own self in language; the narrator anticipates in his language-work the subjective meaning interpretation of the listener. Poetry is always forming of language; narration is always formed language.[13]

In narration, the word presents itself to the listener as objec-   p.18 tive meaning context which has to be interpreted; according to its structure, it is decisively the word heard. Thereby, it is not asserted that the literary representation of prose has the character of communication. On the contrary, narration is essentially different from mere 'communication' - if conversation in daily life is accepted as basic type of the latter.

In contrast to narration, most of all, communication is essentially social oriented. The communicator does not merely presuppose, as does the narrator, the existence of consociates who understand him. Rather, he expects through his communication to induce the person addressed to take some kind of position, to resort to a conduct which is oriented on his communication and is therefore social. He does not merely expect understanding but a conduct which is conditioned by this understanding and oriented toward it. Such conduct may occur in the form of an action (maybe an answer) or in inner conduct (maybe in a motivational change of the affectual situation of the person addressed on the basis of his interpretation of the facts offered to him). Communication is always purposive-rational; it always expects to release a specific effect in the addressed person. Therefore, it is directed to one or several addressed persons who, in the opinion of the speaker, offer a chance to release the conduct which he intended by his   p.19 communication. Even the speaker at a rally considers the given 'mass' whom he addresses and expects from them a specific reaction to his 'communication.'

Not so the novelist as narrator. He directs himself to a listener whose existence he presupposes as much as the chance to be understood by him. But he does not expect social conduct from his listener. His story is not purposive-rational; he does not 'want' to achieve an immediate effect through it - except the esthetic effect produced by any work of art. The listener, whose existence is presupposed, may thus remain anonymous without thereby doing damage to the story. As work of art, the story neither in content nor in intention makes a selection among the circle of all possible readers. It directs itself neither to an individual nor a social group; it merely addresses the listener, whoever he may be. This is contrary to the character of communication. The latter, both in content and form, is always oriented toward the individual situation of the person addressed and wants to release a specific conduct.

From this follows the second difference between narration as work of art and communication. Since the narrator does not direct himself to a specific listener, he alone decides about the subject matter of the story, and that in the widest possible sense. He   p.20

alone selects from all possible contents those which appear to him worthwhile to be told. The person of the listener does not influence the decision. Therefore, the unity of the narration is consistently preserved: The narrator always pays attention to the existence of the listener but never to his orientation.

In contrast to 'expression' and 'communication,' the typical character of the word in narration will be called 'representation' *(Darstellung)*. It has to be stressed that 'representation' is a generic concept. To it belongs, next to narration, a whole series of linguistic objectifications carrying representative character, most of all didactic representations of scientific investigations. But we are not concerned with all types of linguistic forms and abstain from investigating the related forms of representation. Decisive for all of them, ultimately, is the character of the symbol system which is shaped in representation. For instance, in scientific representation the system is that of knowledge, respectively of the particular categories of thinking. Generally what manifests itself in literary narration is the symbol system of the work of art, and more specifically the symbol series of poetry as such. A possible definition of 'epos' is the following: linguistic representation which is subordinated to general poetic laws.

RULES OF UNITY AND UNFOLDING

p.21   According to Goethe's and Schiller's essay, Concerning Epic and Dramatic Literature, the 'general poetic laws' are most of all the laws of unity and unfolding. Their effect on the species 'narration' will subsequently be studied with Goethe's 'Novella.'[14] It will be demonstrated that that which is essentially epic can always be reduced to the specific character of the word in the epos. All distinctions between poetry and drama can be located in the completely different structures of the word material which is the foundation of these species in the sense of the above investigations

According to Goethe and Schiller, the laws of unity and unfolding dominate the epic as well as the dramatic forms. What is the essential content of these laws? But, first of all, what does it mean to pose the question of laws in a form of art?

On the surface, it appears that a law of art is nothing more than a mere pragmatic formula of craftsmanship. It seems to have been found in a purely empirical way providing, so to speak, a recipe for satisfying one esthetical postulate or other. Partly, this view is not unwarranted. This is so because what is generally claimed to be a law of art is of quite heterogeneous nature. Sometimes, laws of 'art' are simply ideal-typical constructions of a specific style period. As examples may serve the laws of a triangular, respectively pyramidal, composite structure of works of
p.22   the fine arts in the Renaissance and Baroque periods, but also Boileau's poetry. Characteristically, this group of laws of art is valid only for a specific, historically limited, realm of style. We do not assert that such laws are merely superimposed upon the

respective works of art by later art analysts. It is also completely irrelevant whether such laws originated in the striving for repeating that which had proven itself as being of beautiful or pleasant effect, or whether a specific creative will of an artistic individuality or a dominant school gave rise to their formulation and development. Essentially it is only that we deal here not with general laws of art but with rules which are particular for a specific group of works of art. Other works of art follow other laws. We will call this group of laws or art style-immanent laws.

Another group of laws produces exclusively formal crafts-rules; to follow them allows the production of effects, which have been intended beforehand, on and through given materials. Such laws, too, are valid only within limited periods and areas. However, they span several style periods: in them, the traditional moment is much more prominent than in style-immanent laws. They also unite geographically larger areas.[15]   p.23

In painting, such laws are the laws of perspective which are valid for Western paintings since the fifteenth century. In music, such laws are the laws of the theory of harmony (in so far as it is not concerned with leading singing voices - *Stimmfuehrung*); they apply only to our occidental rationalized system of sharps and flats in its present form. It is not valid for any other system, for example, the five-tone or the quarter-tone systems. We shall call this group material-rational laws. Such laws are limited to specific materials and display distinctively purposive character. A whole series of other such laws could be mentioned. Essentially, the achievement of the customary history of art, literature, and music consists in nothing else but the postulation of such laws limited to periods and areas. In contrast to them, a group of essential laws of every species of art exist which can be demonstrated to be valid for any work of art beyond all limitations of period and area.

These laws are essential because they contain the categories of   p.24 the understanding of any work as such. They transcend its time-space objectification and contain the presuppositions for the acts of positing meaning by the artist and for the acts of meaning interpretation by the viewer (listener, reader, HRW) both within the symbol series characteristic of the specific artistic material (in which the artists work HRW).

We call these laws the *meaning* laws of the arts. For example, to them belong, in architecture, all those laws which are concerned with the symbolic interpretation of space itself (theory of the relations of dimensions) and, in music, those laws which deal with the symbolic reduction of time sequences in their relation to duration (e.g., theory of melody or of rhythm).

With regard to works of the literary arts, only those laws can be called laws of meaning[16] which reduce the objective meaning content of the linguistic context to the linguistically formed and posited meaning of the writer as well as the meaning interpretation of the linguistic form by the listener. Therefore, they bring both into one single and necessary context. A law which is applicable   p.25

only to the acts of meaning posited by the writer would be a
law of literary fantasy; it would have to be immanent in the consciousness of the writer. Here belong, for instance, all the rules
about literary subjects which have been postulated by Goethe. A
law treating only the act of meaning interpretation could only state
something about the character of the understandability of a
literary object; that is, so to speak, it is a rule for the interpretation of literary meanings in the consciousness of the reader.
Here belong all rules concerning 'effect' and consequences of a
work of art.

One cannot call the two groups 'laws of meaning' because they
remain ever immanent in consciousness. They would belong to the
real duration either of the writer or the listener; it is out of
these durations that the linguistic creation is objectified. And, in
reverse, these durations enter into the literary form as subjective
elements. The laws of meaning of literary creations transcend
these two subjective and thereby real durations. They belong
neither solely to the consciousness of the writer nor exclusively
to that of the listener but to the objective context of language.
For this reason, they are accessible to the act of positing meaning
as well as that of interpreting meaning; thus, they belong to the
consciousness of both. As in the case of all meaning contexts
which transcend individual consciousness, these laws result in
ambivalences. The writer views the law of meaning only in the
specific conscious attitude of the reader toward the objective
p. 26   linguistic context, as it takes place in the act of understanding
and thus in meaning interpretation. The reader cannot possibly
see anything else in the law of meaning than the embodiment of
the conscious processes of the writer which make the literary
creation possible.

This dual aspect is made possible by the fact that, in literature,
each law of meaning[17] [contains the possibility of an objective
linguistic context and with it of language formation and language
form as such. Therefore, every law of meaning concerning the
literary work] postulates a connection between duration and the
space-time existence of the objective language context. This connection is characteristic of the literary symbol series. Only the
phenomenon of duration is common to the consciousness of both
listener and writer. In its essence, each law of meaning will be
anchored in the Thou relation even though it externally establishes
a connection not between two consciousnesses in duration but
only between one such consciousness (of the writer *or* the reader)
and the spatial-temporal objective language context. In other words:
the laws of meaning of the literary work of art are neither normative ought-rules nor empirical propositions. They are of a
purely genetic-explicative nature. They typify the preconditions
for the transformation of literary conceptions, experienced in the
duration of the writer, into the space-time language material
which is endowed with objective meaning. But it does the same
p. 27   also for the possibility of experiencing the objective space-time
language context as a symbol context in the duration of the reader.

Speaking schematically, the following steps result: original experience in duration of the writer - symbolization in the symbol series by the writer - act of positing meaning in the linguistic creation - objective linguistic context (language form) - meaning interpretation of the linguistic form by the reader - reinterpretation of the literary material through reduction to the generally essential (de-symbolization) - reinterpretation in pure experience of duration by the reader. The true meaning law of language has to bring all the mentioned events into a necessary, uninterchangeable, specific, and conscious context which offers their genetic explication.

The laws of unity and unfolding are such laws of meaning. The former aims at the symbolization of duration in a purely spatial-temporal and objective linguistic context. The latter aims at the reinterpretation of the manifold successions of the stream of consciousness into a coexistence which is arranged in a certain way.

According to Schiller and Goethe, the laws of unity and of un-   p. 28
folding are general literary laws. Therefore, they must be valid for every kind of literary creation. This, again, means that the Goethe-Schiller law of unity must be based on another concept than that of the three units of drama: place, time, and action - as postulated by Aristotle, misunderstood and banalized in French poetry, and modified in more recent German but most of all English literature. Yet, as revealed by closer inspection, the law of unity in literature, as law of meaning of the literary work of art, is merely that general proposition of which the three units of the drama are specific applications.

Every artistic creation is a closed symbol system. As such, it tends to interpret primary facts of experience and to endow them with meanings which are specific to the artistic symbol series. It can achieve this only when it is able to contain the basic elements of every experience, even though transformed. Seen from this angle, the conflict between realism and symbolism, which dominates all artistic tendencies of all places and times, is not limited to esthetic evaluations. The general value problem is at its root: what should be achieved by a value system as such? Is the transformation of the content of experience, which occurs in and through the symbol and creates a larger or smaller distance between symbol and symbolized, at all possible without becoming unexperientiable, that is, absolutely irreal?

If one accepts this formulation, realism would mean bringing the   p. 29
literary symbol series closer to the symbol series of our external real life. Symbolism would mean the opposite. But neither artistic realism nor symbolism have ever theoretically or practically denied that the basic facts of our experience of our truly real inner world present the sole foundation for artistic symbolization. Our daily life in the outer world presents itself as a highly complex symbol system which transforms the material of our inner world. Therefore, the postulate of artistic realism signifies only an approximation of the artistic symbol system to the symbol system of our daily life. We are more familiar with the latter than with all other

symbol systems, because we act in it, live in it with our consociates, speak and think in it. Therefore, it appears to be privileged. Consequently, the postulate of realism, aiming at the
approximation of the artistic symbol series to that of daily life,
is only a style-immanent law. The true relation between the meaning of art and the meaning of life must lie elsewhere. The laws,
which deal with this relation, have to be common to all styles and
all periods. They cannot be subjected to evaluations; therefore,
they cannot be concretized, to various degrees, in material works
of art. They have to be absolute because their origin lies where
the symbol series of art and of daily life spring from the basic experience of the inner world, which is common to both.

p.30

What has been explained in the immediately preceding passage
applies to all kinds of art. In the literary work, it becomes difficult because language itself is a symbol series of daily life as
well as of artistic creation. At the beginning of these considerations, it has been explained to what degree the word of daily
speech can be identified with the word of the literary writer. We
deal here not with the material of the given symbol but with the
meaning of the symbol series itself. Namely, if life and poem are
said to issue from a common basic experience, it must be possible,
in an act of self-contemplation, to reduce both symbol systems to
one original experience. In spite of all transformations, the meaning of the final symbolic formulation must be identical with that
of the original experience. Otherwise, no possibility would remain
for meaningfully integrating these symbol series themselves, as
experiences, into the stream of our consciousness. A fundamental
law of all symbolic creation postulates that the symbol must be
experientiable just as meaningfully as that which it symbolizes.
A poem, which would not satisfy this postulate, would be meaningless in itself as soon as it has gained its finished form. We may
say, it would occur in a language we do not understand - even
though we may have understood it when the poem emerged. Thus,
we can risk asserting that the laws of unity in poetry mean nothing else than the postulate of the identity of the poetic object
with the original experience of our inner world which, in turn,
becomes the foundation of poetic creation.

p.31

This thesis seems simple but is exposed to great misunderstandings as soon as one attempts to lift the original experience out of
our familiar symbol series of daily life in order to integrate it into
the symbol series of artistic creation. Again and again the fatal
attempt has been made to form poetic symbol series in the same
fashion in which symbol series of daily life enter into the course
of the latter.

The theory of the three units of the drama may be mentioned as
a typical example of such a misunderstanding, particularly in the
interpretation of French writers. Lessing already realized that,
for the ancient thinkers, the original law was that of the unity of
action. Other unities resulted from it without difficulties, like that
of place and of time. Unity of action means nothing other than a
meaningful course of the dramatic event - meaningful because it

p.32

occurs according to the same laws which govern the successive development of the original experience in our duration. But already here, in this main law of unity, occurs a stupendous misunderstanding.

Within inner duration, the development of our basic experiences occurs in a most variegated manner. We cannot account for it, either in language or in thought, when we try to break through the symbol series of our outer world and to retreat intuitively into the inner world. We may mention the dream as an example. Its apparent meaninglessness can only consist in the fact that succession and unfolding of the dream events occur not according to the categories of the outer world. Thus, they are linguistically not comprehensible. When a writer like Strindberg attempts dramatically to recreate dream events, he apparently destroys the 'unity of action' in the sense of French literature. Yet, he does not violate this basic law. French literary theory demands that the poet establish the unity of action in his poem with the same   p.33 means with which a thinking person in the outer world of his daily life tends to recreate the unity of his basic experience: conceptual and *motivational*.

Thus, it happens that, according to the theory of Boileau and Corneille, unity of action is confused with sufficient motivation – a view which is so deep-rooted that even a mind like Lessing shared it. Like no other writer of his time, he recognized the insufficient and confused conception of the basic laws of drama as displayed by the French dramatists. Yet, he felt he had to defend his Shakespeare against the reproach of insufficient motivation; he attempted to show that real motivational reasons (for Shakespeare's dramatic characters, HRW) can be assumed as possible and are therefore admissible.

Of course, the possibility of confusing the unity of action with the continuity of motivation in the conceptual-linguistic sense exists because 'motivation' is a specific category of the literary symbol function. Yet, it has nothing to do with the conceptual-logical motivation of daily life. If both are identified with one another, it is on the basis of the impossible notion that the relations between literary creations can be exchanged with the re-   p.34 lations in our external life, and this without any adaptation.

This basic misunderstanding also explains the truly curious forms which the postulates of the unity of time and the unity of space have assumed in the course of the history of literature. The unity of the stream of duration represents an irreversible unambiguous relation between our immediate experiences. In outer life, the symbol of this unity of duration is the unity of real time. The latter is nothing else but a projection of duration into space. Nobody has ever thoroughly investigated the transformation of duration in the artistic, and especially the time-bound literary symbol systems of poetry (and other literary art forms, HRW). Erroneously, one has conceived the time concept of daily life as a category of the literary symbol system. Here, Lessing achieved something important. In the 45th piece of his 'Hamburg Dramaturgy,'

he denounced as superstition the notion that dramatic action has to take place within the physical time of a single day, countering it by the demand that one has to consider the unity of moral time
p.35   – which has nothing to do with physical time. This was to mean that the stage events occur in irreal, imaginary time, not experienced by anyone. This time is neither like our duration nor like physical time; it is the projection of duration into the linguistic-literary symbol series (in contrast to the linguistic-conceptual one).

It will not be necessary analogously to demonstrate the same for the unity of place. Here, too, the need for spatial fixation of the basic experience within the literary symbol series is attempted with a means which belongs not to the latter but to the outer world. How much the postulates of the unity of place and of time depend on the – already formulated – law of the unity of action, has been shown on the example of the drama. However, since it is a law of meaning, all kinds of literary creation are subject to it. This is only possible if one sees, in the law of the unity of action, nothing more than the metaphorical expression of the unity of the primary experience.

In this sense, Aristotle's definition of the unity of action, as given in his *'Poetics,'*[18] is only a special case. It pertains to epos
p.36   and drama, but can also be applied to poetry, provided that action, in the broadest sense, is understood as original experience. The Aristotelian definition of the unity of time,[19] too, is only a special application of his law of the unity of action to the factualities of epos and drama. Therefore, in the sense of Goethe and Schiller, our task remains to demonstrate the law of meaning of every form of literature and, within individual kinds of literature – poetry, epos, drama – to reduce it to the meaning structure of the word material as expression, communication, and representation.
p.37   We have stated earlier that, in the literary work of art, the law of meaning displays a peculiar ambivalence. The reader will always presuppose the meaning law within the literary conception, the writer always presupposes the interpretative process of the reader. Actually, both conceptions are deceptive. The essence of the law of meaning transcends consciousness. Therefore, it cannot be anchored in duration but only in the objective reality of language. Applied to the law of unity, this means that, for the reader, the unity seems to be given in the literary conception. Aristotle thought of something similar when he spoke of the action of the poem, whose parts have to cohere in such a fashion that the whole suffers change and transformation even if only one single part is altered or removed. Obviously, this notion refers to the act of poetic conception.

The reconstructing reader may ask himself how the composition would be changed if this or that part had been formed differently. Obviously, this question aims at the creative process of the writer. Yet, it is always presupposed that he, the reader, would subject a thus imaginarily changed literary piece to a specific but different interpretation. For instance, such a task is executed by the

philologist who scrutinizes variations of the same poem with regard
to their esthetic value.

In reverse, the writer apperceives the unity of the object not as
unity of the creative act of its conception. To him, all possibilities
of selection among the experiences on hand are still open. However,
only he can change or correct a poem without violating the law of
unity. He certainly will make such corrections in order to satisfy
this law. This is so because, by unity of the original experience,
the writer understands the unity of the experience in the interpretation of the reader.

After finishing his 'Novella,' Goethe posed the question to
Eckermann whether the owner of the animal show, together with
wife and child, should already appear in the exposition.[20] He rejected this plan for reasons not so much taken from the law of
unity as the law of unfolding. He limited himself to let the lion
roar when the princess and her entourage pass the cages; he
makes these changes with the clear intention to evoke a specific
effect in the reader. This specific effect consists in the adaptation
of the fundamental stratum of the literary symbol series to the
original experience of the reader, which he intends to evoke.

The ambivalence of the meaning laws of literature comprises acts   p.39
of positing meanings and of interpreting meanings, or so it seems.
This leads to the assumption that the essence of the word, as it
reveals itself to naive considerations in the objective reality of
language, must be the carrier of the law of meaning. This notion
is as imprecise as it is incorrect, if one means by objective reality
of language the word as such. The latter could as well be object
of grammar, of conversation in daily life, as of artistic creation.
However, if we take the initially asserted structural change of
the word in each of its material functions, the law of meaning can
very well be transposed into the reality of objective language. In
the sphere of the word as material of literary creation, the law of
unity would assert nothing else than the adequacy of the word to
the original experience of inner duration. The postulate of the
identity of the word with the original experience would be completely unverifiable. Between that which is symbolized and the
symbol exists not the relation of identity but only the relation of
adequacy. Seen from this angle, the differentiation of the meaning
structures of poetry, epos, and drama - which was offered at the
start of this investigation - appears in a new light. It turns out   p.40
that these structural differences issue from the capacity of objective linguistic materials as such to be adequate to experiences.

However, expression, communication, and representation are not
only functions of language; they also designate a specific quality
of the original experiences itself. It follows that some themes are
considered unsuitable for one or the other literary art form. The
basic experiences, to which these themes refer, display specific
affectual tones which push toward one of the given means of
literary creation. If one intends to achieve the adequacy of the
word in objective linguistic reality to the affectually colored original
experience, the word will have to be formed as expression, com-

munication, or representation. Consequently, its form must be the
lyrical poem, the drama, or the epic. All three forms are linguistic
functions subjugated under literary laws of meaning. Thus, they
are all subordinated to the law of unity, because this law is already the foundation of the material which, in its structural differentiation, leads to the origin of the individual species of
literature. To discuss in what manner each literary form, with
its specific material, satisfies the law of unity and how it modifies
it, is a task which goes far beyond the framework of the present
investigation. On occasion of the analysis of the 'Novella,' something will have to be said about this in connection with comparative
references to poetry and drama.[21]

p.41   From our expositions thus far, one may erroneously conclude
that the apparently literary meaning law of unity is either a
general law of language, or else that it amounts to no more than
a tautology: within literature, the objective language material is
reduced to its structural form. By way of a *petitio principii*
(begging the question), the general literary law of meaning is
deduced from this reduction. As to the first objection: we do not
at all deny the possibility of the existence of an analogous law of
meaning of language in other than the literary symbol forms; so
in the logical-conceptual sphere. It is merely excluded from consideration here. As to the second objection: the paradox is (based
on the assumption, HRW) that one makes into a characteristic of
the objective meaning context in poetry what is 'poetic' from the
outset. This (erroneous assumption) can be traced back to the
transposition of the factual configuration into the linguistic-
conceptual sphere.

The experiencing I lives in all systems and thus also in that of
the symbol series and no less in the system of facts which are to
be symbolized. For it, such a paradox cannot appear. However,
the latter must occur in the ideal-typical abstractions of independent symbol series if one does not assume that the symbol function
is exhausted in the act of transforming that which is symbolized
into the symbol. The symbol, too, enters as experience into the
stream of consciousness in no other way than the original experiences which are the ground for the event of symbolization.

A basic experience, which enters into the symbol forms of
language and further into those of literature, does thereby not
dissolve itself into symbols. It remains effective and mixes itself
with newly added experiences of formed symbols; it becomes a new
and third experience. The experience, which is literarily transformed, does not enter memory loosely and unconnected with the
literary symbol series: it mixes itself with it. Within unitary consciousness, it thereby becomes itself literary. Thus, the tautology
is fictitious.[22] At first, the law of unity is a law of the literary
transformation of the basic experience into the symbol form of the
poem. Since the poem, in turn, becomes experience, this law
becomes later a law of the original literary experience as such.

Having concluded the investigation of the literary law of unity
and demonstrated its meaning structure, we can treat the law of

unfolding in shorter form. This law of meaning, too, concerns the essential linkage between the streams of consciousness of the writer and the reader (on the one hand, HRW), and the objective reality of language (on the other, HRW).[23]

NOTES

Schutz provided eight footnotes for this manuscript. The editor added fifteen of his own. They are marked by the initials of their authors: AS and HRW, respectively.

1   AS: This is different when, in another symbol series, one repostulates the meaning of the same factualities with its characteristic means; for instance, musically in song or opera.

2   HRW: This passage alludes to Schutz's theory of the life forms; it has found its elaborate treatment in the main essay of this book: Life Forms and Meaning Structure. The present discussion of literary symbolization may be considered an expansion of the theory of individual life forms, which was not completed in the main essay.

3   HRW: The last two sentences (which are one in the original text) were written on the top of the left-hand margin of p. 4 of the manuscript. They replace a corresponding passage which was rendered partially unreadable in the typescript. Additional text was crossed out diagonally. But passages which were obviously needed for maintaining the meaning of the whole paragraph have been included in the translation.

4   AS: In this context, we ignore that this act is likewise and necessarily yet secondarily combined with an act of meaning interpretation on the part of the speaker.

5   AS: For the sake of the simplification of this exposition, I will refrain from referring either to the I who thinks in words (and thereby in concepts) and who is similar to the speaking I, or to the speaking I who corresponds to the listener. This is the more justified as the word, in every work of the literary arts, has most of all to be seen – not only from the viewpoint of an esthetical appraisal – as tonal creation, as combination of sounds and as combination of letters.

6   HRW: In his later work, Schutz seems not to have reiterated *this* conception of the difference between objective and subjective meaning.

7   HRW: Most likely, Schutz referred here to Husserl's 'Logische Undersuchungen'.

8   HRW: This typological dichotomy was set up by Friedrich Nietzsche in his book on 'The Birth of Tragedy' (1872). Appollinic Man is the artist, thinker, and actor of 'measured constraint,' of calm meditation, of sober rationality. Dionysian Man, by contrast, is the ecstatic enthusiast, the person of emotional exuberance, and the impulsive actor.

9   AS: For the time being, we speak here only of the purely narrative account. For reasons to be explained later, narrations

in I-form, among them letters and diaries, do not fit into these considerations.

10 HRW: Schutz, here, spoke of the 'Praeteritum' in agreement with his preference for grammatical terms in Latin.

11 HRW: The existing text of this unfinished manuscript does not contain a specific discussion of such literary devices as changing the tenses in the course of a narration.

12 HRW: This sentence and the preceding short paragraph were written by hand on the left margin of p. 17 of the original MS. It replaced and in part repeated a crossed-out passage of five lines of plain text and seven lines on which different words were typed on top of each other. This, obviously, was due to an error of the typist. The content of the text of the crossed-out passage, as originally typed, is literally contained in the next paragraph of the MS.

13 HRW: It follows an unfinished sentence which breaks off with the end of the MS page. But it does not connect with the next page, which begins with a new sentence. Either the typist left a gap in the text here, or Schutz omitted to cross out the unfinished sentence.

14 HRW: The quotation marks do not indicate a title but specify a literary device. See the introductory note to this essay. When Schutz broke off his work on this essay, he had not yet reached its main topic.

15 AS: Note: In these considerations, we can neglect the purely technical rules, for instance, of the correct treatment of the palette or the theory of the possibilities for the use of instruments in an orchestra (however not the theory of their harmony). This is merely a matter of rules of everyday experience which are related to art only in a very indirect context.

16 AS: If we speak of meaning laws of language, it should never be forgotten that it is always a matter of laws of art which, within the literary work of art, understand the transformation of the artistic language symbol from the positing of meaning by the writer to the meaning interpretation by the listener. They belong to a completely different complex of problems as the mere meaning laws of language whose basic types are the propositions of grammar.

17 HRW: Here, the manuscript contains a crossed-out passage; I have restored it to the text, setting it between brackets.

18 AS: In all recreating arts, recreation has to present *one* object; the plot of the drama, as recreation, also has to present *one* action, and this one in its totality. Its parts have to cohere in such a way that, if one of them is changed or removed, the whole itself suffers alteration and transformation ('Poetics', chapter 6).

19 AS: The tragedy, as far as possible (limits) its action to one day, or goes as little as possible beyond it. The epos, however, is not tied to any time limits ('Poetics', chapter 4).

20 HRW: That is, whether it should be made a part of the continuously narrated action, as unfolded in the novel itself.

21 HRW: This intention was not carried out.
22 HRW: Schutz, obviously, refers here to what he earlier called begging the question and a paradox: the untenable assumption that objective literary concepts are constructed from literature and not from language itself.
23 HRW: The manuscript breaks off at this point.

Meaning Structures of Drama and Opera

EDITOR'S NOTE

This manuscript, if not written before all the other studies united
in this volume at least conceived and outlined before them, has
been placed last. This is dictated by its content. Its theme both
links it to and places it after the Meaning Structures of Literary
Art Forms. Dealing with the art form of the drama, it reiterates
and expands the discussion of one of the literary art forms
analyzed before. However, the drama, here, occurs as a kind of
substratum and point of origin of the art form of the musical drama
and the opera proper. The latter occurs as a transforming combination of the forms of dramatic stage performance and that of
music, yielding a synthesis which presents itself as an art form
in its own rights.

Again, this thematic expansion gave Schutz the occasion to
apply to the operatic art form the insights presented in the preceding piece: the objectification of the meaning posited by the
artist, the subjective meaning interpretation of the operatic work
by the viewer/listener, and the dramatic treatment of the Thou
problem.

Schutz placed these central themes within a historical framework
and the framework of a comparative analysis of various operatic
forms and styles. Although these considerations are necessarily
sketchy, they betray his quite thorough knowledge both of the
history of the musical art forms and of their structural variations.

ART FORMS AND FORMS OF THE OPERA

p.1 It is necessary to keep the question of the meaning of an art form
separate from the question of the meaning of a work of art. A
work of art may be considered a social product; that is, it can be
studied in its particular relations to the Thou-problem of which it
is a part both with regard to its intention and its effect. The mere
material form of a work of art lends itself to a dual interpretation
of its meaning. On the one hand, an interpretation of the objectified concrete work of art refers to the meaning posited by its
creator. On the other hand, its meaning interpretation finds its
problematics and its limitations in the objective meaning content in
which the work of art presents itself to the art appreciator. [To
distinguish these two forms of interpretation should be the main
task of every aesthetics; up to now, theories of the latter have

unfortunately been permeated with the contradiction between the
work of art to be created and the created work of art.]
   With regard to the genus of an art or, if you wish, the art form,
this duality of interpretation is absent. To both the artist and
the art appreciator, it presents a completely objective type which
has to be filled with a new meaning content. It is difficult to
decide whether a sharply articulated art form is meaningful in
itself, or whether every art form receives its meaning only from
the content with which it is filled and from the specifically given
idea which it concretely presents. However, it seems to me that
this problem issues exclusively from an equivocation of the term
'meaning'. On the one hand, the term signifies the reversal of
attention from the posited symbol to the symbol to be interpreted;   p.2
on the other hand, it is used as expression of the inherent
necessity *(eigene Gesetzlichkeit)* of anything spiritual *(geistig)*.
If one wants to take the term 'meaning' in the first sense, he
encounters no objective units of meaning as such. He finds only
such which had been created before and which, in their given
shape, had been placed into the spatial-temporal world and which,
afterwards, had to be interpreted by another being endowed with
the ability of interpreting and positing meanings. It is always
possible to demonstrate the processes of positing and interpreting
meanings on hand of any single work of art. To inquire merely
about the art form means to neglect the act of positing meaning
or, rather, to blend it with the act of interpretation: the art form
is taken to be something which persists in objective unchange-
ability; it is not accessible to the subjective positing of meaning.
While it can be filled with most different contents, it remains invariable and constant in itself.
   To take the art form of the drama as example: it is certain that
one cannot draw parallels between a drama by Euripides[1] and a
modern drama, say one by Strindberg,[2] if one concerns oneself
with the ideas expressed as well as the style in which the meaning
content is brought into the form. Yet, the technical task characteristic of the drama remains the same in both cases: to present
to the spectator, immediately and without interpretation, relations
between humans through their acting and speaking within a
specific spatial-temporal frame. Among all art forms, only the play
can perform this task; it will be achieved in every drama. Therefore, certain preconditions are common to the whole art form. For
instance, (a) the interpretability of speech or gesture of the individual actor who, again, is symbol for the hero whom he presents to the audience as well as to an interpreter; (b) the understandability of all relations among all persons who constitute the
substance of the drama; (c) the possibility of vicariously experi-   p.3
encing the spatial-temporal development of the acting on the stage;
finally (d) the possibility that all the factors mentioned can be
thought of as means of expression or as symbols of that idea
which determines the specific character of a given drama.
   All these preconditions are demands on the spectator. As said
before, they are made by every drama but only by the drama. A

particular theme *(sujet)* can be seized upon and treated by the
most different art forms; it can serve as theme *(Vorwurf)* not only
for the verbal but all other art forms. Almost every myth has been
object not only for epic, lyric, and dramatic literature; it has
found its concretization also in painting and sculpture and sometimes even in music. However, what difference does exist between
the statue of Laocoon and the account Virgil[3] wrote of his destruc-
tion? Lessing[4] used this example in order to establish the boundaries of painting and poetry. He wished to ascribe development
to literature as adequate expressive content, and state *(Zustand)*
to sculpture. Certainly, he showed strikingly that both art forms
have to emphasize and transform other aspects of their theme as
essential for themselves, lest they will contradict the form which
alone is adequate to them. We do not learn from a concrete work
of art what the proper mode of an art form is; we learn this only
through reflections about the meaning of that which can be presented in the given art form itself.

These general considerations about the actual meaning of an
art form allow us to proceed to the problem of our interest, that
of the opera. At the outset, it must be stated that, in our investigations, we aim at that form of the opera which had been developed
since the middle of the eighteenth century, most of all in Germany.
No attempt will be made to write the history of opera. However,
one has to point shortly to the historical tendencies which con-
verged in order to bring about what we call opera today.

p.4

The place of birth of the opera was Florence, Italy. About
1600, it was created suddenly by a circle of well-known humanists
who, at first for the sake of the social life of nobility, wanted to
revive the antique tragedy. Thanks to the tremendous influence
of Monteverdi,[5] the first opera house was dedicated in Venice.
Soon, the opera became general property; it lost its original
function as performance at festivities of the nobility. It became
cruder and fell under the influence of a peculiar kind of virtuosi;
eventually, it became nothing for them but an occasion to display
their virtuosity. The original intention of reviving the antique
tragedy was more and more forgotten. Even the chorus, at the
beginning the most important exponent of operatic action, disappeared gradually in order to make more and more room for the
artful soloists.

This fate of the serious opera *(opera seria)* was not shared by
the comic opera *(opera buffo)*. The latter was not rooted in the
artistic speculations of the circles of nobility but in the comedy
of the common people, the *commedia dell'arte*. Like all popular
art forms, in contrast to the serious opera, it always managed to
preserve a refreshing diversity: in the libretto through the
continuation of the typifications which were popular in Italian
comedies; and in the musical score through the inclusion of dance
forms and folksongs. Thus, in comparison with the serious opera,
it gained more and more importance. Not only did the comic opera
absorb the specific characters of the comedy; from the outset, it
provided a home for the lyrical pair of lovers. The latter was given

more and more room; eventually, it became necessary to accept into the comic opera all those aspects of the serious opera which had maintained their value.

The relationship between these two kinds of opera may be compared to the attempt at continuing the tragedy according to the antique three laws of unity *(Einheitsgesetze)*. The heroic character of the serious opera, soon, yielded to boring and empty schema-   p.5 tization; the products of this art form became more and more identical and typical; the situations resembled each other as much as the plots (almost every composer of serious operas composed an Orpheus and an Alceste). Finally, the whole art form was frozen into a barren formula. One may contrast this with the development of the English theater up to Shakespeare's time: a development from the original folk comedy *(Ruepelspiel)*[6] to 'Hamlet' or   p.6 'King Lear'. Here, any schematization had already been prevented by the inclusion of ever new popular aspects. It can be clearly seen how the living popular play gradually pulled the art drama with its best elements into its sphere. Thus, contrary to the so-to-speak retrogressive development of the art drama, it brought about that tragedy which, possibly, the initiators of the art drama had in mind.

But the serious opera did not perish without having found successors outside of Italy. According to the different social and spiritual cultures into which the serious opera had been transplanted, these successors developed their own characteristics. Most of all, France has to be named here, where the serious opera was converted into the lyrical tragedy through Lully,[7] Rameau,[8] and eventually Jean-Jacques Rousseau.[9] It found its revivor in Gluck.[10] Meanwhile, the more popular successor of the comic opera accepted the nationally formed stamp of the French comedy merely by replacing the figures of the Italian comedy by the types of the French comedy. Only the great reform work of Gluck, whose significance is fully recognized today, created the musical drama out of the lyrical tragedy. The struggle between the so-called Piccinists and Gluckists is music-historically known and has often been described.[11] In it occurs the actual birth of the modern opera, the development from the lyrical but contentless stories of Metastasio[12] to the real tragedies of Gluck's librettists. Mozart came to Paris[13] during the time of the first struggle between the two camps; it was eventually lost by the Piccinists. He knew how to combine these forms with the musical play *(Singspiel)*, which had followed the short spring time of the opera after Heinrich Schütz.[14] Mozart now created that kind of opera whose interpretation shall be subsequently attempted. [First, we shall try to understand the opera as means of expression. Secondly, with Mozart's and Wagner's operas, we shall show the possibilities which this (operatic, HRW) form can do justice to and what changes it undergoes due to most different meaning contents.]

THE DRAMA

Possibly, it will be useful preliminarily to subject the drama alone
to a minimum of consideration, thus following the procedure which
Richard Wagner adopted in his main theoretical work on 'Oper und
Drama'.[15]
What means of expression are at the disposal of the drama? Most
of all, the word. The word, however, not as the expression of a
single person, of an I who objectivizes his experiences in the
symbol series of language; rather, the word spoken to someone
and understood by him. Language itself presupposes the Thou;
[concepts cannot be formed without the Thou relationship]. If
one ignores this and accepts the word simply as given material,
one could rightfully consider the word of the poet as pure expression: it is meaningful in itself without having to be heard or
understood by somebody else. Poetry is an art form which satisfies
itself. Maybe, aside of absolute music, it is the loneliest of all art
forms. The word of the dramatist is of a completely different
character. It is not the statement of an experiencing I who arti-
p.7   culates his experiences to himself. Rather and always, it is communication, word spoken to someone else, word destined to be
heard, understood, and interpreted: to be interpreted not only
by the audience but also by the co-actor, the consociate
(*Nebenmensch*) or better the actor as symbol of the consociate who
finds himself simultaneously on the stage. (Here, the monologue
is ignored. We refrain from inquiring whether this factor actually
belongs to the art form of the poet. In any case, the positing of
the Thou has been nowhere better achieved than in the dramatic
monologue. In the monologue, too, speaks one human to another
for whose understanding he hopes. But he speaks in order to
gain clarity about himself, he reflects on actions done or actions
planned and, thus, fills his loneliness with his own past or
future.)
    An essential, nay, the most important precondition of the drama
is the Thou-relationship. Certainly, it is the Thou-relationship
merely made concrete or, if you wish, symbolized in the social
acting first of the heroes and then in the roles (*Masken*) of the
actors. This, too, is an essential difference from poetry and epos.
The ideal listener of a poem or a tale must needs depend on the
word material offered. He has to limit himself to perceiving the
idea of the work of art, to interpreting immediately the subjective
meaning of the author. If it is permissible to say so, he has to
deal with a linguistic reality. The spectator of a drama sees before
him two actors who speak with one another, although not as actor
A and actor B, but as Hamlet and Horatio. The scene of the actors
is merely a symbol for the scene which occurred between Hamlet
and Horatio; it is the symbol of the scene which occurred or,
better, could have occurred somewhere sometime between someone
called Hamlet and someone called Horatio.
p.8   In other words: the Thou problem as such is presented by two
humans speaking with one another, but not as their real psycho-

physical egos would speak with one another, but as symbolization of any kind of Thou relationship at any time. The existence of such a Thou relationship, which can be clearly understood, is an essential precondition of the drama. If, in an epos, a novel, or a poem a Thou relationship is described, it of course presupposes the objective chance of the understandability of such a relationship. But these presentations are basically solitary; the relationship does not become clearly visible. Description merely offers mediate knowledge. In the drama, nobody speaks actually about the Thou relationship. It is neither described nor told - which already would be an appeal to interpret it subjectively. Rather, it is placed before the spectator without any further hint for its interpretation. The precondition for this is immediate evidence: both figures on the stage understand each other reciprocally in a similar fashion in which the spectator understands them. The partner of the actor cannot perceive the player in a fashion different from that in which we, the onlookers, could understand him. Both are humans and consociates, intelligent beings who resemble us, who use the same symbol series we use. While the writers of an epos and even the poets supply us with part of the interpretation, the dramatist leaves the interpretation completely to us. This is the more so as we not only hear the two actors speak, we also see them acting. It is not that two heroes act in their bodily existence; but two temporal-spatial physical persons act as we would act ourselves with the same understandable gestures and bodily expressions. Actually, the drama is made   p.9
possible by the silent conclusion that actor A and actor B act and move before our eyes as Hamlet and Horatio acted and moved. In the novel, Hamlet and Horatio would be integrated into the meaning relationship of the writer. He would *tell* about their gestures and movements, their appearances and their expressions. The dramatist *presents* them through the medium of the actors, who themselves are only symbols of the heroes. He leaves to us the task of grasping the symbols of the acting heroes in the symbols of the acting players. Since gesture and word, in the drama, belong originally and in a basic sense together, we have already established two essential means of expression in this art form. Both are based on the Thou-relationship and serve one and the same task.

The art form of the drama is a sole unity in duality *(en dia dyoin)*. It takes place in the space-time world in which we live and places acting persons before our eyes. They breathe the same air as we: living persons who speak the same language and understand each other as we understand one another. It is our life which is lived and presented to us on the stage; it is the same Thou relation in which we live which is used, by the drama, as means of expression. The basic precondition of the drama is that this life, this time, this space, the Thou, the gesture, the word are generally authentic because generally understandable. The drama *symbolizes* living persons, presents them to us through other psycho-physical unities, and takes place not in a one-

dimensional but the spatial-temporal sphere. Nevertheless, it is
the ultimate and most artistic illustration of inner duration which
we can achieve: In every one of its elements, its form contains in
itself pure duration as an understandable precondition of every
interpretation. To clarify this idea completely is of greatest
importance for the considerations which follow.

p.10   The symbolization of inner duration is made solely possible by
this transplantation into the world of space and time. No other
art form can bring it so vividly before our consciousness as the
drama - even though its means are apparently the extreme
opposite of pure duration; they are of purely spatial-temporal
and conceptual nature. Reasons for this phenomenon are: the
living movements and actions of the actor, which we understand;
the inclusion of the spectator into the Thou relationship with the
hero; and the ability to understand action and life in sympathetic
introspection.

What constitutes the meaning of an actual drama depends on
the external *(fremde)* material which enters into or, better, is
seized by this art form.[16] This material itself is already endowed
with meaning. The same plot could also be the material for a novel
or a poem. But only the drama can present it in *this* fashion: in
the particular duality of the relationship between heroes, actors,
and audience on the one hand, and the meaningful pre-artistic
material, the author, and the stage-setting on the other.

However, one could object that the drama does not represent
our reality; it merely shows slices of time, space, and Thou
relationship: slices which can serve as symbols in the sense of
the action (outlined in the dramatic plot, HRW). In the world of
our real life, no curtain falls over a scene in order to be lifted
for a new one. In our world (usually, HRW) the arena of our life
does not change suddenly. Our experience of space is continuous.
When we leave our room and enter the street, it occurs in a continuous transition not, as in the theater, in a (sudden complete,
p.11   HRW) change of scenery. In our world unexplainable events do
not occur, events not subordinated to the law of causality, as
they may occur on the stage, for instance, in a magical or a
mystery play. Even our affects, our passions, our feelings occur
differently, develop differently, display transitions, and do not
have the characteristic high points which the drama exclusively
presents. We live continuously; we live in our duration. Even
though we are placed into time and space, we are conscious of the
identity of our experiencing I in every Now and Thus.

Certainly, the dramatic happenings which we witness as spec-
tators are different from all other happenings. They are devoid
of that duration which would be ours. The time and space world
of the theater may be very similar to our temporal-spatial world.
Yet, the event of the stage, in all efforts to be a true symbol of
our experience, remains a symbol. In every history of literature
occur periods in which, characteristically, these connections have
been forgotten: periods of naturalism or of an artificial classicism
which attempts to make the difference between our life and the life

on the stage disappear by either offering a truthful picture of reality or else by certain theatrical tricks. The well-known three laws of Aristotle[17] or those of Boileau,[18] concerning the unity of space and action in the tragedy, find their explanation here. The law of the unity of space is supposed to help us – deceptively – to overcome the misgivings which occur with the realization that our duration, when placed into space, cannot change the place of action without transition while, by contrast, this is possible in the world of the stage. In a compromise, the law of the unity of time demands that the stage action occur without interruption, at least, within the course of one day. The time spent on the stage should be close to the time of our duration, otherwise the listener would conclude that our life and our duration flow more slowly than that of the acting hero. Finally, the law of the unity of action p.12 aims at the consistency of affects and demands, at their presentation in gradual separation and integration *(auseinander und ineinander)*, thereby postulating the identity between our own actual experiencing and that on the stage.

The three laws (were and, HRW) remained a genial error; more than anything else they contributed to making the form of the classical tragedy superficial. Necessarily, the drama moves toward selected high points. It establishes an ideal continuity, which is not our own. It jumps, so to speak, from positing meaning to positing meaning without showing all the intermediate stages. But the latter are the essentials of our life, of our ego. Certainly, we would all be capable of the same affects, the same feelings, the same actions and words, as those presented on the stage. However, one affect would relieve the other, one action would emerge from the other, and one word would gain its meaning only from that word which was spoken before. The time in which the drama takes place is not our time; it is not duration. It is an imaginary time, as Bergson called the time which can be experienced neither by me, nor by you, nor by anybody else. The persons on the stage live in duration, but it is not our duration but an imaginary one: a duration in which, we assume, the other lives. But nobody lives through it, not even the actor who seems to live in it. For him, the drama no more signifies a continuity than it does for us. These statements about time and drama are of extraordinary importance for our theme; it is just this aspect which, through the introduction of music, makes the opera possible. We will speak about this later.

The manifoldness of the criteria of the dramatic form is almost p.13 inexhaustible. To add something characteristic to it, one has to keep in mind that not only man and consociate but also their spatial-temporal surroundings are theatrically symbolized. The stage may be as simple as in Greece or in Shakespeare's England. The palace, in which the action takes place, is not at all a palace, does not even try to be one. Never could a castle look like this; it is *a place beyond all reality which can symbolize reality only because the actor, that is the hero, pretends to experience it as real.* This curious relativity shows that, what the hero *assumes*

as real, impresses and surrounds us in the same manner as our
own surroundings. We accept the latter as real; maybe, a spectator of the play whose actors we are, could doubt it as much as
we doubt the reality of the stage. In so far as spatial surroundings
influence our life and our actions, they do so to no greater degree
than the stage scenery influences the actor. Essential for both
is not being-real but being-taken-for-real. This alone creates the
possibilities for all action and sensory impression. Whether the
room exists, or whether the acting person assumes it to exist,
makes no difference: the room becomes surrounding, place of
action, object of my acting, cause of my sensory impressions.

But this typification is not exhausted by time, space, and
causality. The Thou-relation itself and the individual oriented toward it are typified; thereby, they become more general yet more
individual. In his conclusion to 'Miss Julie,' Strindberg[19] ingeniously
contrasted his own manner of bringing individuals on the stage
with that of Molière[20] and other writers of older comedies. Harpagon
is presented to us as a miser, and displays no other traits. Aside
from his avarice, he might have been a good merchant, a tender
father, a caring son. All this is irrelevant for the character
comedy. The personification of one trait demands a one-sided
illumination out of the perspective of this single trait. Strindberg,
by contrast, insists that the dramatic author make an effort to
present the variability of every single possibility (of character,
HRW). With this rule, Strindberg believes he has become a natural-
ist in a true and higher sense. Is this correct? I believe that every
hero of the drama necessarily becomes a type; essentially, it
makes no difference at which point one ceases the approach to real
life and turns away from the acting, speaking, and thinking human
being who simultaneously abandons himself to his sensory impressions. This is particularly well demonstrated in those manifestations of life which issue exclusively from Thou: the life of
emotions, the affections, the passions and, therefore, the word.
Up to now, we have not sufficiently stressed that this word is not
written; it is heard and spoken. It is the word in which the tone
of voice reveals more about the inner state of the speaker than
the underlying term. Or the affectual word immediately emerges
from the Thou relationship, whose conceptual content and signification comes much later to our attention than its effects upon
the consociate and ourselves. This characteristic of the word
makes it possible to use rhymes and verses in dramas without
making them appear unnatural [provided one wants to discover a
contradiction in the experience of the existence of heroes and
villains with exaggerated one-sided characteristics, which we do
not encounter in life even though we never doubt the possibility
of seeing them, in the next moment, before us as living realities].

p.15   But the drama brings not merely persons on the stage; it also
shows the collective, the masses, the people and - most of all in
the antique drama - the chorus. The role of the chorus in Greek
tragedy has been subject of many investigations and has caused
the greatest differences of opinion. Well-known is Schlegel's[21] idea

p.14

of the chorus as the ideal spectator. Nietzsche[22] objected correctly
that a spectator never conducted himself as the chorus does. He
leaned toward the view of Schiller[23] that the chorus, so to speak,
forms a wall which separates the spectator from the stage. Thereby, it erects a barrier between the apparent reality of stage
action and the reality of the spectator. There seems to be no
basic contradiction between these two opinions. The chorus is
spectator in so far as it accompanies the actions on the stage with
reflections; for itself, it clearly speaks about the inclusion of the
Thou into the events on the stage. Thus, it urges the actual
spectator affectually to follow the stage action in the same manner.
And it thereby separates the stage events from real life.

If, in order to use Nietzsche's expression, the actor alone is the
true Dionysian man, the chorus alone makes possible the Apollinian
stance. It presents to us a mass which is one with us, the audience, yet belongs to the sphere of the stage; it illustratively
presents to us that effect which the actual action of the tragedy
is supposed to evoke in us. A new interpretation of meaning
results from our seeing in the chorus our own reflection and a
model for ourselves; through it, we are forced to interpret the
stage events in a new manner which, however, is related to us.
We welcome this the more because, in addition, the chorus indicates to us one single motivation for otherwise disjointed events.
Frequently, it becomes active just when the supernatural and the
miracle call for translation into human terms *(Vermenschlichung)*.
Every miracle creates such realities and strongly demands motivation. The 'realistic' drama, too, no longer manages without   p.16
miracle. According to Goethe,[24] the actual dramatic conflict may
be rooted in the struggle of man against fate, as in the Greek
tragedy; or it may issue in the entanglement with one's own
guilt brought about by one's own will, as in Shakespeare. The
actually mythical, all guilt and atonement, the conflict with
heavenly or mundane law, the struggle against fate, destiny, and
doom - all are in need of motivation. Therefore, French tragedy
sought a way out by replacing the chorus with a series of characters: servants, friends, or persons trusted by the hero; their
sole task is to be witness of his life and, thus, to explain to us
the stages of his life, to show where the tragic conflict started
and over which stages it led to the final catastrophe.

In these few points we have tried to develop some of the essential characteristics of the drama, upon which the actual possibility
of the opera depends. It is solely the integration of drama and
music, being based on completely different preconditions, which
yields the meaning of that art form which we call opera.

MUSIC, LYRICS, DIALOGUE

This self-determined world of the stage and the dramatic event
enters into a relationship with a world which, likewise, is self-
determined and stands in sharpest contradiction to our life in space

and time: the world of music, bringing about the art form of the opera. Music is linked to the two main characteristics of the drama: the word and the gesture. Each of these categories can enter individually into a relationship with music. Song and dance are the two poles of this unification. [Since its earliest beginnings, the operatic action proper - as operatic drama - was tied to both; and it will remain tied to them. Most important (of the two, HRW), it seems to us, is the possibility of setting words to music. Yet, in recent times, in the works of Schoenberg, Stravinsky, and Alban Berg,[25] the opera has moved in the direction of a predominance of the gesture,] be it in the form of ballet or the mimical drama.

p.17   Before dealing with the possibility of setting to music first the word and then the action, it must be established which place music occupies in the layers of our experiences. All philosophers who occupied themselves with this problem agree that music is an event in our inner world which takes its course independent of the events of our life. According to Schopenhauer,[26] music is will, not idea. But, added Nietzsche, will is object of music but not its origin; what we call feeling and what is brought to us, beyond all ideas, is only object of music in so far as it is not permeated with, and saturated by, conscious or unconscious ideas. According to him, music originated not at all in the will; it is beyond all individuation. All affects yield only ideas of manifestations of the will. Affects are schemes of interpretation which we impose upon music. [These schemes represent the symbolized world of affects;] through them, the listener interprets the music which deals with affects. (He does this, HRW) in the calmness of Apollinian reflection and bare of all affects.[27]

Richard Wagner occupied himself repeatedly with this problem, most impressively in his essay about Beethoven, written in 1870. He stands completely on the ground of Schopenhauer's philosophy. For him, too, music was universal will. It is melodious world-idea in Schopenhauer's sense, and it seizes that side of consciousness which is not directed upon the perception of other things but upon the own self. This consciousness alone has the ability to see as clearly on the inside as perceptual cognition will manage when seizing ideas directed toward the outside. One is curiously touched by Wagner's likening of the effects of music to those of the world of dreams. He justifies this by saying that our relations with the forms of outside cognition, of space and time, do not apply to

p.18   either music or dream. Music is the highest excitement of the will, while all spatial arts are the deepest calming of it. Only the state of working is able to surpass the wide-awakeness (*Hellsichtigkeit*) of the musician in an ever-returning state of individual awareness. Only religion and church lift the individual above the whole state of individuality; this is the reason for the fact that music has always been granted churchly functions. It is the task of the musician to grasp the innermost dream image. His attempt to communicate it forces upon him the notion of time. He keeps the notion of space under an opaque veil; its removal would immediately make unrecognizable the dream image which he has envisioned. Wagner says literally:

The harmony of sounds, which belongs neither to space nor time, remains the most essential aspect of music. But the creative musician, so to speak, offers his hand to the changing world of phenomena through the rhythmic time sequence of his manifestations. He does this in the same fashion in which the allegoric dream fastens on the habitual ideas of the individual: the wide-awake awareness, turned toward the outer world, can hold on to the dream image even though it immediately recognizes the great difference of this image from the event in daily life. The musician, through the rhythmic order of his sounds, makes contact with the clearly articulated world - and this by virtue of a similar kind of law as that according to which the movement of visible bodies manifests itself understandably to our perception.

In the dance,[28] the human gesture tries to make itself understandable through impressive *(anschauungsvolle)* regular movements. It seems to be for music what bodies are for light; the latter too would not shine were it not broken by objects. We can say *that, without rhythm, music would not be perceivable by us.*

This conception of music also explains Wagner's conception of melody. In his book 'Opera and Drama' he says that harmony and rhythm are organs of forming music, but melody truly forms music itself. Harmony and rhythm are like blood, nerves, and bones with all inner organs, which remain hidden to the onlooker when he sees the finished living human being. By contrast, melody is like this full human being as he presents himself to our eyes. p.19 Melody is the most definite, most convincing, manifestation of the life of the real, living, inner organism of music. In every music is inherent the will to ever greater clarity, to ever greater manifestation of the actual ideal intention. In its need for greater clarity, music reaches for language, the medium which is higher and clearer because it is more closely related to our world of perception and ideas. For this reason, in his Ninth Symphony, Beethoven inserted the word after the stirring recitative. The whole meaning and content of the work can be summed up, through Beethoven's genius, in the words of Schiller's poem.[29] The ideal creator of operas simultaneously has to be poet and musician; he has the task of putting the unity of word and melody into the place of the infinite melody, as found in pure (absolute) music. This unity is rooted both in meaning and content of the word and in its sound, in the combination of consonants and vowels. The origin of language itself is to be explained in terms of assonances and acoustic reproductions. The other dramatic element, expressive movement and gesture, is acquired from music itself. The actual dramatic design *(Vorwurf)* has to manifest itself in the element of the word: over and over again and in ultimate intention, it has to accomplish anew the forming of the myth. This is the highest achievable idea of poetry as such.

Long before Nietzsche turned against Wagner . . . he raised important objections against this conception of Wagner. However,

in order not to insult his friend, he did not include them in his first publication, 'The Birth of Tragedy'. Nietzsche contests the primacy of the word. He wants to see the origin of all lyrics in a basic musical feeling; and he points to Schiller who insisted that he had observed this in his own processes of lyrical creation. When we listen to the last movement of Beethoven's (Ninth, HRW) Symphony, we in no way hear Schiller's poem. Nietzsche says: only for him who sings along there is a text, there exist word and verse. For the listener, only the music exists; it is the creator, the mother of all lyrics. Music can never become a means; even the worst forces the best text under its spell. Therefore, for the *listener*, a '*drama*' within the opera is impossible. The listener forgets it. He awakens to it only after the Dionysian magic leaves him. Dramatic music is thinkable only as music of excitement in the guise of a symbolics which is purely conventional. For music, drama exists only in so far as it is action but not as literary work *(Dichtung)*. In this case, a kind of pre-established harmony rules between true tragedy and true music. The tragedy absorbs music into itself. Thereby, it brings music to perfection; it places a sublime allegory, the mythos, between the universal validity of its music and the Dionysian receptive listener. It awakens the illusion in the latter, that music is merely the highest means of the presentation of the animated, articulated world of the mythos. Music, in appreciation, offers a reciprocal present to the mythos of the tragedy: a metaphysical significance, as impressive and convincing as that which word and picture may achieve without

any help. Nietzsche's notions of the unconditional primacy of music and of the dissolving of the contrast between word, action, meaning, and mythos is supported by a well-known statement by Mozart. In a letter to his father, he wrote: The word, at all times, has to be the obedient servant of music. [A whole world separates this conception of Nietzsche and Mozart from the notion of Wagner.]

Now, we will try to delineate, in a few words, the true place of music *as experience*. The viewpoint found thereby shall give us the occasion to demonstrate the most different attempts at a solution of this problem on hand of the operas of Mozart and Wagner.

Thanks to its spacelessness and its continuity, the melody is more closely related to our duration than any other phenomenon of our inner and outer experiences. Whenever Bergson tries to present the nature of inner duration as an allegory, he by necessity falls back upon the example of the melody. It is continuous and manifold, even if its manifoldness is limited. It does not know of things appearing side-by-side and in succession; it becomes and passes away like something genuinely alive without being forced to objectify itself in space and time. Harmony and polyphony, too, do not break through the limitations of our inner duration. As said before, music is the most lonely art. It does not call for a Thou because it does not call for interpretation. But inner duration is the most primitive and original experience of man; he can go beyond it only because, by being aware of his body as something extended, he arrives at the establishment of space and time. The latter, again, are necessary preconditions for Thou, language, and concept. Therefore, every higher stratum of consciousness which is built upon inner duration[30] can come in contact with melody which lives solely in inner duration: the acting I in dance, expressive movement, and gesture; the speaking I in song, the   p.22 conceptually-thinking I in those great symbolizations which are musically known to us as incidental music *(Programmusik)*. However, the truly original experience remains rooted in inner duration: the word can be set to music only in so far as its elements, in their deepest meaning relation, reach into inner duration.

Nevertheless, music is vividly evident *(anschaulich)*; it necessarily leaves the realm of inner duration. It possesses rhythm; it knows repetitions and even specific repetitions which become forming elements. Thus, so to speak, it knows things side-by-side and things being simultaneous. It is completely clear that the phenomena of inner duration are intuitively recognizable by us only in an act of self-reflection but have to be abandoned in every objectification. Our own self steps out of the realm of inner duration by acting, by moving, by the extensity of its body. Thereby, it also creates space and time for itself; time being nothing but duration projected into space. Movement, through continuity and manifoldness, belongs to inner duration but the path travelled belongs to space and time. Music belongs to inner duration through melody, harmony, and harmonizing, interweaving voices *(Stimmführung)*. But it belongs to outer time through rhythm.

However, how does rhythm come about? Obviously, it is nothing but the distribution of a melody over space-time. The precondition of rhythm is a melody which became and passes away. Something melodic becomes so only in comparison to something melodic which already passed away. The earlier cited sentence of Wagner hits the essential point: without rhythm, music could not be recognized by us. One should not forget that, when hearing a musical work which we already know, we assume an entirely different stance than when we hear everything, for the first time, as something becoming.

We may, so to speak, move within a piece of music from the first p.23 to the last tone without burdening ourselves with extra-musical processes of consciousness, memory, and associatively grasped ideas and concepts; we may simply enter the musical stream and thus . . . experience music as something becoming. If the piece is purely musical – not dramatically accompanied by gestures, bodily movements – there does not occur the idea of rhythm. The power of music to immediately excite feelings, to agitate the will, stems predominantly from the possibility of apperceiving any melody, like our duration, as something continuously growing and becoming. Music is not forced to abandon the direction in which our duration leads. We can speak of rhythm only when we, amidst this onrushing stream, stand still and stop, and direct our atten-

tion no longer upon the streaming music but upon that which has
elapsed, upon the music passed away. It is rhythmical in so far
as it has passed away, like movement becomes space only after it
has ceased. Thus, we see that, for us Apollinic listeners, the
rhythmical element comes only into view when the melody has
faded away. For Apollinic man, remembered music is rhythmical.
For Dionysian man - for the acting, dancing person who moves to
music, who experiences the rhythm also in his body - this difference becomes blurred. The temporal-spatial element, alien and
hostile to true duration, actually does not enter his consciousness
by way of the music but most of all through his body. The latter
is extended; its position in space and its movement remain in consciousness, it is manifest any time, and creates space only through
its finished movement.

p.24   It cannot be the purpose of these investigations to pursue this
difficult question to its final points. We have to be satisfied to
state that no revelation of our being is so closely related to our
true inner duration as music. Even rhythm, when it is felt and
becomes conscious, offers only the idea of time but not the idea
of space. However, it must be emphasized that, here, we speak
exclusively of musical rhythm and not of the rhythm of a poem or
the rhythm of the word. The word is most deeply rooted in the
spatial-temporal sphere, nay, more, in a sphere which is populated
with similar intelligent beings, with consociates, with a Thou.
Rhythmic arrangement must coincide with meaningful arrangement.
The word, rhythm, is truly corporeal. Rhythm divides space into
sequences of verse - a space which is traversed by the walking
or speaking person. Rhythm, here, is actually external; it issues
from time and enters into space. Characteristically, it is impossible
to sing a song in which this external rhythm is not destroyed
and subjugated to that true inner rhythm of music in which alone
occurs the inclusion of the outer world into the realm of our
duration.

In this sense, lyrics are always subjugation of the word to music.
This also explains the form of the verse song in which one and
the same melody does justice to the most different contents of the
words. This applies to most folk songs. Now, as mentioned before,
language is dually determined: first, through the meaning which
conceptually inheres in the word; and second through the tone
of voice of the speaker. The latter alone mediates and makes understandable the affect which is expressed in words. Generally
p.25   accepted theory states that any musical symbolic procures its
meaning content from the world of poetic moods. This cannot mean
anything else but: either music has its conceptive origin in the
meaning content of the word, in the affect which is expressed in
the context of the word; or, if one accepts Nietzsche's view of
the relationship between word and tone, the effort is made to
grasp the basic mood which preceded the creation of the lyrics
by a poet.

What actually is composed in a song? This question is one of the
most difficult ones; it is hardly answerable. Let us look at one and

the same poem, maybe Goethe's Mignon songs, in the composition
of different masters like Schubert,[31] Beethoven, Hugo Wolf.[32] In
itself, each composition would be perfect. But each illuminates
only certain aspects of Goethe's poem. One understands the com-
plaint of Hugo Wolf that really good and perfect poetry simply cannot be set to music. The particularity of the process of musical
creation shows itself (in a dual manner, HRW): the sound accen-
tuations of speech, of recitation, enter into the music; simultaneously, this music itself is occasioned or improvised by the meaning
content of the word or of a line of poetry. This can be especially
observed in the early period of musical lyrics, so by Bach.[33]
Albert Schweitzer undertook highly pertinent investigations of
this.[34] He shows, with Bach's cantatas,[35] that a composer often
receives a rhythmic or melodic inspiration from a single word.
For the earlier times of the opera and even for Mozart, we can
establish that the basic musical form had been derived not only
from the spiritual meaning content and not merely from the outer
and inner rhythms of the word sequence, but often simply from
a specific metaphor. This type of allegoric aria, as it is called,   p.26
can be demonstrated on many examples. In part, this phenomenon
may be explained in terms of the fact that nature itself produces
acoustic phenomena; maybe, in her rhythms, one can find melody.
Therefore, spatial-temporal appearances can be integrated into
the musical realm [which belongs to inner duration but can never
be completely divested of its spatial-temporal character]. This
problem has occupied theorists for a long time; it is generally
known in the form of a question about the acceptability of musical
accompaniment.
   From earliest times, the attempt has been made to describe individual events musically. One tries musically to imitate actions,
movements, events of acoustic or visual nature. A continuous line
leads from there to Bach's capriccio about the departure of his
brother and to Beethoven's Pastoral Symphony. In modern music,
(the line reaches, HRW) from the great program-musical tone
poems of Liszt and Richard Strauss[36] to Stravinski's 'Firebird'[37]
and so on. The essence of this music consists in the attempt to
strip music of its melodic function, of its belonging to inner duration. This unheard-of process of rationalization took place and
spread; in it, associative events of the outer world were imputed
to the phenomenon of music. Elements which belong to the outer
world are treated as if they would belong to inner duration and
the lines of melody. For the old masters, this was 'still more feeling than painting,' as Beethoven said about his Pastoral Symphony.
In the new tendency, it has already become total illustration and
something actually alien to music. This is especially so because
everything programmatic takes place in the realm of absolute music;
it finds its solution neither in word nor gesture. Yet, here also lies   p.27
the origin of the great innovation of (the form of, HRW) the opera,
which Richard Wagner initiated: the Leitmotiv.[38] To be sure, this is
connected with the whole transformation of the meaning of the art
form of the opera, which Richard Wagner intended and carried out.

However, before we discuss this in detail, we have to try to
inspect the individual categories of the drama, which we enumer-
ated earlier, with regard to their relationship to the true essence
of music so as to establish the possibilities which offer themselves
for the art form of the opera pure and simple.

OPERA AS DRAMA AND MUSIC

Our basic presupposition of the drama was that it symbolizes the
Thou problem and presents it. In the spatial-temporal world of
the stage, the illusion of true duration is achieved because our
life in duration - even though interpretatively transferred into
the spatial-temporal sphere - precisely assumes the character of
continuity which it already seemed to have surrendered to objectification. If music is added to the played, spoken, and acted
stage dialogue, two functions may be served. First, music could
assume the function which corresponds to the composition of the
song. In the spoken drama, verse occurs not as unnatural and
contrary to the meaning of this art form; on the contrary, it most
clearly fathoms the spatial-temporal world in contrast to inner
duration, which is more understandable for us. Similarly, rhythmic
speech *(gebundene Rede)* could be expanded into the song which
is sung. It would be possible to interweave songs as high points
of lyrical nature, supported by gestures, enlivened by actions.
The actually spatial-temporal moment would emerge from rhythm
and expressive movement, while inner duration is preserved in
melody. Or, the opera could find the fulfilment of its meaning in
the emphasis on those elements of spoken words in ordinary speech
which are brought close to us in affects, in the tone of voice,
and the context of words and sentences. They all remain closely
related to musical experience.

p. 28   related to musical experience.
    The first form makes understandable the origin of the aria; the
second explains the so-called recitative. The main achievement of
the old opera, most of all of the comic opera, was the transition
of the spoken word into the - at first unaccompanied - secco
recitative,[39] the elevation of the secco recitative into the recitative
accompanied by instruments, the development of the latter into
the arioso,[40] and in conclusion the aria proper. This articulation
can be of great help for a clever stage director.
    The development (from recitative to aria, HRW) becomes still
more visible if we choose the structure of, say, a Passion by
Bach.[41]
    Up to Mozart, the actual dramatic part occurred mainly in
recitatives. Arias were monologues or addresses of a more lyrical
nature. Through them, the hero expressed his real affects. The
music had a relationship to action only in so far as it was mundane
only in so far as soldiers marched or peasant girls danced to it.
Here, significant stylistic elements for the whole development of
the opera reveal themselves. Various kinds of operas differ from
another not so much in the treatment of the word; they are dis-

tinguished by the elements of dramatic action which are mobilized in their compositions.

Beyond this, the opera is not solely borne by singing voices; the continuity of the music is secured by the accompaniment of instruments - even if the latter, as in the secco recitative, is reduced to a most modest form. In one important respect, the role of the orchestra makes the opera really into a successor of the Greek tragedy. As pointed out earlier, the role of the ancient Greek chorus consists in separating our world from the world on the stage and making the events of the actual tragedy more understandable for us. If the chorus is not the ideal spectator it is the   p.29 ideal interpreter of the stage events. Thereby, it both separates us from the stage and links us with it. The orchestra is the actual expressive means of pure absolute music, and the latter belongs completely to our duration. The orchestra accompanies the events on the stage in a dual sense. It interprets the gesture of the actor and it links the song to that element of inner duration access to which is denied to the spoken word. [From this angle, we gain a perspective on the possibility of composing the song. The unaccompanied song, even the recitative, remains still captured by, and limited to, space-time.]

Pure duration is introduced into the stage events exclusively by the orchestra. A triple complex of symbol and interpretation is offered to the opera audience: the visible actor, whose gesture can be understood; the words of the actors which we have to interpret linguistically and conceptually; their speech and inflexion which allows us to understand their affects and motives. The orchestra, however, seizes all three complexes of interpretation. It preforms the gesture and alludes to its origin in events within the stream of our duration. It strips the word of its conceptual character and reduces it to an expression of the will to a Thou, which is rooted in inner duration. It relates all events of feeling, life, tone modulation and tone intensity to the unitary interpretative scheme of the melody.

Here, also, the necessity of an overture which intends to be more than a preparation for the events on the stage reveals itself: musical sounds before the first gesture is made and before the first word enters into our consciousness. Through it, we are urged into a state of submersion into our inner life; it enables us to sympathetically experience (*nacherleben*) in our duration all other events in the spatial-temporal world (placed before us on the stage, HRW). Where the orchestra transcends this task, where it programmatically imitates the actual musical-dramatic   p.30 happenings, the word of Nietzsche applies: in the real drama, music actually seizes only the acting but not the lyrical work. Here, music functions secondarily and solely as music of excitement. Essentially, music does no lyrical work. It sorts out those elements which belong to the space-time world; it allows them to disappear and limits itself to the pursuit of the true inner meaning in the continuity of pure duration for which all poetry is only a superstructure.

During our analysis of the drama, we established that meaning
is conveyed to it only by the Thou relation: the monologue is an
exception since it presupposes the doubling of the I, representing
a special case of the Thou problem.[42] The Thou problem, too, is
contained in pure duration. It is, so to speak, a symbolization of
affectual experiences and of actions which are oriented upon consociates. Consequently, it should be possible to grasp it in the
melody, which is related to inner duration. More: music offers,
beyond the word of Shakespeare, a simultaneity, a side-by-side,
and a together which the word could never reach. This makes for
the creation of the ensemble which, it seems to me, owes its existence not to musical reasons but exclusively to the compulsion
issuing from the meaning of the opera (as art form, HRW). Thus,
we have established, even though only sketchily, what the inclusion of music into basically dramatic phenomena may offer to (the
art form of, HRW) the opera.

These theoretical assertions will become clearer when we [now
try to explain the meaning of two styles, namely, the styles of
Mozart's and Wagner's operas, on hand of the tenet we have
postulated. First, however, we shall] say a few words about the
oratorium: that art form in which seem to be unified almost all of
the elements which we before called characteristics of the opera.
Thereby, we will make clear the differences between the essence
of dramatic and of epic music. So far, music history has not been
successful in establishing a tenable criterion for differentiating
between opera and oratorio. The last attempt was made by the
Viennese music historian Adler[43]; it does not penetrate below the
surface. Adler sees the main difference in the place of the chorus,
which is dominant in the oratorio. In fact, an opera by Handel[44]
is hardly distinguishable from an oratorio by Handel. For a modern
audience, the difference rests solely in the recognition that his
operas found a scenic structure under all circumstances, his
oratorio only occasionally. It appears to me that the place of the
chorus is completely irrelevant for the epic character of both.
Essential is the deep difference in the stance of the audience.
The oratorio is without gesture and representation of action. It
tells about actions, but nobody acts in it. Usually, it entrusts the
narrating part to a specific person in the testa.[45] It compels the
listener to follow the narration by the insertion of lyrical and
dramatical illustrations. Each of them, however, interrupts the
continuity. The audience is not immediately included in the Thou
relation which unrolls among the persons on stage on the one
hand, and between each of them and the audience on the other.
The listeners[46] do not face the subjective but an objective meaning
content. They participate in the act of meaning interpretation
but not that of positing meaning; the latter is undertaken by the
storyteller or the stage character who anticipates it singingly.

By contrast, it is the essence of the opera to place the Thou
relation before my eyes and to interpret it before my eyes. This
occurs in an unheard-of complicated manner in which the word is
attached to meaning content, the gesture to the understandable

p.31

space-time world, the music to inner duration. Thus, as spectator, p.32
I can understand what actor A means when addressing actor B;
I can follow how actor B accepts this address; and I can observe
how a meaning content grows between A and B which can be interpreted only by me. Always, the audience must know more than the
actors: this is an old rule of French dramatic theory. That it
actually knows more, in an opera, comes to pass because the
orchestra betrays to me a specific scheme of interpretation which
must needs be hidden from (the stage figures, HRW) A and B.
The dominant role of the orchestra in opera goes back to the
implicit *(unbedingte)* inclusion of the apperceived space-time
world into my inner duration. In addition, the physical-psychic
impressions of the actors which are optically and acoustically perceived by me, are also symbols of the true meaning content. This
is of greatest importance for my attitude (toward the opera, HRW).
It is common to say: this actor is so brilliant, one almost forgets that one is in the theater. Truly understood, this means
nothing but that understandability has reached an optimum of
evidence; it has evoked an illusion of reality in which the space-
time world, in which our life occurs, and the fictive unreal
space-time world of the stage which cannot be experienced, have
come together as close as possible. However, this mediating power
is at all times inherent in music. It ties the ribbon of its melodies,
of inner duration, around actors and speakers on the one hand,
and the listeners on the other. This ribbon is common to all,   p.33
understandable by all; it is fundamentally evident.
    While the opera demands this trifold complex of symbol inter-
pretation, the oratorio stops with mere reporting. The singer in
the oratorio, even if the role of the hero has been assigned to him,
first of all remains a singer. We do not see the hero living before
us. In order to grasp the meaning (he has been assigned in the
oratorio, HRW) it suffices for us to know that he could have lived,
worked, acted, and spoken. In any case, we are satisfied with
the objective chance (of his existence, HRW). We are never urged
to develop the illusion of a real event from an unlivable fictitious
reality. This, of course, does not prevent the understanding of
the events of this irreal world; they are and remain understandable.

THE MEANING CONTENT OF THE OPERA

The character of the opera has been indicated by differentiating
it from the oratorio. Now, its meaning content can be filled with
diversified contents. Thoroughly different, also, are the elements
which are mobilized for reaching this goal. (In this respect, HRW)
some of the characteristic differences between Mozart and Wagner
(shall be discussed in order to, HRW) bring to greater clarity
what has been said before.

(1) *Subject matter*

Mozart relied on other librettists. For his operas, he pulled together the most differentiated subject matters ranging from the
lighthearted comedy action of 'Die Entführung' ('Il Seraglio': 'The
abduction from the harem') to the actually tragic 'Don Juan' ('Don
Giovanni'). Hermann Cohen devoted a nice essay to the subject
matter of Mozart's operas.[47] He said, apparently correctly, that
Mozart composed love. All his operatic subject matters deal with
it. The milieu may be oriental, as in 'Die Entführung'; Spanish, as
in 'Don Juan'; the world of contemporary nobility, as in 'Figaro';
or imaginary as in 'The Magic Flute'. But the composer, more than
the librettist, is interested in placing living, natural persons on
the stage instead of historical masks. What is of interest on the
fate and the happenings of these heroes is certainly not given in
the librettist's themes. With the exception of 'The Magic Flute'
and the ending of 'Don Juan' - actually unimportant for the meaning content (of Mozart's score, HRW) - it is the fates of the figures
of the comic operas which could occur to every one of us. [Music,
however, can occupy itself only with the extraordinary with its
in one or other respect superior climax.] However, it so happens
that Mozart, amidst the most ridiculous situations, develops the
meaning of the whole scene far beyond the milieu and the framework of the plot, aiming at the generally important. In the midst
of an act of 'Figaro', which is filled with conventional intrigue,
the chambermaid Susanna sings the well-known aria of the roses.
One forgets that it is a chambermaid who sings; one forgets the
cheerfulness and subtlety she displayed in earlier acts: one knows
only that it is an evening in spring on which a young girl waits
for her lover. Papageno, the farcical figure of 'The Magic Flute',
plays a scene with the Moor in the good old tradition of the harle-
quinade only in order to join Pamina in a duet which is the most
moving expression of erotic communion. It betrays a feeling which
is adequate [neither to his prior nor] to his [subsequent] completely comical and funny role. But precisely these moments, in
which Mozart completely reversed the lyrical action, are the truly
touching ones in his operas. Obviously, Mozart did not compose
figures or characters; no action and, therefore, no drama. He
composed situations in spite of all individualization which he granted
his figures within *one* scene, *one* situation. In his operas, these
situations are interchangeable. Arias like that of the roses could
be sung as well by Zerlina or Pamina as by Susanna.

By contrast, Wagner's ideal is the true tragedy. In his librettos
something miraculous occurs; it is just this miracle which he composes. Captivated by Schopenhauer's philosophy, he saw the
meaning of his work in the genuine salvation from the suffering
of the world, the negation of the will to live, the turning-away
from reality, and the belief in the miracle. Therefore, he started
from mythos and ever again returned to it. The unique 'Meister-
singer', who seem to assume a more earthly character, are still
placed into a mythical context through the immense human deepen-
ing of the person of Hans Sachs, through the connection between

p.34

p.35

work of art and creator amidst a protestant sanctification of work
[by the mastercraftsman who is also an artist]. Wagner's figures
are clearly delineated on the stage. Their fates are not destined
in advance; they develop before our eyes. The tragedy of man,
who is cursed in solitude, repeats itself time and again, often in
the most cruel manner. With the exception of Erda in the 'Ring of
the Nibelungs', no female figure created by Wagner leaves the
drama unbroken.
    For this reason, Wagner composes the whole tragedy. Mozart,
as stated, merely composes given dramatical situations. Wagner
is the composer of the myth; he believes only in the miracle and
drapes it in music. The miracle comes from the outside, from a
meaning content which, in itself, could be familiar to the listener
and which can be grasped solely by the listener, not by the hero.
This is the reason that Wagner could rightfully say about himself   p.36
that his works are to a high degree German and could be understood only by Germans. Mozart also knew of the miracle, but not
that which comes from the outside. The emergence of human feelings was enough for him; it was these feelings which he composes.
Everything else was accidental and secondary.

(2) *Continuity*
Mozart's attitude toward his subject matter shows itself clearly in
its musical treatment. He uses music at high points. For the
secondary work, the recitative suffices; often only the spoken
word. Wagner, not incorrectly, demanded and carried out the
completely composed opera: an opera in which, (at least in principle,) exists nothing but music. His whole conception of the
development of the tragedy is responsible for the fact that he
never omits its inclusion into the (musical, HRW) realm of duration. Mozart does not reach beyond the Now and Thus which
rings out over a given scene. He does know neither a before nor
an after because the action, for him, is only an inducement for
giving his heroes an occasion to express what just moves their
hearts.
    By Wagner, the orchestra gains a dominant position because it
brings a running commentary to the dramatic happenings. It does
not only reach beyond a given scene but spans several complete
acts, and sometimes several complete tragedies, as in the 'Ring
of the Nibelungs'. This is the meaning of Wagner's so-called technique of the Leitmotiv. With it, a completely extraordinary unity
of meaning is created. Originally it is based on extraordinary
associative and cognitive functions. Through the reduction of one
situation to another one, it gains a kind of fateful significance.
The latter provides the rigid and solid background for the actual
theme of Wagner's operatic lyrics: the miracle. It is, so to speak,
a revival of the antique idea of fate.
    A Leitmotiv belongs not only to persons or individual fates, to
props like the sword of Siegfried or the ring of the Nibelungs;
whole situations, experiences, happenings will be compressed into   p.37
a musical theme. Leitmotives replace reports about the motives and

significances which, otherwise, would have to be dramatically
presented by auxiliary characters.
   Wagner introduces individuality into the opera; Mozart knows
only characters. The typical in Wagner's figures, which bestows
general validity upon them, is their general human tie to fate.
The typical which brings Mozart's figures close to us in their
relation to their own spontaneity, the relation of their lives to
their surroundings, their knowing about their feelings, their
actions, their words. Therefore, Mozart does not know the pathos
which is typically Wagnerian: a pathos which is permanently
imputed to speakers and actors. Mostly, Mozart's pathos is limited
to instrumental interludes or else to the rare moments in which
actual, real life allows, nay, demands it. Mozart is realist to an
incomparably higher degree than Wagner, even though his technique - the number opera,[48] - seems to create the actually operatic
(components of his work, HRW), the unbelievable and incredible.
For realistic reasons, Mozart adopts the inflexion of conversation
in his recitatives. The gestures, which he demands from his
singers, are the natural movements of persons who are moved by
passion. By contrast, the main thing by Wagner is declamation,
that is, the adaptation of musical modulation to the meaning content
of the sentence. His gestures are rhythmically conditioned by
passionately exalted states of his heroes which are constantly in-
creased.

(3) *Thou problem*
The world of Mozart, which actually seems to unravel reality, is
nothing else but the elementary and innermost experience of our
surroundings. It seizes the Thou to a degree which Wagner never
strove to reach and which he never reached. Earlier, we saw the
nature of the drama in the Thou relationship, which is the most
important precondition of every dramatic event. Concerning Mozart,
we can assert that he derived his dramatic inspiration - and formed
it musically - out of the actual existence of two persons in space
and time. Thus, he reached his greatest achievements in the ensemble, in the simultaneous singing and acting of several persons
who express their different attitudes toward the same situation.
In his grandiose finales occur the final solutions of the conflicts
(of his operatic characters, HRW). In these finales, Mozart uses
in unsurpassable mastery the old elements of the finale-technique
for new dramatic effects. He does this merely by completely ex-
hausting the in-each-other, the against-each-other, and the
together-with-one-another of the individual characters. By Wagner,
we find only an after-another - with the exception of the 'Meister-
singer' quintet and the duet in the second act of 'Tristan and
Isolde'. (In his operas, HRW) it simply does not happen that
several persons simultaneously experience the same: by the mere
fact that one person has spoken, the world has changed in the
lives of the others. Thus, Wagner cannot develop an ensemble
technique; more, he rejects it. (Even the exception of the 'Meister-
singer' could be explained in this way.) Alone in 'Tristan' did the

p.38

true and deep devotion to the Thou force the composer to contradict the theorist; it is the only genuine duet in Wagner's work.
  Summing up, we could say that, by Mozart, the dramatic conflict issues always from the original source of the drama: from the
fact that a Thou exists, that we live in a social world, that we
depend on consociates and orient ourselves toward them. Nothing   p.39
special occurs by him, but everything occurs in our world in the
truest sense. It is not the world in which we live, act, and think;
it is that world which is simultaneous with our duration. Mozart
makes us aware, in a touching and for everyday-man rare clarity,
of the Thou-relationship. The subject matter of Mozart's compositions is not love but the knowledge of a Thou. In it is included
the true acceptance of life, the modest renunciation of events
occurring outside of this world, the marvellous naturalness and
self-evidence of his tonal language. Wagner, on his part, places
us outside this world and into a world of struggles and of the
fate of miracle and salvation. He forgoes the immediate evidence
of the Thou relationship; he appeals to the reason of the listener
for cooperation; he demands that he, the listener, never forgets
that he too has suffered and suffers and knows about symbol
relations which belong to the mythos and, thus, are alien to
stage and music.
  The opera can serve both goals. It can do this because it
accepts from drama the illusion of the identity of our space-time
world with the space-time world of the stage. It does not kill the
meaning content of the word; it heightens the effect of the word
through music. On the other hand, it finds in music a medium
which makes understandable, capable of being experienced, and
evident the original experiences of pure duration and the Thou
relationship in a manner which cannot be achieved by any other
form of art.

NOTES

All footnotes have been added by the editor. They provide a bare
minimum of information on writers and composers mentioned or
explain the meaning of technical musical terms which may not be
generally known. In addition, some comments on the translational
procedure have been made.
Four major sources have been used:
'Encyclopaedia Britannica.' Vols 1-24. Chicago: 1946.
'The Encyclopedia of Philosphy.' Vols. 1-8. New York: Macmillan
1967.
Apel, Willi and Ralph T. Daniel, 'The Harvard Brief Dictionary of
Music.' New York: Simon & Schuster, 1961.
Gilder, Eric and June G. Port, 'The Dictionary of Composers and
Their Music.' New York: Random House, 1978.
Since the information culled from these sources is quite elementary,
I have refrained from identifying them in the notes.

204 *Part II*

1 Euripides (c. 484-407 BC) possibly the greatest of the Greek playwrights who helped bringing Athenian culture to its unsurpassed heights.
2 Johan August Strindberg (1849-1912), the Swedish playwright, pioneered European theatrical realism.
3 Virgil (70-19 BC), well-known Roman poet.
4 Gotthold Ephraim Lessing (1729-81), German thinker, critic, and dramatist. In 1766, he wrote his famous art critical-esthetical essay about 'Lakoon oder die Grenzen der Malerei und Poesie.'
5 Claudio Monteverdi (1567-1643) the first composer of the Italian Renaissance.
6 'Ruepelspiel', literally 'play of the louts', is a short and coarse comedy. It was brought to its most popular form by Hans Sachs (1494-1576), the Nuremberg shoemaker and poet. Shakespeare integrated an English version of the Ruepelspiel into his 'A Midsummer Night's Dream' in form of the play within the play, which Bottom the Weaver and his friends perform for the Duke and his guests.
7 Jean Lully (1632-87) another of the early Italian composers.
8 Jean Rameau (1683-1764), French composer.
9 Jean Jacques Rousseau (1712-78), the Swiss-French exponent of the philosophy of enlightenment.
10 Christoph Willibald von Gluck (1714-87), Bavarian composer.
11 The Piccinnists were followers of the Italian composer Niccola Piccinni (1728-1800) who was called, in 1776, to the French court. In Paris, he was made the center of a raging controversy with the followers of Gluck.
12 Metastasio was the assumed name of Pietro Trapassi (1698-1782), Italian poet and writer of plays which were partially set to music.
13 Wolfgang Amadeus Mozart (1756-91) lived in Paris during the years of 1778-9.
14 Heinrich Schutz (1585-1672) was the first of the German composers of lasting significance.
15 Richard Wagner (1813-83) wrote the study on 'Oper und Drama' during his exile in Switzerland (1849-59).
16 By material Schutz means here the dramatic plot, the story to be dramatized; usually pre-existing as legend, as story, as historical report, or at least provisionally outlined by the author before writing the drama.
17 In his 'Poetics', Aristotle (348-322 BC.) postulated the 'unity of the plot' as the crucial criterion of a good tragedy. His main requirement is that the tragedy 'must represent an action, a complete whole, with its several incidents so closely connected that the transposal or withdrawal of any one of them will disjoin and dislocate the whole' ('De Poetica' 8: 1451a. W.D. Ross (ed.) 'The Student's Oxford Aristotle'. vol. VI. London: Oxford University Press.) The 'Poetics' contain no explicit 'law' of the 'unity of space and time.' As one old but most reliable source informs us, it is 'very doubtful' that

Aristotle ever spoke of such a combined law; but if so, 'rather as an observance than a strict law.' (Johann Eduard Erdmann: 'A History of Philosophy', vol. I: 176. London: Swan, 1893). The law, then, seems to be the product of later Aristotelians.

18 Nicolas Boileau-Despréaux (1636-1711), an outstanding French writer of his period, published his 'L'Art poétique' in 1674. In its third book, he dealt with tragic and epic poetry.

19 Strindberg wrote 'Froeken Julie' in 1888. This drama is considered the prototype of the realistic tragedy.

20 Jean Baptiste Poquelin (1622-73) became famous under the assumed name, Molière. An actor of wide experience, he became one of the greatest playwrights of Europe.

21 Friedrich von Schlegel (1772-1829), one of the main exponents of German literary Romantic, published a two-volume 'History of Ancient and Modern Literature' in 1815.

22 Friedrich Nietzsche (1844-1900) was the first German thinker in existential revolt against philosophical rationalism. His first book, written in 1872, dealt with 'The Birth of the Tragedy out of the Spirit of Music.' It gave rise to violent controversies.

23 Friedrich Schiller (1759-1805). Next to Goethe, he was the main figure of the classical period of German literature. Like Goethe, he was involved with the theater in Weimar. In 1803, he wrote an essay about 'The Use of the Chorus in Tragedy.'

24 Johann Wolfgang von Goethe (1749-1832) wrote various notes on the drama; notably 'On Epic and Dramatic Poetry' (1797) and 'Supplements to Aristotle's Poetics' (1827).

25 The Viennese composer Arnold Schoenberg (1874-1951) opened up the era of 'modern' music with the introduction of the twelve-stone scale. Among his earlier works is the musical drama, 'The Lucky Hand' (1913). The Russian composer, Igor Stravinsky (1882-1971), is best known for his ballet scores. He produced a 'lyrical tale in three acts' ('The Nightingale') in 1914, a 'Cantata Ballet' ('The Marriage') in 1917, and a comical opera ('Mavra') in 1922. Alban Berg (1885-1935), another Austrian composer, wrote the opera 'Wozzeck' in 1921.

26 Arthur Schopenhauer (1788-1860), the German philosopher generally labelled as philosopher of pessimism, broke with the prevailing Kantian and Hegelian traditions. Centering his philosophy on The Will, he called his major work 'The World as Will and Idea' (1819). In its third volume, he developed his theory of music, which greatly influenced Richard Wagner.

27 Nietzsche's critical response to Schopenhauer's theory of music is contained in a fragment, 'About Music and Word,' which he wrote in 1871.

28 This paragraph was written by hand on the left margin of the MS.

29 This poem is Schiller's An die Freude, a rhapsodic praise of joy.

30 The strata of consciousness, to which Schutz alludes here, are identical with the life forms which he treated at length

in the main part of his projected study. (See 'Part I'
and the early sections of the first two pieces of 'Part
II.')

31 Franz Schubert (1797-1828), the Austrian composer, set
various poems of Goethe to music.

32 Hugo Wolf (1860-1903), also Austrian, wrote the music for
more than fifty poems of Goethe.

33 Johann Sebastian Bach (1685-1750), the greatest German composer of the Baroque period, brought polyphonic techniques
to perfection.

34 Albert Schweitzer (1875-1965) wrote a two-volume study of
'Johann Sebastian Bach', which, in 1938, appeared in English
translation (New York: Macmillan).

35 Cantatas are vocal compositions including arias, duets, recitatives, and choir presentations.

36 Franz Liszt (1811-86), Hungarian composer and pianist, wrote
various compositions which are classified as 'symphonic poems'
or 'tone poems.' Richard Strauss (1864-1949), the German
composer, created his own operatic form. Among his earlier
works are a 'Don Juan' (1888) and a 'Till Eulenspiegel' (1894),
prime examples of the symphonic poem.

37 In Schutz's MS, the title of this score was given as 'Fire-
works.' There are indications that, at the time, he disliked
Stravinsky's program music more than that of any other
composer.

38 One of the most characteristic operatic innovations of Wagner,
a Leitmotiv is a short musical theme standing for a character
or object fraught with symbolic significance. It is introduced
in the overture and appears throughout the opera whenever
the action brings the character on the stage or refers to the
symbolic object.

39 The secco recitative is recited in irregular rhythmic patterns
and delivered in deliberately inexpressive manner (secco =
dry).

40 Arioso is a recitative of pronounced lyrical expressiveness.

41 This statement occurs in the original MS in the midst of a
very long paragraph (which I have divided into several sections). Yet, it does not precede a discussion of a Passion by
Bach; it is merely a hint at the possibility of such an illustration. When Schutz, later in the essay, returned to the topic
announced here, he chose Handel, not Bach, as model.

42 Here, Schutz aimed at the fact that, in a monologue, a person
(actor) addresses himself as if he were two persons. This
'doubling of the I,' of course, is nothing but an incipient
form of the juxtaposition of the 'I' and the 'Me' in the sense
in which Schutz should later encounter it in the writings of
William James and George Herbert Mead.

43 In 1923, Guido Adler published his lectures about Richard
Wagner, which he offered the University of Vienna. He wrote
various historical essays about composers and musical styles,
among them 'heterophony.' His main work was the 'Handbook

of Music', the first edition of which appeared in 1924.

44 Georg Friedrich Handel (1685-1759), another outstanding German composer of the German Baroque period, wrote mostly church music. His oratorio 'The Messiah' (1741) is his most famous work.

45 The testa is presented by a testo, that is, a singer who narrates the story of the oratorio.

46 In the original MS, the reference to the audience *(das Publikum)*, here, is erroneously given with the masculine pronoun for the third person singular (er); in the next sentence, the correct German neuter-pronoun (es) is used. I have replaced 'Publikum' by 'listeners,' setting the whole statement in the plural.

47 Hermann Cohen (1842-1918), the leading figure of the Marburg School of neo-Kantianism, published a book on 'The Dramatical Idea in the Texts of Mozart's Operas' (1916). Schutz discussed it, in some detail, in his American essay on 'Mozart and the Philosophers' (1956a).

48 'Nummernoper' is a generic designation of the early operatic style which consisted largely of a succession of disconnected pieces (arias, duets, songs for chorus, recitatives) written for and presented by different singers. As Schutz pointed out with regard to the early Italian operas, this style amounted to what I am tempted to call a kind of musical variety show in which individual singers offered their 'numbers' for the benefit of the display of their vocal virtuosity. Mozart's operas, of course, are not of this extreme type. But they preserved something of the number style in the alternation of what Schutz called operatic high points and musically unemphasized passages (recitatives or spoken dialogues) but also in his treatment of individual scenes as musical unities in themselves.

PART III
Object and Methods of the Social Sciences

Editor's note

Aside from a seven-point outline, Schutz left no documents whatever whose content would correspond to the topic of the planned third and final part of his Bergson project. There exist three short outline-collections, which originated after 1927 but before 1932; they deal with: Pragmatism and Sociology, Understanding and Action, and Relevance. Parts of each of them seem to be related to the topics of Part III. However, they do no longer properly belong to Schutz's Bergson period and thus cannot find consideration here.

Outline for Main Part III

Object and method of the social sciences

especially of the sociology of understanding

1 Theory of the social person; collectives and duration
2 Meaning interpretation and meaning positing; understanding
3 Objective chance and adequate causation
4 Social action and its kinds, especially rational action
5 Concerning the understandability of meaning contexts without visible Thou
6 The intimate person of the individual and of the collective limits of understanding
   Race, nation, and historism[1]
   Sex differentiation
7 The historical individual[2] and the historical event

NOTES

1 The term seems to be unknown in the English language. In contrast to 'historicism,' which refers to a theory of the teleologically predetermined course of history as a whole, 'historism' denotes theories which assume that larger social events are sufficiently explained by an analysis of the historical circumstances and contexts in which they appear.

2 The meaning of this term is not clear. It was seldom if ever again used by Schutz. In the German text, it reads 'historisches Individuum.' This is an expression used by Max Weber *not* as a label for a person playing a role in history or seen in historical perspective, but as a combination of a multiplicity of spiritual-evaluative traits shared by many and being effective in the shaping of the course of history. In its uniqueness, it may appear in different social settings and reappear in different historical periods. The prime example of a 'historical individuum' is Weber's famous ideal-typical concept of the Protestant Ethic. Even though there can be no doubt that Schutz accepted the term from Weber together with other conceptions which determined the topics of some points of the present outline (notably (2) and (3)), it is not a foregone conclusion that he intended to use it in its Weberian sense. He may have wished to set up the ideal type of a social actor in historical context and as maker of or contributor to historical events. This possibility must be raised in view of the fact that Schutz never displayed a genuine interest in the analysis of large-scale historical events, which was a trade mark of much of Weber's work.

NAME INDEX

SUBJECT INDEX

Routledge Social Science Series

Routledge & Kegan Paul   London, Henley and Boston

39 Store Street,
London WC1E 7DD
Broadway House,
Newtown Road,
Henley-on-Thames,
Oxon RG9 1EN
9 Park Street,
Boston, Mass. 02108

Contents

*Authors wishing to submit manuscripts for any series
in this catalogue should send them to the Social Science Editor,
Routledge & Kegan Paul Ltd, 39 Store Street,
London WC1E 7DD.*
● *Books so marked are available in paperback.*
○ *Books so marked are available in paperback only.*
*All books are in metric Demy 8vo format (216 × 138mm approx.)
unless otherwise stated.*

International Library of Sociology
General Editor John Rex

GENERAL SOCIOLOGY

Barnsley, J. H. The Social Reality of Ethics. *464 pp.*
Brown, Robert. Explanation in Social Science. *208 pp.*
●   Rules and Laws in Sociology. *192 pp.*
Bruford, W. H. Chekhov and His Russia. *A Sociological Study. 244 pp.*
Burton, F. and **Carlen, P.** Official Discourse. *On Discourse Analysis, Government Publications, Ideology. About 140 pp.*
Cain, Maureen E. Society and the Policeman's Role. *326 pp.*
● **Fletcher, Colin.** Beneath the Surface. *An Account of Three Styles of Sociological Research. 221 pp.*
Gibson, Quentin. The Logic of Social Enquiry. *240 pp.*
Glassner, B. Essential Interactionism. *208 pp.*
Glucksmann, M. Structuralist Analysis in Contemporary Social Thought. *212 pp.*
Gurvitch, Georges. Sociology of Law. *Foreword by Roscoe Pound. 264 pp.*
Hinkle, R. Founding Theory of American Sociology 1881–1913. *About 350 pp.*
Homans, George C. Sentiments and Activities. *336 pp.*
Johnson, Harry M. Sociology: *A Systematic Introduction. Foreword by Robert K. Merton. 710 pp.*
● **Keat, Russell** and **Urry, John.** Social Theory as Science. *278 pp.*
Mannheim, Karl. Essays on Sociology and Social Psychology. *Edited by Paul Keckskemeti. With Editorial Note by Adolph Lowe. 344 pp.*
Martindale, Don. The Nature and Types of Sociological Theory. *292 pp.*
● **Maus, Heinz.** A Short History of Sociology. *234 pp.*
Myrdal, Gunnar. Value in Social Theory: *A Collection of Essays on Methodology. Edited by Paul Streeten. 332 pp.*
Ogburn, William F. and **Nimkoff, Meyer F.** A Handbook of Sociology. *Preface by Karl Mannheim. 656 pp. 46 figures. 35 tables.*
Parsons, Talcott and **Smelser, Neil J.** Economy and Society: *A Study in the Integration of Economic and Social Theory. 362 pp.*
Payne, G., Dingwall, R., Payne, J. and **Carter, M.** Sociology and Social Research. *About 250 pp.*
Podgórecki, A. Practical Social Sciences. *About 200 pp.*
Podgórecki, A. and **Łos, M.** Multidimensional Sociology. *268 pp.*
Raffel, S. Matters of Fact. *A Sociological Inquiry. 152 pp.*
● **Rex, John.** Key Problems of Sociological Theory. *220 pp.*
  Sociology and the Demystification of the Modern World. *282 pp.*
● **Rex, John.** (Ed.) Approaches to Sociology. *Contributions by Peter Abell, Frank Bechhofer, Basil Bernstein, Ronald Fletcher, David Frisby, Miriam Glucksmann, Peter Lassman, Herminio Martins, John Rex, Roland Robertson, John Westergaard and Jock Young. 302 pp.*
Rigby, A. Alternative Realities. *352 pp.*
Roche, M. Phenomenology, Language and the Social Sciences. *374 pp.*
Sahay, A. Sociological Analysis. *220 pp.*
Strasser, Hermann. The Normative Structure of Sociology. *Conservative and Emancipatory Themes in Social Thought. About 340 pp.*
Strong, P. Ceremonial Order of the Clinic. *267 pp.*
Urry, John. Reference Groups and the Theory of Revolution. *244 pp.*
Weinberg, E. Development of Sociology in the Soviet Union. *173 pp.*

FOREIGN CLASSICS OF SOCIOLOGY

● **Gerth, H. H.** and **Mills, C. Wright.** From Max Weber: *Essays in Sociology. 502 pp.*

● **Tönnies, Ferdinand.** Community and Association *(Gemeinschaft und Gesell-schaft).|Translated and Supplemented by Charles P. Loomis. Foreword by Pitirim A. Sorokin. 334 pp.*

SOCIAL STRUCTURE

Andreski, Stanislav. Military Organization and Society. *Foreword by Professor A. R. Radcliffe-Brown. 226 pp. 1 folder.*

Broom, L., Lancaster Jones, F., McDonnell, P. and **Williams, T.** The Inheritance of Inequality. *About 180 pp.*

Carlton, Eric. Ideology and Social Order. *Foreword by Professor Philip Abrahams. About 320 pp.*

Clegg, S. and **Dunkerley, D.** Organization, Class and Control. *614 pp.*

Coontz, Sydney H. Population Theories and the Economic Interpretation. *202 pp.*

Coser, Lewis. The Functions of Social Conflict. *204 pp.*

Crook, I. and **D.** The First Years of the Yangyi Commune. *304 pp., illustrated.*

Dickie-Clark, H. F. Marginal Situation: *A Sociological Study of a Coloured Group. 240 pp. 11 tables.*

Giner, S. and **Archer, M. S.** (Eds) Contemporary Europe: *Social Structures and Cultural Patterns, 336 pp.*

● **Glaser, Barney** and **Strauss, Anselm L.** Status Passage: *A Formal Theory. 212 pp.*

Glass, D. V. (Ed.) Social Mobility in Britain. *Contributions by J. Berent, T. Bottomore, R. C. Chambers, J. Floud, D. V. Glass, J. R. Hall, H. T. Himmelweit, R. K. Kelsall, F. M. Martin, C. A. Moser, R. Mukherjee and W. Ziegel. 420 pp.*

Kelsall, R. K. Higher Civil Servants in Britain: *From 1870 to the Present Day. 268 pp. 31 tables.*

● **Lawton, Denis.** Social Class, Language and Education. *192 pp.*

McLeish, John. The Theory of Social Change: *Four Views Considered. 128 pp.*

● **Marsh, David C.** The Changing Social Structure of England and Wales, 1871–1961. *Revised edition. 288 pp.*

Menzies, Ken. Talcott Parsons and the Social Image of Man. *About 208 pp.*

● **Mouzelis, Nicos.** Organization and Bureaucracy. *An Analysis of Modern Theories. 240 pp.*

● **Ossowski, Stanislaw.** Class Structure in the Social Consciousness. *210 pp.*

● **Podgórecki, Adam.** Law and Society. *302 pp.*

Renner, Karl. Institutions of Private Law and Their Social Functions. *Edited, with an Introduction and Notes, by O. Kahn-Freud. Translated by Agnes Schwarzschild. 316 pp.*

Rex, J. and **Tomlinson, S.** Colonial Immigrants in a British City. *A Class Analysis. 368 pp.*

Smooha, S. Israel: Pluralism and Conflict. *472 pp.*

Wesolowski, W. Class, Strata and Power. *Trans. and with Introduction by G. Kolankiewicz. 160 pp.*

Zureik, E. Palestinians in Israel. *A Study in Internal Colonialism. 264 pp.*

SOCIOLOGY AND POLITICS

Acton, T. A. Gypsy Politics and Social Change. *316 pp.*

Burton, F. Politics of Legitimacy. *Struggles in a Belfast Community. 250 pp.*

Crook, I. and **D.** Revolution in a Chinese Village. *Ten Mile Inn. 216 pp., illustrated.*

Etzioni-Halevy, E. Political Manipulation and Administrative Power. *A Comparative Study. About 200 pp.*

Fielding, N. The National Front. *About 250 pp.*

● **Hechter, Michael.** Internal Colonialism. *The Celtic Fringe in British National Development, 1536–1966. 380 pp.*

Kornhauser, William. The Politics of Mass Society. *272 pp. 20 tables.*

Korpi, W. The Working Class in Welfare Capitalism. *Work, Unions and Politics in Sweden. 472 pp.*

Kroes, R. Soldiers and Students. *A Study of Right- and Left-wing Students. 174 pp.*

Martin, Roderick. Sociology of Power. *About 272 pp.*

Merquior, J. G. Rousseau and Weber. *A Study in the Theory of Legitimacy. About 288 pp.*

Myrdal, Gunnar. The Political Element in the Development of Economic Theory. *Translated from the German by Paul Streeten. 282 pp.*

Varma, B. N. The Sociology and Politics of Development. *A Theoretical Study. 236 pp.*

Wong, S.-L. Sociology and Socialism in Contemporary China. *160 pp.*

Wootton, Graham. Workers, Unions and the State. *188 pp.*

CRIMINOLOGY

Ancel, Marc. Social Defence: *A Modern Approach to Criminal Problems. Foreword by Leon Radzinowicz. 240 pp.*

Athens, L. Violent Criminal Acts and Actors. *104 pp.*

Cain, Maureen E. Society and the Policeman's Role. *326 pp.*

Cloward, Richard A. and Ohlin, Lloyd E. Delinquency and Opportunity: *A Theory of Delinquent Gangs. 248 pp.*

Downes, David M. The Delinquent Solution. *A Study in Subcultural Theory. 296 pp.*

Friedlander, Kate. The Psycho-Analytical Approach to Juvenile Delinquency: *Theory, Case Studies, Treatment. 320 pp.*

Gleuck, Sheldon and Eleanor. Family Environment and Delinquency. *With the statistical assistance of Rose W. Kneznek. 340 pp.*

Lopez-Rey, Manuel. Crime. *An Analytical Appraisal. 288 pp.*

Mannheim, Hermann. Comparative Criminology: *A Text Book. Two volumes. 442 pp. and 380 pp.*

Morris, Terence. The Criminal Area: *A Study in Social Ecology. Foreword by Hermann Mannheim. 232 pp. 25 tables. 4 maps.*

Rock, Paul. Making People Pay. *338 pp.*

● Taylor, Ian, Walton, Paul and Young, Jock. The New Criminology. *For a Social Theory of Deviance. 325 pp.*

● Taylor, Ian, Walton, Paul and Young, Jock. (Eds) Critical Criminology. *268 pp.*

SOCIAL PSYCHOLOGY

Bagley, Christopher. The Social Psychology of the Epileptic Child. *320 pp.*

Brittan, Arthur. Meanings and Situations. *224 pp.*

Carroll, J. Break-Out from the Crystal Palace. *200 pp.*

● Fleming, C. M. Adolescence: Its Social Psychology. *With an Introduction to recent findings from the fields of Anthropology, Physiology, Medicine, Psychometrics and Sociometry. 288 pp.*

● The Social Psychology of Education: *An Introduction and Guide to Its Study. 136 pp.*

Linton, Ralph. The Cultural Background of Personality. *132 pp.*

● Mayo, Elton. The Social Problems of an Industrial Civilization. *With an Appendix on the Political Problem. 180 pp.*

Ottaway, A. K. C. Learning Through Group Experience. *176 pp.*

Plummer, Ken. Sexual Stigma. *An Interactionist Account. 254 pp.*

● Rose, Arnold M. (Ed.) Human Behaviour and Social Processes: *an Interactionist Approach. Contributions by Arnold M. Rose, Ralph H. Turner, Anselm Strauss, Everett C. Hughes, E. Franklin Frazier, Howard S. Becker et al. 696 pp.*

Smelser, Neil J. Theory of Collective Behaviour. *448 pp.*

Stephenson, Geoffrey M. The Development of Conscience. *128 pp.*

Young, Kimball. Handbook of Social Psychology. *658 pp. 16 figures. 10 tables.*

SOCIOLOGY OF THE FAMILY

Bell, Colin R. Middle Class Families: *Social and Geographical Mobility. 224 pp.*
Burton, Lindy. Vulnerable Children. *272 pp.*
Gavron, Hannah. The Captive Wife: *Conflicts of Household Mothers. 190 pp.*
George, Victor and **Wilding, Paul.** Motherless Families. *248 pp.*
Klein, Josephine. Samples from English Cultures.
  1. Three Preliminary Studies and Aspects of Adult Life in England. *447 pp.*
  2. Child-Rearing Practices and Index. *247 pp.*
Klein, Viola. The Feminine Character. *History of an Ideology. 244 pp.*
McWhinnie, Alexina M. Adopted Children. *How They Grow Up. 304 pp.*
● **Morgan, D. H. J.** Social Theory and the Family. *About 320 pp.*
● **Myrdal, Alva** and **Klein, Viola.** Women's Two Roles: *Home and Work. 238 pp.*
  27 tables.
Parsons, Talcott and **Bales, Robert F.** Family: Socialization and Interaction Process. *In collaboration with James Olds, Morris Zelditch and Philip E. Slater. 456 pp. 50 figures and tables.*

SOCIAL SERVICES

Bastide, Roger. The Sociology of Mental Disorder. *Translated from the French by Jean McNeil. 260 pp.*
Carlebach, Julius. Caring For Children in Trouble. *266 pp.*
George, Victor. Foster Care. *Theory and Practice. 234 pp.*
  Social Security: *Beveridge and After. 258 pp.*
George, V. and **Wilding, P.** Motherless Families. *248 pp.*
● **Goetschius, George W.** Working with Community Groups. *256 pp.*
Goetschius, George W. and **Tash, Joan.** Working with Unattached Youth. *416 pp.*
Heywood, Jean S. Children in Care. *The Development of the Service for the Deprived Child. Third revised edition. 284 pp.*
King, Roy D., Ranes, Norma V. and **Tizard, Jack.** Patterns of Residential Care. *356 pp.*
Leigh, John. Young People and Leisure. *256 pp.*
● **Mays, John.** (Ed.) Penelope Hall's Social Services of England and Wales. *368 pp.*
Morris, Mary. Voluntary Work and the Welfare State. *300 pp.*
Nokes, P. L. The Professional Task in Welfare Practice. *152 pp.*
Timms, Noel. Psychiatric Social Work in Great Britain (1939–1962). *280 pp.*
●   Social Casework: *Principles and Practice. 256 pp.*

SOCIOLOGY OF EDUCATION

Banks, Olive. Parity and Prestige in English Secondary Education: a Study in Educational Sociology. *272 pp.*
● **Blyth, W. A. L.** English Primary Education. *A Sociological Description.*
  2. Background. *168 pp.*
Collier, K. G. The Social Purposes of Education: *Personal and Social Values in Education. 268 pp.*
Evans, K. M. Sociometry and Education. *158 pp.*
● **Ford, Julienne.** Social Class and the Comprehensive School. *192 pp.*
Foster, P. J. Education and Social Change in Ghana. *336 pp. 3 maps.*
Fraser, W. R. Education and Society in Modern France. *150 pp.*
Grace, Gerald R. Role Conflict and the Teacher. *150 pp.*
Hans, Nicholas. New Trends in Education in the Eighteenth Century. *278 pp. 19 tables.*
●   Comparative Education: *A Study of Educational Factors and Traditions. 360 pp.*
● **Hargreaves, David.** Interpersonal Relations and Education. *432 pp.*
●   Social Relations in a Secondary School. *240 pp.*
  School Organization and Pupil Involvement. *A Study of Secondary Schools.*

6

- **Mannheim, Karl** and **Stewart, W. A. C.** An Introduction to the Sociology of Education. *206 pp.*
- **Musgrove, F.** Youth and the Social Order. *176 pp.*
- **Ottaway, A. K. C.** Education and Society: An Introduction to the Sociology of Education. *With an Introduction by W. O. Lester Smith. 212 pp.*

Peers, Robert. Adult Education: *A Comparative Study. Revised edition. 398 pp.*

Stratta, Erica. The Education of Borstal Boys. *A Study of their Educational Experiences prior to, and during, Borstal Training. 256 pp.*

- **Taylor, P. H., Reid, W. A.** and **Holley, B. J.** The English Sixth Form. *A Case Study in Curriculum Research. 198 pp.*

SOCIOLOGY OF CULTURE

Eppel, E. M. and **M.** Adolescents and Morality: *A Study of some Moral Values and Dilemmas of Working Adolescents in the Context of a changing Climate of Opinion. Foreword by W. J. H. Sprott. 268 pp. 39 tables.*

- **Fromm, Erich.** The Fear of Freedom. *286 pp.*
- The Sane Society. *400 pp.*

Johnson, L. The Cultural Critics. *From Matthew Arnold to Raymond Williams. 233 pp.*

Mannheim, Karl. Essays on the Sociology of Culture. *Edited by Ernst Mannheim in co-operation with Paul Kecskemeti. Editorial Note by Adolph Lowe. 280 pp.*

Merquior, J. G. The Veil and the Mask. *Essays on Culture and Ideology. Foreword by Ernest Gellner. 140 pp.*

Zijderfeld, A. C. On Clichés. *The Supersedure of Meaning by Function in Modernity. 150 pp.*

SOCIOLOGY OF RELIGION

Argyle, Michael and **Beit-Hallahmi, Benjamin.** The Social Psychology of Religion. *256 pp.*

Glasner, Peter E. The Sociology of Secularisation. *A Critique of a Concept. 146 pp.*

Hall, J. R. The Ways Out. *Utopian Communal Groups in an Age of Babylon. 280 pp.*

Ranson, S., Hinings, B. and **Bryman, A.** Clergy, Ministers and Priests. *216 pp.*

Stark, Werner. The Sociology of Religion. *A Study of Christendom.*
  Volume II. *Sectarian Religion. 368 pp.*
  Volume III. *The Universal Church. 464 pp.*
  Volume IV. *Types of Religious Man. 352 pp.*
  Volume V. *Types of Religious Culture. 464 pp.*

Turner, B. S. Weber and Islam. *216 pp.*

Watt, W. Montgomery. Islam and the Integration of Society. *320 pp.*

SOCIOLOGY OF ART AND LITERATURE

Jarvie, Ian C. Towards a Sociology of the Cinema. *A Comparative Essay on the Structure and Functioning of a Major Entertainment Industry. 405 pp.*

Rust, Frances S. Dance in Society. *An Analysis of the Relationships between the Social Dance and Society in England from the Middle Ages to the Present Day. 256 pp. 8 pp. of plates.*

Schücking, L. L. The Sociology of Literary Taste. *112 pp.*

Wolff, Janet. Hermeneutic Philosophy and the Sociology of Art. *150 pp.*

SOCIOLOGY OF KNOWLEDGE

Diesing, P. Patterns of Discovery in the Social Sciences. *262 pp.*

● **Douglas, J. D.** (Ed.) Understanding Everyday Life. *370 pp.*
● **Hamilton, P.** Knowledge and Social Structure. *174 pp.*
  Jarvie, I. C. Concepts and Society. *232 pp.*
  Mannheim, Karl. Essays on the Sociology of Knowledge. *Edited by Paul Kecskemeti. Editorial Note by Adolph Lowe. 353 pp.*
  Remmling, Gunter W. The Sociology of Karl Mannheim. *With a Bibliographical Guide to the Sociology of Knowledge, Ideological Analysis, and Social Planning. 255 pp.*
  Remmling, Gunter W. (Ed.) Towards the Sociology of Knowledge. *Origin and Development of a Sociological Thought Style. 463 pp.*
  Scheler, M. Problems of a Sociology of Knowledge. *Trans. by M. S. Frings. Edited and with an Introduction by K. Stikkers. 232 pp.*

URBAN SOCIOLOGY

  Aldridge, M. The British New Towns. *A Programme Without a Policy. 232 pp.*
  Ashworth, William. The Genesis of Modern British Town Planning: *A Study in Economic and Social History of the Nineteenth and Twentieth Centuries. 288 pp.*
  Brittan, A. The Privatised World. *196 pp.*
  Cullingworth, J. B. Housing Needs and Planning Policy: *A Restatement of the Problems of Housing Need and 'Overspill' in England and Wales. 232 pp. 44 tables. 8 maps.*
  Dickinson, Robert E. City and Region: *A Geographical Interpretation. 608 pp. 125 figures.*
  The West European City: *A Geographical Interpretation. 600 pp. 129 maps. 29 plates.*
  Humphreys, Alexander J. New Dubliners: *Urbanization and the Irish Family. Foreword by George C. Homans. 304 pp.*
  Jackson, Brian. Working Class Community: *Some General Notions raised by a Series of Studies in Northern England. 192 pp.*
● **Mann, P. H.** An Approach to Urban Sociology. *240 pp.*
  Mellor, J. R. Urban Sociology in an Urbanized Society. *326 pp.*
  Morris, R. N. and **Mogey, J.** The Sociology of Housing. *Studies at Berinsfield. 232 pp. 4 pp. plates.*
  Mullan, R. Stevenage Ltd. *About 250 pp.*
  Rex, J. and **Tomlinson, S.** Colonial Immigrants in a British City. *A Class Analysis. 368 pp.*
  Rosser, C. and **Harris, C.** The Family and Social Change. *A Study of Family and Kinship in a South Wales Town. 352 pp. 8 maps.*
● **Stacey, Margaret, Batsone, Eric, Bell, Colin** and **Thurcott, Anne.** Power, Persistence and Change. *A Second Study of Banbury. 196 pp.*

RURAL SOCIOLOGY

  Mayer, Adrian C. Peasants in the Pacific. *A Study of Fiji Indian Rural Society. 248 pp. 20 plates.*
  Williams, W. M. The Sociology of an English Village: *Gosforth. 272 pp. 12 figures. 13 tables.*

SOCIOLOGY OF INDUSTRY AND DISTRIBUTION

  Dunkerley, David. The Foreman. *Aspects of Task and Structure. 192 pp.*
  Eldridge, J. E. T. Industrial Disputes. *Essays in the Sociology of Industrial Relations. 288 pp.*
  Hollowell, Peter G. The Lorry Driver. *272 pp.*
● **Oxaal, I., Barnett, T.** and **Booth, D.** (Eds) Beyond the Sociology of Development.

> *Economy and Society in Latin America and Africa. 295 pp.*

Smelser, Neil J. Social Change in the Industrial Revolution: *An Application of Theory to the Lancashire Cotton Industry, 1770–1840. 468 pp. 12 figures. 14 tables.*

Watson, T. J. The Personnel Managers. *A Study in the Sociology of Work and Employment, 262 pp.*

ANTHROPOLOGY

Brandel-Syrier, Mia. Reeftown Elite. *A Study of Social Mobility in a Modern African Community on the Reef. 376 pp.*

Dickie-Clark, H. F. The Marginal Situation. *A Sociological Study of a Coloured Group. 236 pp.*

Dube, S. C. Indian Village. *Foreword by Morris Edward Opler. 276 pp. 4 plates.*
India's Changing Villages: *Human Factors in Community Development. 260 pp. 8 plates. 1 map.*

Fei, H.-T. Peasant Life in China. *A Field Study of Country Life in the Yangtze Valley. With a foreword by Bronislaw Malinowski. 328 pp. 16 pp. plates.*

Firth, Raymond. Malay Fishermen. *Their Peasant Economy. 420 pp. 17 pp. plates.*

Gulliver, P. H. Social Control in an African Society: a Study of the Arusha, Agricultural Masai of Northern Tanganyika. *320 pp. 8 plates. 10 figures.*
Family Herds. *288 pp.*

Jarvie, Ian C. The Revolution in Anthropology. *268 pp.*

Little, Kenneth L. Mende of Sierra Leone. *308 pp. and folder.*
Negroes in Britain. *With a New Introduction and Contemporary Study by Leonard Bloom. 320 pp.*

Tambs-Lyche, H. London Patidars. *About 180 pp.*

Madan, G. R. Western Sociologists on Indian Society. *Marx, Spencer, Weber, Durkheim, Pareto. 384 pp.*

Mayer, A. C. Peasants in the Pacific. *A Study of Fiji Indian Rural Society. 248 pp.*

Meer, Fatima. Race and Suicide in South Africa. *325 pp.*

Smith, Raymond T. The Negro Family in British Guiana: *Family Structure and Social Status in the Villages. With a Foreword by Meyer Fortes. 314 pp. 8 plates. 1 figure. 4 maps.*

SOCIOLOGY AND PHILOSOPHY

Adriaansens, H. Talcott Parsons and the Conceptual Dilemma. *About 224 pp.*

Barnsley, John H. The Social Reality of Ethics. *A Comparative Analysis of Moral Codes. 448 pp.*

Diesing, Paul. Patterns of Discovery in the Social Sciences. *362 pp.*

● **Douglas, Jack D.** (Ed.) Understanding Everyday Life. *Toward the Reconstruction of Sociological Knowledge. Contributions by Alan F. Blum, Aaron W. Cicourel, Norman K. Denzin, Jack D. Douglas, John Heeren, Peter McHugh, Peter K. Manning, Melvin Power, Matthew Speier, Roy Turner, D. Lawrence Wieder, Thomas P. Wilson and Don H. Zimmerman. 370 pp.*

Gorman, Robert A. The Dual Vision. *Alfred Schutz and the Myth of Phenomenological Social Science. 240 pp.*

Jarvie, Ian C. Concepts and Society. *216 pp.*

Kilminster, R. Praxis and Method. *A Sociological Dialogue with Lukács, Gramsci and the Early Frankfurt School. 334 pp.*

● **Pelz, Werner.** The Scope of Understanding in Sociology. *Towards a More Radical Reorientation in the Social Humanistic Sciences. 283 pp.*

Roche, Maurice. Phenomenology, Language and the Social Sciences. *371 pp.*

Sahay, Arun. Sociological Analysis. *212 pp.*

● **Slater, P.** Origin and Significance of the Frankfurt School. *A Marxist Perspective. 185 pp.*

Spurling, L. Phenomenology and the Social World. *The Philosophy of Merleau-Ponty and its Relation to the Social Sciences. 222 pp.*
Wilson, H. T. The American Ideology. *Science, Technology and Organization as Modes of Rationality. 368 pp.*

International Library of Anthropology
General Editor Adam Kuper

● Ahmed, A. S. Millennium and Charisma Among Pathans. *A Critical Essay in Social Anthropology. 192 pp.*
Pukhtun Economy and Society. *Traditional Structure and Economic Development. About 360 pp.*
Barth, F. Selected Essays. *Volume I. About 250 pp.* Selected Essays. *Volume II. About 250 pp.*
Brown, Paula. The Chimbu. *A Study of Change in the New Guinea Highlands. 151 pp.*
Foner, N. Jamaica Farewell. *200 pp.*
Gudeman, Stephen. Relationships, Residence and the Individual. *A Rural Panamanian Community. 288 pp. 11 plates, 5 figures, 2 maps, 10 tables.*
The Demise of a Rural Economy. *From Subsistence to Capitalism in a Latin American Village. 160 pp.*
Hamnett, Ian. Chieftainship and Legitimacy. *An Anthropological Study of Executive Law in Lesotho. 163 pp.*
Hanson, F. Allan. Meaning in Culture. *127 pp.*
Hazan, H. The Limbo People. *A Study of the Constitution of the Time Universe Among the Aged. About 192 pp.*
Humphreys, S. C. Anthropology and the Greeks. *288 pp.*
Karp, I. Fields of Change Among the Iteso of Kenya. *140 pp.*
Lloyd, P. C. Power and Independence. *Urban Africans' Perception of Social Inequality. 264 pp.*
Parry, J. P. Caste and Kinship in Kangra. *352 pp. Illustrated.*
Pettigrew, Joyce. Robber Noblemen. *A Study of the Political System of the Sikh Jats. 284 pp.*
Street, Brian V. The Savage in Literature. *Representations of 'Primitive' Society in English Fiction, 1858–1920. 207 pp.*
Van Den Berghe, Pierre L. Power and Privilege at an African University. *278 pp.*

International Library of Phenomenology and Moral Sciences
General Editor John O'Neill

Apel, K.-O. Towards a Transformation of Philosophy. *308 pp.*
Bologh, R. W. Dialectical Phenomenology. *Marx's Method. 287 pp.*
Fekete, J. The Critical Twilight. *Explorations in the Ideology of Anglo-American Literary Theory from Eliot to McLuhan. 300 pp.*
Medina, A. Reflection, Time and the Novel. *Towards a Communicative Theory of Literature. 143 pp.*

International Library of Social Policy
General Editor Kathleen Jones

Bayley, M. Mental Handicap and Community Care. *426 pp.*
Bottoms, A. E. and McClean, J. D. Defendants in the Criminal Process. *284 pp.*
Bradshaw, J. The Family Fund. *An Initiative in Social Policy. About 224 pp.*

Butler, J. R. Family Doctors and Public Policy. *208 pp.*
Davies, Martin. Prisoners of Society. *Attitudes and Aftercare. 204 pp.*
Gittus, Elizabeth. Flats, Families and the Under-Fives. *285 pp.*
Holman, Robert. Trading in Children. *A Study of Private Fostering. 355 pp.*
Jeffs, A. Young People and the Youth Service. *160 pp.*
Jones, Howard and Cornes, Paul. Open Prisons. *288 pp.*
Jones, Kathleen. History of the Mental Health Service. *428 pp.*
Jones, Kathleen with Brown, John, Cunningham, W. J., Roberts, Julian and
    Williams, Peter. Opening the Door. *A Study of New Policies for the Mentally
    Handicapped. 278 pp.*
Karn, Valerie. Retiring to the Seaside. *400 pp. 2 maps. Numerous tables.*
King, R. D. and Elliot, K. W. Albany: Birth of a Prison—End of an Era. *394 pp.*
Thomas, J. E. The English Prison Officer since 1850: *A Study in Conflict. 258 pp.*
Walton, R. G. Women in Social Work. *303 pp.*
● Woodward, J. To Do the Sick No Harm. *A Study of the British Voluntary Hospital
    System to 1875. 234 pp.*

International Library of Welfare and Philosophy
General Editors Noel Timms and David Watson

● McDermott, F. E. (Ed.) Self-Determination in Social Work. *A Collection of Essays
    on Self-determination and Related Concepts by Philosophers and Social Work
    Theorists. Contributors: F. P. Biestek, S. Bernstein, A. Keith-Lucas, D. Sayer,
    H. H. Perelman, C. Whittington, R. F. Stalley, F. E. McDermott, I. Berlin, H. J.
    McCloskey, H. L. A. Hart, J. Wilson, A. I. Melden, S. I. Benn. 254 pp.*
● Plant, Raymond. Community and Ideology. *104 pp.*
Ragg, Nicholas M. People Not Cases. *A Philosophical Approach to Social Work.
    168 pp.*
● Timms, Noel and Watson, David. (Eds) Talking About Welfare. *Readings in
    Philosophy and Social Policy. Contributors: T. H. Marshall, R. B. Brandt, G. H.
    von Wright, K. Nielsen, M. Cranston, R. M. Titmuss, R. S. Downie, E. Telfer, D.
    Donnison, J. Benson, P. Leonard, A. Keith-Lucas, D. Walsh, I. T. Ramsey.
    320 pp.*
● Philosophy in Social Work. *250 pp.*
● Weale, A. Equality and Social Policy. *164 pp.*

Library of Social Work
General Editor Noel Timms

● Baldock, Peter. Community Work and Social Work. *140 pp.*
○ Beedell, Christopher. Residential Life with Children. *210 pp. Crown 8vo.*
● Berry, Juliet. Daily Experience in Residential Life. *A Study of Children and their
    Care-givers. 202 pp.*
○ Social Work with Children. *190 pp. Crown 8vo.*
● Brearley, C. Paul. Residential Work with the Elderly. *116 pp.*
● Social Work, Ageing and Society. *126 pp.*
● Cheetham, Juliet. Social Work with Immigrants. *240 pp. Crown 8vo.*
● Cross, Crispin P. (Ed.) Interviewing and Communication in Social Work.
    *Contributions by C. P. Cross, D. Laurenson, B. Strutt, S. Raven. 192 pp. Crown
    8vo.*

● **Curnock, Kathleen** and **Hardiker, Pauline.** Towards Practice Theory. *Skills and Methods in Social Assessments. 208 pp.*

● **Davies, Bernard.** The Use of Groups in Social Work Practice. *158 pp.*

● **Davies, Martin.** Support Systems in Social Work. *144 pp.*

Ellis, June. (Ed.) West African Families in Britain. *A Meeting of Two Cultures. Contributions by Pat Stapleton, Vivien Biggs. 150 pp. 1 Map.*

● **Hart, John.** Social Work and Sexual Conduct. *230 pp.*

● **Hutten, Joan M.** Short-Term Contracts in Social Work. *Contributions by Stella M. Hall, Elsie Osborne, Mannie Sher, Eva Sternberg, Elizabeth Tuters. 134 pp.*

Jackson, Michael P. and **Valencia, B. Michael.** Financial Aid Through Social Work. *140 pp.*

● **Jones, Howard.** The Residential Community. *A Setting for Social Work. 150 pp.*

● (Ed.) Towards a New Social Work. *Contributions by Howard Jones, D. A. Fowler, J. R. Cypher, R. G. Walton, Geoffrey Mungham, Philip Priestley, Ian Shaw, M. Bartley, R. Deacon, Irwin Epstein, Geoffrey Pearson. 184 pp.*

Jones, Ray and **Pritchard, Colin.** (Eds) Social Work With Adolescents. *Contributions by Ray Jones, Colin Pritchard, Jack Dunham, Florence Rossetti, Andrew Kerslake, John Burns, William Gregory, Graham Templeman, Kenneth E. Reid, Audrey Taylor. About 170 pp.*

○ **Jordon, William.** The Social Worker in Family Situations. *160 pp. Crown 8vo.*

● **Laycock, A. L.** Adolescents and Social Work. *128 pp. Crown 8vo.*

● **Lees, Ray.** Politics and Social Work. *128 pp. Crown 8vo.*

● Research Strategies for Social Welfare. *112 pp. Tables.*

○ **McCullough, M. K.** and **Ely, Peter J.** Social Work with Groups. *127 pp. Crown 8vo.*

● **Moffett, Jonathan.** Concepts in Casework Treatment. *128 pp. Crown 8vo.*

Parsloe, Phyllida. Juvenile Justice in Britain and the United States. *The Balance of Needs and Rights. 336 pp.*

● **Plant, Raymond.** Social and Moral Theory in Casework. *112 pp. Crown 8vo.*

Priestley, Philip, Fears, Denise and **Fuller, Roger.** Justice for Juveniles. *The 1969 Children and Young Persons Act: A Case for Reform? 128 pp.*

● **Pritchard, Colin** and **Taylor, Richard.** Social Work: Reform or Revolution? *170 pp.*

○ **Pugh, Elisabeth.** Social Work in Child Care. *128 pp. Crown 8vo.*

● **Robinson, Margaret.** Schools and Social Work. *282 pp.*

○ **Ruddock, Ralph.** Roles and Relationships. *128 pp. Crown 8vo.*

● **Sainsbury, Eric.** Social Diagnosis in Casework. *118 pp. Crown 8vo.*

● Social Work with Families. *Perceptions of Social Casework among Clients of a Family Service. 188 pp.*

Seed, Philip. The Expansion of Social Work in Britain. *128 pp. Crown 8vo.*

● **Shaw, John.** The Self in Social Work. *124 pp.*

Smale, Gerald G. Prophecy, Behaviour and Change. *An Examination of Self-fulfilling Prophecies in Helping Relationships. 116 pp. Crown 8vo.*

Smith, Gilbert. Social Need. *Policy, Practice and Research. 155 pp.*

● Social Work and the Sociology of Organisations. *124 pp. Revised edition.*

● **Sutton, Carole.** Psychology for Social Workers and Counsellors. *An Introduction. 248 pp.*

● **Timms, Noel.** Language of Social Casework. *122 pp. Crown 8vo.*

● Recording in Social Work. *124 pp. Crown 8vo.*

● **Todd, F. Joan.** Social Work with the Mentally Subnormal. *96 pp. Crown 8vo.*

● **Walrond-Skinner, Sue.** Family Therapy. *The Treatment of Natural Systems. 172 pp.*

● **Warham, Joyce.** An Introduction to Administration for Social Workers. *Revised edition. 112 pp.*

● An Open Case. *The Organisational Context of Social Work. 172 pp.*

○ **Wittenberg, Isca Salzberger.** Psycho-Analytic Insight and Relationships. *A Kleinian Approach. 196 pp. Crown 8vo.*

Primary Socialization, Language and Education
General Editor   Basil Bernstein

Reports of the Institute of Community Studies

Reports of the Institute for Social Studies in Medical Care

Cartwright, Ann, Hockey, Lisbeth and **Anderson, John J.** Life Before Death. *310 pp.*
Dunnell, Karen and **Cartwright, Ann.** Medicine Takers, Prescribers and Hoarders. *190 pp.*
Farrell, C. My Mother Said. . . *A Study of the Way Young People Learned About Sex and Birth Control. 288 pp.*

Medicine, Illness and Society
General Editor W. M. Williams

Hall, David J. Social Relations & Innovation. *Changing the State of Play in Hospitals. 232 pp.*
Hall, David J. and **Stacey, M.** (Eds) Beyond Separation. *234 pp.*
Robinson, David. The Process of Becoming Ill. *142 pp.*
Stacey, Margaret *et al.* Hospitals, Children and Their Families. *The Report of a Pilot Study. 202 pp.*
Stimson, G. V. and **Webb, B.** Going to See the Doctor. *The Consultation Process in General Practice. 155 pp.*

Monographs in Social Theory
General Editor Arthur Brittan

● **Barnes, B.** Scientific Knowledge and Sociological Theory. *192 pp.*
Bauman, Zygmunt. Culture as Praxis. *204 pp.*
● **Dixon, Keith.** Sociological Theory. *Pretence and Possibility. 142 pp.*
The Sociology of Belief. *Fallacy and Foundation. About 160 pp.*
Goff, T. W. Marx and Mead. *Contributions to a Sociology of Knowledge. 176 pp.*
Meltzer, B. N., Petras, J. W. and **Reynolds, L. T.** Symbolic Interactionism. *Genesis, Varieties and Criticisms. 144 pp.*
● **Smith, Anthony D.** The Concept of Social Change. *A Critique of the Functionalist Theory of Social Change. 208 pp.*

Routledge Social Science Journals

The British Journal of Sociology. *Editor – Angus Stewart; Associate Editor – Leslie Sklair. Vol. 1, No. 1 – March 1950 and Quarterly. Roy. 8vo. All back issues available. An international journal publishing original papers in the field of sociology and related areas.*
Community Work. *Edited by David Jones and Marjorie Mayo. 1973. Published annually.*
Economy and Society. *Vol. 1, No. 1. February 1972 and Quarterly. Metric Roy. 8vo. A journal for all social scientists covering sociology, philosophy, anthropology, economics and history. All back numbers available.*

Ethnic and Racial Studies. *Editor – John Stone. Vol. 1 – 1978. Published quarterly.*
Religion. Journal of Religion and Religions. *Chairman of Editorial Board, Ninian Smart. Vol. 1, No. 1, Spring 1971. A journal with an inter-disciplinary approach to the study of the phenomena of religion. All back numbers available.*
Sociology of Health and Illness. *A Journal of Medical Sociology. Editor – Alan Davies; Associate Editor – Ray Jobling. Vol. 1, Spring 1979. Published 3 times per annum.*
Year Book of Social Policy in Britain. *Edited by Kathleen Jones. 1971. Published annually.*

Social and Psychological Aspects of Medical Practice
Editor   Trevor Silverstone

Lader, Malcolm. Psychophysiology of Mental Illness. *280 pp.*
● **Silverstone, Trevor** and **Turner, Paul.** Drug Treatment in Psychiatry. *Revised edition. 256 pp.*
Whiteley, J. S. and **Gordon, J.** Group Approaches in Psychiatry. *240 pp.*

Printed and bound in Great Britain by
Redwood Burn Limited, Trowbridge & Esher